Wanting

ALSO EDITED BY MARGOT KAHN
AND KELLY McMASTERS

This Is the Place:
Women Writing About Home

Women Writing About Desire

Wanting

Edited by Margot Kahn
and Kelly McMasters

Catapult New York

Please see permissions on page 335 for individual credits.

ISBN: 978-1-64622-011-3

Library of Congress Control Number: 2022944797

Cover design by Nicole Caputo
Book design by Laura Berry

Catapult
New York, NY
books.catapult.co

Printed in the United States of America

10 9 8 7 6 5

I am free to be sung to;
I am free to sing. This woman
can cross any line.

—JOY HARJO, "ALIVE"

Contents

Introduction

DESIRE IS NOT NEW, BUT OUR UNDERSTANDING OF the experience and the way we're willing to reveal it is constantly shifting. In "A Song in the Front Yard," Gwendolyn Brooks writes:

> *I've stayed in the front yard all my life.*
> *I want a peek at the back*
> *Where it's rough and untended and hungry weed grows.*
> *A girl gets sick of a rose.*

Most of us can identify in our bodies a memory of that first spark of reckless desire, of wanting the rough and the untended, of feeling like that hungry weed. As we age, of course, our desires layer and change, but the base experience of *want* remains the same. Desire is messy. And raw. And irrational. And often embarrassing in its effacement, in the way it takes over and leaves us cracked open.

In thinking about desire while coediting this anthology, we've come to understand that desire lives in both the body and the brain. Unattainability—in a person, a paycheck, an object, an orgasm—stokes the flame, while getting what we want extinguishes it, though not its memory. "When I desire you, a part of me is gone," the critic and poet Anne Carson once wrote. The vulnerability involved in wanting something—often to the exclusion of everything else—is inherently risky because the allure hinges on not knowing if you will attain the quarry.

So what do women want? Hopefully, by now, we all know there is no easy answer to that question. Historically, of course, female desire was defined by men; women's voices on this subject were conspicuously absent from the page. But women want to want. And wanting—which demands hunger and requires autonomy—remains, for women, a dangerous concept.

When we first set out to collect these essays, we had a basic sense of the shape of the book we hoped to create: a space for women to interrogate and luxuriate in their desire—not as a means to an end, but as the main subject. We knew that we wanted to include a cross section of voices representing a variety of races, religions, ages, socioeconomic realities, and geographies, as we did with our first anthology, *This Is the Place: Women Writing About Home*. We knew loosely the topics we hoped to cover but were mostly focused on getting the longing, beauty, seduction, fear, and introspection that desire often demands onto the page.

What we didn't realize was how difficult it would be for many writers to claim these things without the cloak of fiction, poetry, or reportage. So often, our brainstorming discussions with contributors would tread into fascinating territory but end with a writer shaking their head, saying, *Oh, but I could never publish a nonfiction essay on that. My family/children/partner/ parent might read it!*

In these pages, thirty-three writers were brave enough to explore the primal, the abiding, the illicit. Our writers want to belong and to escape, to dominate and submit, to fuck and feel and be free. Some ache to be alone and others ache for the full feeling of another person inside them. They want abortions and they want babies, have addictions and affairs; there are things they want to ravage and things they want to cleave from themselves. Some want partners they've lost to return; others want to lose the partners they have. Some just want to remember what it feels like to want to live.

Often, when we talk about desire, the impulse is assumed to be an active one, focused on the object of desire, and dichotomous: you are either the desired or the one desiring. But this is a reductive trap. We hope this collection complicates that notion, pushing beyond this simple math equation and shifting our attention to the ache of absence required in order to desire. This is where our collection's title comes from: it can mean, in one way, the act of wanting, but it also reflects the lack that is often overlooked in the process.

The majority of these essays are original, written specifically for this anthology. The women writing are parents and pilots, PhDs and porn connoisseurs, liars and thieves in the most vital and human ways. Sexual appetites and attractions range, but what we found was that the experience of desire—the pleasure and the pain of it—ultimately came down to something one experiences alone. It is this relationship—between wanting and the body, wanting and the brain, wanting and the heart—that binds these women and their experiences. For an impulse that inherently requires another object or person or idea, the experience of desire is internal and intimate. Ultimately, there is nothing more personal than one's desire, except sharing it. Our desires—and speaking them aloud—make us powerful. We hope this book creates a space for you, lights a fire.

—MARGOT KAHN AND KELLY McMASTERS

Wanting

When I Imagine the Life I Want

Larissa Pham

I LIKE TO TELL PEOPLE I WANT A HOUSE SOMEWHERE by the ocean with a Morandi in the study. I want a place to write, I say, and a place to paint, even though I haven't painted in years. I want to get it back. I want a garden, with peonies, because those are the flowers my grandfather raised, and a big kitchen, with a big, solid butcher block, where I'll be able to prep ingredients for all the meals I want to make. I'll have enough space to have friends over, and enough space for the ones I love to work beside me. I'll have a reading nook. I'll have light in every room.

In this fantasy I'll have enough time to take care of the garden, which will be full of vegetables and flowers. Not just peonies, but tomatoes, lettuce, kale, radishes, roses, quince. Maybe I'll have some chickens, and I'll have time to take care of them too—to scatter feed and set out water and collect their speckled eggs. I'll write every day—I'll still be writing, in the world where this fantasy takes place. I'll wake up and make tea and I'll sit down at my desk and write.

I'll live somewhere nice. I already mentioned the ocean, but I want trees too. I also want the city, so in this fantasy, I'll be close, close enough to go to bars, and restaurants, and the places where people dance. I'll have plenty to do, being so close, and so closely involved, and I'll be writing, but I'll have time to teach, and write criticism, and go to see a show not because of work but just because. I'll see art, and I'll be inspired, and I'll go home and think of things I want to make.

And if I allow myself—if I think about material things, things that I've held in my hands—I picture, yes, a desk. And a row of books, some of which are mine. And a cup—maybe two cups, because it means I'm not lonely. The nice kind that are a double layer of blown glass, so drinks stay hot.

But after a point my fantasy winds down. I can't imagine picking out a backsplash, or the color of paint on my studio walls. The image wavers, then grows hazy and thin. Because these are all, when I think about it, adornments. They're trappings of a life I've made into something I want to be mine. They're symbols, comforts, material things I've imagined looking at in catalogs and Instagrams. When I really think about this fantasy, this small life I want to live with the life that is mine, what I want, more than anything, is time. That's what the house, the study, the garden represent: time.

When I say I want a house with a Morandi in the study, what I'm saying is that I want to be able to afford a house with a Morandi in the study, because if I can afford that, I can afford anything. A lost job, an accident, a medical emergency—money erases problems the way nothing else can. But that's not really what I want. (The garden, the studio, the desk.) What I want is more than money. (The chickens, the easel, the sink.) What I want most of all is to have the freedom to imagine a large and ambitious life. (The art, the food, the care.) I want to work because I love work, because there is joy in purpose, in making and growing things; I want to caretake because I love care, because there is fulfillment in sharing love with others. I don't want to have to balance what I want with what is attainable because I want it all. I want it all.

Let me revise my fantasy. When I imagine the life I want, I imagine the world changed. No jails, no fossil fuels, no billionaires. No private insurance, no fracking, no food instability. Living wages, dignified work, decency toward all living things.

I imagine a world completely different from the one we have now, broken and remade. It's a world so different it's almost hard to believe it could exist. But, for now, and for a long time, I want to believe. In that world, I have time. And so do you. So do we all. Time to think, and care for each other, and create.

Appetite

Michelle Wildgen

THE FIRST MEAL I EVER WANTED TO COOK FOR MY-
self was a pasta recipe I found in a stray issue of *Bon Appétit* at a
friend's house. It was fettuccine with crab meat, saffron butter,
and shiitakes, with a handful of scallions. Nowadays, this dish
does not appeal to me—it seems random and formerly trendy,
like that three-month period when we all went nuts for elf boots
and oversized sweaters—but at the time I just had to have it. It
wasn't that I thought this dish would taste delicious. It was that
I had no clue *what* this dish would taste like. That was the part
that got me: that I could not even guess.

I took the magazine home and asked my mom how to pro-
nounce *shiitake*. It was the 1980s in suburban Ohio; she didn't
know either. But we found the shiitakes and the saffron at the
Acme Click, a store where we also picked up the occasional
beach towel and soccer ball, and I made that dish. The saffron
stained the butter a woodsy golden color, the shiitakes were
musky and velvety, the seafood (later I often subbed in shrimp)
was sweet and coral white. Even the scallions suddenly felt
new—they were brighter and more herbal than I recalled.

More than I liked eating this dish, I craved the process of
cooking it. Each time, it was confirmation of a question I'd answered, a task I'd completed successfully. Enjoying the food was
almost beside the point. I made some version of it for years, into
college, until it started to seem a little dated. Besides, by then,
there were so many other things I had to eat. I had to know about

foie gras and why drinking late harvest wine with it made for an entirely different taste. I had to try sweetbreads and chanterelles and fresh wasabi root, which for some reason I ordered off the nascent internet. (Did I know what to do with fresh wasabi root besides grate it? I did not. But I thought it might be interesting.) I had to stand on the street corner outside Murray's Cheese Shop on Bleecker and eat a few ounces of chilly Alsatian Muenster cheese all by itself. A heel of baguette might have been nice, and in truth I wasn't hungry for Muenster right then, but I was visiting New York, and the cheese I'd always heard was so much better than its bland American sandwich slice was right there in front of me, so I stood there on the cobblestones and ate cold cheese and I did it all because I could not refuse the opportunity.

Several years later, when my boyfriend and I ate a four-course meal after consuming a pile of seafood appetizers we'd thought were our dinner, we did it for the same reason: this place on Cornelia Street made its own pasta, which was something I had long wanted to try, and handmade pasta wasn't thick on the ground where we lived back then, so it had to be done. The handmade tortelloni was rustic and tender and toothsome; I never forgot it and I stand by every bite.

I had the sense that out in the world there was a vast cloud of knowledge, of what was good and what was special and what could be combined with what to *become* special, but I could only see a few little objects floating in the general fog. I suppose it's telling that while some people vanquish their educational shortcomings with daunting piles of books and maps and lists, I decided my ignorance was something I'd just have to eat.

The more I think about those years in my teens and twenties that were powered almost entirely by hunger, the clearer it is to me that my appetite was not about wealth, though I had to work to save the money to buy the things I hoped to eat or to journey to the places where I could eat them. And it was not exactly about seeming worldly or well traveled, though I wanted to be both. It was the prospect of French food that drove me in college to close my eyes and buy my first plane ticket to France before I could get nervous and back out. And it's not that I was a snob about simple food, or the Midwestern food I'd grown up on: one of my most enduring obsessions was a three-ingredient fresh tomato pasta dish from Nora Ephron's *Heartburn*, and I will still throw down over my hometown hamburger drive-in, which is manifestly superior to my husband's hometown burger drive-in, no matter what he says.

I wanted to eat, yes, but more than anything I was hungry to *know*. I wanted to know about foods I'd never heard of, but I also wanted to know about the best versions of food I already knew. Surely the cheese you ate in France was different from the Brie we bought at the supermarket? Because I thought that supermarket Brie was pretty damn good. The notion that there existed some version of this delight that I couldn't even grasp until I consumed it was the tantalizer that spurred me into nearly everything I did for about twenty years. Each new flavor felt like a dare and an impossible promise. All my books were telling me there were transporting versions of everything I knew out in the world. It was all—MFK Fisher's paean to ultra-fresh peas, Ephron's description of cool ripe tomatoes hitting hot linguine—about magic, not stumbling on it but learning how to conjure it. Sometimes I think I only started ordering wasabi and raw milk cheese online when I was too old to look for paths to Narnia in the back yard.

There is a downside to a hunger like this. When traveling, you fret over whether That One Dish was the Very Best Version of that dish, that you had your shot and missed it. You become humorless and fascistic about restaurants, because the familiar is a wasted meal and other people's toddlers can just get their shit together and eat squid tentacles with the rest of us. Maybe don't tote up all the time you spent standing in line at a fabled burger joint or trekking out to distant neighborhoods to lose an hour to the fugue state in which you observed an old man making pizza. I know that was time I could have spent reading books, seeing plays, cultivating deeper friendships, and learning to identify grackles. But I spent it asking unfriendly countermen for chunks of guanciale and persuading myself it was justified to bring my own anchovies to restaurants that served the crappy ones.

Anyway. The years passed and all the same changes have happened to me and to my obsessions that happen to a lot of people. My siblings had babies and even I got tired of antagonizing their children with food they feared and loathed. At forty, retirement no longer seemed like a wispy dream, and the ungodly amounts I'd once serenely dropped at a big-event restaurant like Alinea now seemed unjustifiable. I had a baby and I worked a lot more and suddenly I didn't care so much about finding out what stinky tofu tasted like either.

But I miss that appetite. I miss the sense of discovery it was grounded in and the pleasure and energy it both fed and generated. I still spend a lot of time thinking about what I will cook next, and I still devote my disposable time and income more to travel and meals than anything else. (A conversation last night at dinner: "Do you treat yourself to massages?" "No." "Facials?" "No." "Manicures, pedicures?" "No. I color my hair and I eat.") But sometimes it feels as if the reason I spend so much time planning meals is not because I still get joy out of it but because I am trying to get that joy back. In some ways, that sense of discovery is simply gone and not returning—you can only read food magazines for so many years before suspecting you've entered a time loop—but I hope my old appetites don't surrender entirely to jadedness or age. I don't know if eating for the sake of knowledge will ever feel as important and meaningful as it once did. I find pleasure in eating for different reasons: because I'm grateful to have it, because my child asked what falafel tasted like, because the seasons shift and this is how I mark their passage. But these days, I have no desire to eat cheese on the street. And that cannot help but feel a little like loss.

Sex in the Suburbs

Angela Cardinale

THE FIRST SUMMER OF THE PANDEMIC, I SPEND A weekend with a chef ten years my junior. When I arrive at his sleek downtown L.A. loft, he's heavily cologned, shirt unbuttoned three down, dark chest hair sprouting forth. He smirks then reaches for the nape of my neck. He pulls me in and kisses me hard before we can get through the door.

I try not to say too much about what I do on the weeks without my children to the other moms in my suburban Saturday morning running group. I'm divorced, while they're in long-term marriages with seemingly supportive spouses and children the same age as mine, teens. We've seen each other for years, at pick-ups and drop-offs and booster meetings and Christmas parades and open houses. We talk about Zoom school, upcoming holiday plans, home projects. One woman's husband is replacing the carpet with laminate. One woman's husband is tackling a rat infestation in their yard, brought about by citrus and palm trees. To fit in, I discuss changing out the pulls on my kitchen drawers. Too 1980s, I say. It's still deep pandemic times, so we run with our masks, sweat clinging to fabric clinging to faces. We raise our voices to hear one another in between heaving breaths. It's warm already on this early Saturday summer morning, and we wave at old couples walking dogs, passing cyclists, young couples with strollers. We run down the center of the street, knowing few cars will be out this early. Our feet hit the asphalt, and the rhythm of movement and small talk reassures me. They ask me about my dating life, but I provide only general answers.

I keep it *Lifetime* quality, PG. I don't tell them he chopped paper thin garlic in nothing but boxer briefs and a leather apron. I don't tell them we didn't get to the food until 2:00 a.m., we were so busy fucking. I don't tell them I tried molly for the first time with him, and we spent hours running our fingers over each other's skin, marveling at the sensation. I tell them, instead, that he was handsome, that he made me dinner, that he provided a range of beverage options.

Everyone I've dated this past year lives in L.A. Most suburban married couples my age seem to stay in their marriages, even the unhappy ones. There are few suitable men to date here. I know much of the gossip—who's illicitly sleeping with whom, who's near divorced but hanging on for the kids. Us single parents are the anomaly, at least in this particular suburb, especially among the parents of my children's friends. Mostly, I can't tell who's happy and who's trapped—it all looks the same on Instagram.

My boyfriend of five years, whom I loved fucking, who could be both extraordinarily kind and extraordinarily cruel, broke up with me a month into the pandemic. We lived together in a suburb a bit farther west, closer to L.A., where he worked. As a result of the breakup, I moved, twice, with my kids, during the pandemic, which I don't recommend. I'm back in the town in which I met my sons' father, where I graduated high school, where my sons will soon do the same. I often feel trapped in the stucco homes and palm trees and smog and summer fires, like some magnet keeps drawing me back despite my efforts to break free. I find myself here once again, freshly dumped, with no ability to socialize with friends or work colleagues, in the brutal heat of another inland Southern California summer. Zoom is no substitute for human contact.

In the initial aftermath of the breakup, when the kids were

at their dad's, I'd curl into the sad brown apartment carpet and let my body heave with grief. I felt like someone had scraped out my insides with a sharp scoop. I'd never felt like this before, not even after my divorce. I decided to go back to therapy, and we talked about attachment. I learned about Harlow's experiments on infant monkeys, in which they'd seek the tactile comfort of a fabricated cloth mother, though the wire mother had the food. I'd been seeking affection from a source that would never provide. My mother left me when I was young. My stepmother abused me. My father was in his own world, oblivious. Some core layer of me will always crave that love I lacked.

My mother had been married five times and had five children by the time she died at thirty-six. She was a purported sex maniac. That's what all the men she'd married told me. She'd always been a mystery, so a few years ago I tracked them down. She'd met two of them hitchhiking on the freeway, the first when she was only fifteen. They were all still haunted by her, whether they hated her or loved her or some mixture. Many of them kept her possessions for decades. One gave me a Polaroid of her she'd torn into twenty-one pieces. He'd painstakingly glued it back together.

She attacked and cheated on all of them. She destroyed herself and those in her path. She tried marriages, she tried casual sex, she tried children, she tried many drugs, she tried evangelical Christianity. She bashed herself up against that cloth mother but she never got what she needed. Her parents were distant and cold, and it left a hunger inside her. She, in turn, bestowed that onto me.

Isolated, not knowing any other way, I download dating apps. Bumble, Hinge. Then, shamefully, Tinder. It's been years and I'm unsure how this works during a pandemic.

That's how I meet the chef. After a month or so, I end it. He is too young and going to too many parties and he doesn't text me back as much as I would like. I want more than I can get from him.

Next, I meet a man I will call Nate. The text banter is excellent. There is nowhere to go, so after substantial time on the phone, I invite him to my home. The first time we meet in person, we spend nearly two days together. I love the way he looks at me, like he can really see me. My body pulses when he touches me. When he leaves, my face is raw, we've kissed for so many hours.

A couple of months in, Nate says he doesn't see how it can work. I live too far away, and he's decided he definitely wants a baby.

"I want you," he says, "but I don't want your circumstances."

It stings. It's why my ex-boyfriend left me. He, too, wanted a child at first, and back then, I was open to it. He said he would've married me if I didn't have children of my own, if I wasn't tied to this region. It was the deepest I'd ever loved someone, but he could only reciprocate with his version of love, with an asterisk.

I go on a dating spree. I meet all kinds of men—younger, older, rich, struggling, sober, wild. I try to choose people who don't seem to go out too much, who work remotely, but I am not as pandemic-safe as I should be. I have a few COVID scares, pay hundreds for rapid tests before my children return. I just want someone to touch me, to sleep in my bed, to want me. There's a vacuum I want desperately to fill.

I date some nice men. But I also meet a man who takes his condom off when we are having sex without telling me, what I later learn is called stealthing. I am wracked with worry that I've contracted an STI. Fortunately, I have not.

I delete the apps. I get lonely and add them back.

I date a man who tells me he's slept with over eight hundred women, who tells me he would never drive to where I live.

I date a man for a month who writes an eight-page erotic story about me, in which my name is misspelled, as is the word *masturbate*.

I date a man who at first seems uninterested. He is wealthy and lives in a beautiful home in Laguna Hills. The ocean spreads into the horizon as we sit on the deck and eat appetizers he's prepared: hummus, olive tapenade, precisely cut pita. He's had a designer decorate his home for him, all midcentury furniture, with massive, expensive art. He's had a landscape architect plant his plants for him. He asks me if I approve. He hurries me out after dinner, though, and our lips hardly touch when he kisses me goodbye. A week later, he invites me over again. He cooks for me in his dazzling kitchen, and we climb into his jacuzzi after. When he removes his towel, I'm startled to discover he's already nude. I'm attracted to him, so we kiss in the hot water, then move to the patio sofa, then move to the indoor sofa. He moves my feet onto his penis, and I realize he expects me to move both feet up and down, for which I definitely do not possess the core strength. He then puts his foot on my crotch, and to my horror, puts his big toe in my vagina. He begins fucking me with his toe. It takes me aback, but I let him. I don't see him again. It's a little much for a second date.

I date a man who asks me if I want to come back to his place and hold his Emmy. His *daytime* Emmy.

I don't tell my married mom friends about any of this. It's too humiliating. I live my life of Zoom meetings and family dinners one week, and a life of semidebauchery in a desperate search for love another. When they chatter about their weekend plans with their husbands, jealousy flashes through me. I'm returning to an empty home, with a cat who meows loudly all day and night since we moved. I have somehow become a *Cathy* cartoon, albeit a version with lots more sex.

I delete the apps. I reinstall.

Nate and I continue texting, nearly every day. We can't find anyone we connect with as well as we connect with one another. We miss the sex. We do it over the phone sometimes.

When L.A. allows restaurants to open patios, a friend and I drive the hour and a half to eat the chef's pizza. I dress in a black mini skirt with a zipper running thigh to hip. I am drunk on the wine he recommends, the roasted squash and sage and onions on the pizza, the way he looks at me when he serves us. That night, after work, he drives to the suburbs and we fuck for hours, first by my fireplace and then in my bedroom. He will never love me, but his lust is a temporary salve.

I despair that I will never be in love again. I still miss the man who occupied my bed for nearly five years. I force myself to remember the bad names he called me, the way he turned cold on me every month or so, for seemingly no reason, how it activated an alarm deep within that I hadn't known was there. I write this all down so I can refer to it in moments of weakness.

By the time the pandemic wanes in the spring and I become vaccinated, I am weary from the disappointments of dating. I begin taking trips alone. I buy a couple of single concert tickets for the fall, when things are supposed to open up again. I've never been to a concert alone before. I buy a body pillow. I adopt a dog.

Many of the men I've dated in the past several months want to love me. My phone fills with their texts. What am I doing this weekend? Do I want to go camping, platonically? Do I want to FaceTime, just to chat? Am I having a good morning? A good week? A good weekend? The weather seems to have shifted inside of me, and I'm no longer desperate for just any man's love. I do want romantic love, badly, that original wound still pulsing. I just don't want it with any of them. I wonder why I can't just make it easy on myself. I wonder if I am more like my mother than I thought, hurting people who want to care about me, hurting myself.

Nate and I decide to continue fucking whenever we are both

not seeing anyone. The way his hands move along my hips, the way he makes me laugh, the way he kisses my ribs and tells me I am beautiful. I think, this is what I'm looking for, with someone who doesn't want a baby, who doesn't think I live too far away. It seems impossible to find.

When I was a child, we were poor and lived on an isolated rural road. I found a bike someone had dumped in the brush down the way, a man-sized bike with no brakes. I'd push that thing to the top of the big hill, hoist myself over the top, and fly. I loved the wind, the speed, the danger. I was only five and too small for the bike. To stop, I'd have to wait until I slowed and crash into something, a tree or a fence or a wall. Then, timing it carefully, I'd tip over and land on one foot so as not to hit my crotch against the top tube. I loved the feeling of flying down that hill, the thrill of how alone I was, that the bike was all mine, that I could protect myself from harm.

Sometimes I want to be wild and powerful and alone, like that child version of me. Sometimes I want to be loved again and grow patio plants with someone, and drink coffee together, and touch each other for hours, and tell jokes only we understand. I want to be loved in a sometimes quiet way and in a sometimes big bold beautiful way by someone who fucks me well, who really sees me, who doesn't try to contain me in order to love me.

We are contradictions, living one life, secretly desiring another, in a battle with ourselves. In *O Pioneers!*, the main character, Alexandria, has led a life of hard work and responsibility working the land. On the surface, she seems like a woman without time for frivolous desires. But her whole life, she has a recurring dream, a sexual one: "It was a man . . . who carried her, but he was like no man she knew; he was much larger and stronger and swifter, and he carried her as easily as if she were a sheaf of wheat. She never saw him, but, with eyes closed, she could feel that he was yellow like the sunlight, and there was the smell of ripe cornfields about him." She scours her body angrily after this dream, furious for allowing herself to fantasize. She's a practical woman who knows she's too heavy for any man to lift. She settles for a boring local, Carl. When I read this in college, it felt so tragic, like a death. I thought, I don't want to settle for Carl. I still don't.

I have come to accept that I might not ever find the deep romantic connection with the kind of partner I seek. An L.A. man tells me I'm "cute but geographically undesirable." After weeks of texting, another tells me he likes me a lot but he's disappointed I'm not Jewish. A bunch of them want babies. It doesn't faze me anymore. I now know I may be alone here in the suburbs, an island on an island, for possibly many years. In the meantime, I have my children, my friends, my dog, spectacular trips into nature, good food, good sex.

I take a trip to New Mexico, alone. In the dark of morning, I wake and drive to the Alkali Flats Trail in White Sands National Park. The sun rises against my back as I climb the brightening dunes, up and down, up and down. The sky is orange and pink and the shadows on the sand are gray and blue. The sand is whiter than I could have imagined. The air grows warmer as I march forward, from orange marker to orange marker, dune to dune. I am the only one I see until the end of the hike, nearly three hours and five miles of pure white sand against deep blue sky. I turn to see the trail my feet have made. Mine are the only tracks, save for some small animal I can't identify, a mouse maybe. The footprints from previous days are already only faint dimples. The night before, an upswell of loneliness made me cry in my Airbnb. Today, I am grateful for my body, for the quiet, for the privilege of having this magical place to myself.

The next day, I drive to the Carlsbad Caverns, three hours from where I'm staying. Though the drive through Lincoln National Forest is pretty, the leaves bright yellow and orange against muted green pine trees and gray cliffs, the rest of the drive is mostly unremarkable—aging strip malls, drooping houses, oil drilling into miles of flat land. Finally, the road rises, and I drive up a hill covered in stones and sagebrush and cactus, dusty and basic. It's hard to believe the caverns are tucked inside. A flock of cave swallows flutter up from the entrance as I descend a steep 750 feet into the belly. Inside the caverns, rocks that began forming half a million years ago twist and jut from every direction, in every shape, the ceiling a cathedral of shimmering minerals. The air is cool, the handrails slicked with moisture. An entire ecosystem thrives here—bats and ringtail cats and snails. A couple of hours later, I step into the parking lot, startled by the contrast of the cool, complex darkness against the sparse, bright desert morning. I know I may be alone, possibly for many more years, and the longing is there, a kind of companion I carry with me. I'll own what I lack and what I do to get by. Like these caverns, we have whole worlds hidden inside.

Pleasure Archive:
Notes on Polyamory, History, and Desire

Keyanah B. Nurse, PhD

WHEN I AM IN THE THICK OF FUCKING, HISTORY weaves itself between my body and the bodies of my lovers. Some of those bodies have been like my own. They too have been marked as Black despite the wide-ranging hues of their skin tones. They too have been gendered as female, despite the nuance of a more colorful lived reality. But other bodies have been different from my own. They have been assigned male at birth. They have been defined as white. They have come into this world on different shores, kissing me and eating me out with entirely different mother tongues.

I have had the luxury of experiencing the variety of these bodies simultaneously. This is my highbrow way of saying that I've fucked a lot of different kind of people, some individually and some as part of group play. And while sex with this broad swath of individuals has taught me many lessons about what I like and how I like it (nipple play is . . . whew), it has also turned my body into a way of asking questions about history.

If history is felt in and through the body, then sex is an archive. It is the collection of kisses, caresses, moans, and fluids that carry within them the particular truths of who we are and how we came to be. Just like an archive, so too does sex feature its own set of invisible power dynamics that inform, for better or for worse, how we occupy our pleasure. While there are plenty of us who would like to believe the myth that our sexual "preferences" are neutral, unbiased choices, I echo the many others who have demonstrated that they are not. Who and how you fuck, and even better, who and how you *want* to fuck, is a function of history. Those desires offer a roadmap across time and space, illuminating what turns us on and why.

As a Black polyamorous woman, I often sit in the historicity of my sex because it happens at different cultural, racial, generational, and national intersections. With two of my partners—D, of ten years, and K, of four—I experience a sexual variety and volume that highlights the juicy differences and surprising similarities between each encounter. With each lover, I discover different versions of myself in my own sexual archive, an indulgence that polyamory affords me as I, to quote Gabriel García Márquez, "[know] the wonder of fucking with love."

When I am with my partner D, himself a product of his parents' decision to emigrate from Guyana to the United States, I find comfort in our shared racial kinship. Despite playing for different teams within the global Black diaspora, my flesh recognizes itself in him, the varying hues of our brown skin creating that feeling of home.

But beyond both being Black, we meet at other intersections: we are both millennials, we both attended the same bougie-ass Ivy League university, and we both have similar politics. Although we grew up in different parts of the country, me in New Jersey and him in Georgia, we both reminisce about our love of Barney as little kids or the *Tom Joyner Morning Show* playing on the radio as our parents drove us to school. I say all of this to note that we have a degree of familiarity, of sameness that translates itself sexually as radical comfort. There are no pretenses, no performances, no projections. When I cum with D, it usually happens when he is inside me, a symbol, no doubt, of how much of ourselves we see in each other.

Our build-up to sex is usually playful and direct. "Wanna fuck?" may be a punchline in a joke to highlight someone's lack of finesse, but for us, it's par for the course. It's the appetizer that precedes the entrée of D's thick lips moving across my neck and collarbone; the giggles I release as he moves down to my breasts; the satisfaction of my plump ass filling his large hands. His strength facilitates a welcome aggression during our lovemaking, which is only made hotter by his anticipation of my commands. "Look at me," I whisper to him. "Say my name," I coax him. "On your knees," I challenge him. His physical power, his handling of my body—all of it is a feast that I ravenously consume as he awaits dessert: the permission I give him to orgasm.

This particular feature of our sex is impossible to translate to someone else's bedroom. I can only find this version of myself with him. To be girlish and commanding is how I express my femininity with D; that dance between power and softness is nothing short of intoxicating. It is only made possible because of D's willingness to be vulnerable, to follow, to bend, to enjoy the ways that femininity can be an expression of dominance. *That* is a function of history, of our history; the micro history of our love, which began as college students trying to survive an unforgiving predominantly white institution, continued into young adulthood as we navigated new professional challenges and frontiers, and persists into the present as we challenge the bounds of marriage within polyamory and make room for our respective autonomy.

But the trust required for this kind of sex is also made possible by a macro history. After all, migration, imperialism, and anti-Black racism coalesced such that two Black millennials could find each other as they both tried to make sense of the scam called American meritocracy. It is the history of how we have navigated the paradoxical *similar difference* of Blackness in diaspora.[1] Our differences appear within the small moments of me trying roti for the first time or the shock of D admitting that he's never seen *The Fresh Prince of Bel-Air*. But our sameness always shows up with *the look*. If you're Black, regardless of where you're from, you know it to be that existential recognition another Black person gives you whenever you've stumbled into a space that's just way too . . . white. It is both a calling and a recognition of your shared discomfort, as well as your resiliency, to find humor in such a situation. Such is the beauty of our millennial, diasporic love, and such is the way that history shows up in our sex.

The richness of these shared histories with D became clearer to me as my relationship with K, my other long-term committed partner, took up more space within my life. On a balmy late summer evening, a mere two weeks after D and I married, I met K. Although I initially teased him about questioning whether or not he was a serial killer (his Tinder profile pics were very intense; luckily, he smiles in them now), I felt instantly attracted to his quirky yet direct way of speaking. The sharp jawline and silver hair also did it for me, which is why he's been my silver fox ever since. We shot the shit over drinks and some laughs, developing the smart-ass, flirty banter that would, unbeknownst to us at the time, blossom into a life-altering love. Kissing him for the first time felt like seeing new colors, and that has always been the disruptive, challenging, profound impact K has had on me.

The beginning of my romance with K was a whirlwind. Until that point in my nonmonogamous journey, I had only desired an open relationship with D. Although I dated other people consistently and grew fond of them, those connections never lasted beyond three or four months. But more importantly, I never felt myself "in love" with anyone else besides D. K changed that in a big way. When I realized I was in love with him, the move from an open relationship to polyamory followed shortly thereafter. I consider myself fortunate that D was also grappling with similar questions about what it might mean to love another person, just as he remained in love with me; I never had to enter polyamory with an unconvinced or otherwise reluctant partner. Nevertheless, the transition forced me to face a lot of internalized ugliness, including assumptions around hierarchy, self-worth, compromise, and communication. The process was, and remains, a journey of profound anguish and immeasurable joy. Unlearning monogamy is, as it turns out, hard as fuck. And precisely because so much of the challenge of this unlearning is rooted in misogyny, racism, classism, and any other *-ism* you can think of, the work is never done.

But back to the story. Like most folks in the throes of NRE, or new relationship energy, I was absolutely smitten with K. Every week, I eagerly waited for him to pull up to my building in his black Mazda and swoop me away to whatever adventure he had planned. Although there are certainly grand gestures that spark falling in love, I have found that it happens more slowly over time. It's hidden within the small quotidian moments that perhaps mean nothing from the outside looking in but eventually change the path of your life. With K, that meant admiring his strength and discipline as an accomplished martial artist, while also seeing the tender moments he shared with his two cats. It meant appreciating the focus with which he listened to my thoughts and opinions, the reverence he displayed for my intellectualism. It meant listening to the small anecdotes about his upbringing in Russia and his early days in the United States.

Born in the former Soviet Union in 1982, K immigrated to Brooklyn with his mother and two sisters in 1996. As he explained to me, his insular upbringing within the Russian Jewish communities of Brighton Beach made it such that his first substantial interactions with Black people didn't happen until college. There, he took a class on the history of the Holocaust and learned about the parallels between it and Jim Crow in the United States. That sense of historical solidarity became the space between me and K. I felt K understood and validated me in a way that the white American men I occasionally dated never could. He never boasted to me about his family's Virginia plantation, or tried to convince me that Trump supporters weren't all so bad. Given his upbringing in an entirely different cultural context, he also couldn't make sense of the stories I shared with him about people telling me I was pretty . . . "for a Black girl." He just thought I was pretty, period. As we first got to know one another, his comparisons between the marginalization that he and his family experienced as Jews in the Soviet Union and what he saw Black people experiencing in Brooklyn resonated with me. Oddly enough, they made me feel seen. In fact, his historical awareness empowered me to be more open in expressing to him my hidden sexual desires. He was the first man to ever choke me, slap me, cum on my face. The first to call me a slut, tie me up, use me.

I wish I could say that when K chokes me or spanks me or slaps me, I don't see a white man. I see the love of my life, or at least one of them anyway. I see someone who has supported my freedom, autonomy, and self-expression. I see someone who has shown up for me in countless ways, big and small. And while this love and devotion are all well and good, simply leaving our relationship in those simplistic and idealistic terms doesn't quite do justice to the broader history at play here. Our relationship is not a neoliberal, colorblind fantasy, wherein love conquers all. We cannot, as individuals, triumph over our various intersecting identities—my Blackness, his whiteness, my Americanness, his Russianness—solving the historical, structural inequalities of our day. We are simply two people, in different bodies from different parts of the world, deciding to wade through all this history, together.

Part of that, however, is my own reckoning with a quiet but deeply held and multifaceted shame. I can neither deny nor divorce the reality of my partner's whiteness from the visceral pleasure of calling him Daddy whenever we fuck. When we are in the middle of that tender violence, I crave the sting across my face as he crashes into me. I melt into the way he lovingly, yet decisively, wraps his hands around my throat. I revel in his possession of my flesh, cradled in those three sacred words: you. are. mine.

Of course, we negotiate and consent to all these actions. And it is precisely in dialogue that I have expressed to K how the ability to opt into and out of this violence at any point is what gets me wet. It is also the place where I exercise my own agency as a young Black woman who is learning to inhabit the messiness of her desires. History and circumstance have given me the privilege to *choose* to have my ass beat, and fucked, and licked, and worshipped by a white man. In that way, the kind of sex we have is grounded, ironically, in my own empowerment. I am choosing this violence, and it is the choice—the exercise of my own will and volition—that transforms a slap in the face, a degrading name, into a flex of my own power.

In wading through this messiness with K, in playing with gendered sexual agency with D, I revise the story of who I'm supposed to be in the bedroom, one that I had absolutely no hand in drafting myself. As a Black woman, I am cast as the hypersexualized Vixen, an insatiable woman incapable of being sexually violated. It's a trope that runs deep, one of the contradictory pillars of the construction of Black American female sexuality.[2] But in choosing to be a Vixen, a slut, in "asking for it" from multiple partners no less, I center my own pleasure. I take back some of my power.

1. Hall, Stuart. "Cultural Identity and Diaspora." *Identity: Community, Culture, Difference.* Jonathan Rutherford, ed. (Chadwell Heath, UK: Lawrence & Wishant, 1990).

2. Harris-Perry, Melissa. *Sister Citizen: Shame, Stereotypes, and Black Women in America* (New Haven, CT: Yale University Press, 2011).

An SUV Named Desire

Jennifer De Leon

THIS IS WHAT I WANTED: A NEW CAR—AN SUV—
with a sunroof, tan seats, a CD player, windows that rolled up
and down with the tap of a button. I was twenty-two years old,
a recent college graduate, shopping for cars with my immigrant
parents on a hot June afternoon. My mother wore black leather
sandals. My father crossed his arms. I didn't focus on interest
rates or gas mileage; I just knew I'd be responsible for making
the monthly payments, that my parents would lend me their
immaculate credit. That was the plan.

The first car we test-drove was a silver Nissan Pathfinder.
My father shook his head and mumbled his way through the
whole process—the boyish car dealer with sandy blond hair taking my driver's license and making a photocopy of it, returning
with a set of keys and my license. I shut out my parents' voices,
the two of them seated in the surprisingly snug backseat, argu-
ing about how I should instead rent their Toyota Camry. They
spoke in Spanish, as if the car dealer dude couldn't make out
the tone of what they were saying. I refused to let their doubts
seep in. I clutched the steering wheel, checked my lip gloss in
the rearview mirror, and pressed my right foot down on the gas.

Every family has a place on a map, it seems, one where all stories take root, the nesting doll at the center, the source of all
beginnings. For my family, this point is a country in Central

America, a nation the size of the state of Louisiana, a home to generations—all of them—before me. Both my parents and their parents and their parents and their parents and, as far as we know, their parents before them, were born and raised in Guatemala. Even now, I struggle to distill my mother's story into a sentence. My mother fled Guatemala. My mother left for the United States for work opportunities. And my father? He moved from Guatemala to the United States temporarily. My father always wanted to come back home. Unlike my mother, who boarded a one-way flight from Guatemala City to Los Angeles at the age of eighteen, looking to squeeze all the juice from the lime that is the United States of America, my father came to L.A. with the goal of making enough money to buy a new motorcycle, after which he would return home. He was twenty. The two of them met and fell in love. The rest isn't so much history as it is an extension of the map. My father got word of a job in Boston, one that was too good to pass up, so he moved first. They wrote love letters for a year, and eventually my mother boarded another one-way flight, this time to Massachusetts. Boston is where I was born, the suburbs are where my sisters and I grew up. Ours was one of two Latinx families in the entire north side of town (the other family a single mom with five kids, all Jehovah's Witnesses).

I grew up, like many children of immigrants, trying to fit in. I pretended to love peanut butter and Fluff sandwiches; I wasn't a good swimmer. No way was I allowed to sleep over at a friend's house, double-pierce my ears, or talk to boys on the phone. I eventually picked my way through all those locks, and more. But what matters, I think, is this: it was never enough.

As a kid, every meal, movie stub, and TrapperKeeper represented a sacrifice—nothing was taken for granted. Nothing was wasted. We reused yellow margarine tubs before it was the cool thing to do on Earth Day. We hung clothes outside to dry even when snow patches blotched the stiff grass on the side of our house. My grandmother kept plastic on her couches to preserve them for (or perhaps protect them from) all her grandchildren and great-grandchildren. My father worked in a steel-manufacturing factory and my mother as a housekeeper. They urged my sisters and me to study hard, earn good grades, graduate from high school, go to college. To them, it was simple—education was an iron-proof protection plan. If we were educated we could always find work. We would always be able to support ourselves. We wouldn't have to rely on anyone else. Certainly not *a man*. "Go to school so you can get a job where you don't have to work with your hands," my father always said. I am a writer and I work with my hands every day. But I know what he meant.

Still, all I wanted was to be like my friends. Their parents seemed to encourage their innocent crushes. They drove them to the mall to get their noses pierced. They picked them up from the movie theater and gave boyfriends rides home. I couldn't *imagine* my father doing that, ever. I was well into my twenties before I brought a boyfriend home, and even then, my mother referred to him as "el amigo de Jennifer."

Yet when it came to school all bets were off. My parents allowed me to spend entire afternoons at the library, picked me up from after-school clubs, and even drove me to visit college campuses during my junior and senior years of high school. They supported any and every activity or field trip or project that fell under the canopy of "school." After I caught on to this, the road ahead had no limit. Once, my father dropped me off at a classmate's house where a group of us (including boys) would work on an *Othello* presentation. Another time, I even convinced my parents to let me travel to Zimbabwe on a community service trip because it would look good on my college application. When it came time, they let me go to college, extending the map even wider.

After I test-drove the silver Nissan Pathfinder, I was confident this was the car I wanted for-real for real. My mother called me crazy. My father said you should never, *ever* buy a car the same day you test-drive it. The young salesman adjusted his tie, said that this year's models were the way to go, that this was the only silver Pathfinder on the whole East Coast. Dad brought up the used Toyota Camry again. I wanted to scream. Or whine. I knew I shouldn't behave this way. After all, my parents were giving me a down payment of three thousand dollars for my college graduation gift, still about twenty thousand less than I needed. I'd graduated just a month ago and had been living in their house since. I slept in the basement where a blue helium balloon—*Congratulations!*—swayed a little less each day. Inside the box that was college: study abroad in twelve countries, including Vietnam, France, and Nigeria. An internship at the United Nations in Lagos. Another internship at *Ms.* magazine in New York City. Nights of chugging Red Bull vodkas with friends and, during senior week, running half-naked across campus at 4:00 a.m. Writing papers about the globalization of Levi's. Seminars in French. Speaking up in class. Inside the box that is home: you will do as we say.

In the showroom my mom sipped coffee from a Styrofoam cup. We sat on gray plastic chairs, waiting to see if the dealer could get his boss to lower the sticker price on the Pathfinder, while I flipped through a magazine, reading an article about J-Lo. My dad said matter-of-factly, "Well, hopefully when you get a better job you can make higher payments."

"At least they have free coffee," I snapped.

"Free?" My mother stood up. "That cup of coffee is costing you twenty thousand dollars."

My first week in college I met with the financial aid director, who informed me that I needed a work-study job on campus because it was part of my financial aid package. I had a scholarship for the majority of the tuition and room and board, but I needed to make up the difference. In high school I worked a ton (retail, babysitting, offices), but in college, I hadn't planned to earn money. What would I need money for? All meals were included. Most of the college events had cookies or wine or both. My friends and I rarely left campus, and even if we did, we'd take the shuttle van which was free. Work? None of my friends had to work. To add to my anxiety, the woman with short hair and dark suit in the financial aid office told me that all the work-study jobs had been filled (later, I'd realize she meant the good ones—working at the library, checking IDs at the Athletic Center); the only one left was the dining hall. I would need to wear a hair net and a blue apron and serve food in the hot line to my roommate, friends, and classmates, who would hold trays and give me awkward stares. Isn't there another way? I pleaded. No, she said. I'm sorry.

When you grow up in a working-class immigrant household in the United States, there are a certain set of unspoken rules to follow. Don't talk back to your parents in public. Don't act like a spoiled American brat. Be grateful for every last drop of goodness in your life because just one generation ago we suffered beyond your privileged brain's comprehension. And always, these were the phrases they wrapped around us like scarves as we stepped into the outside world: Remember to say please and thank you and clear your plate, and don't ask for seconds. Once we returned home—Shut off the light.

My mother, in particular, was exceptionally thrifty. She could win a gold medal in the category, actually. Clip coupons? Check. Used clothing? Check. Kids eat free on Sundays? Check. But she took it to another level, often lifting free packets of ketchup and mustard at fast food restaurants, taking wads of napkins from Papa Gino's, Dunkin', or McDonald's, and setting them on our brown round kitchen table where they belonged. Friends would come over and we'd set the table with these napkins, never knowing which ones you'd get that particular night. She hemmed our pants, ones she'd bought on sale. She cut our hair in the kitchen after we showered and sat in our pajamas, newspaper on the floor. We didn't spend money on items we could otherwise get for free. Books fell into this category. For a while, the only books in our house were the Yellow Pages and the Bible. Luckily, we lived down the street from the library. Heat in the car was rare. AC was out of the question. At department stores she'd happily accept the free samples while spraying herself with enough perfume to last the entire month. She'd spray us too.

I get it. It's why I worked so hard in high school, why I applied for dozens of scholarships, including one from an Association of Cranberry Country Chamber of Commerce, for which I had to write a 250-word essay about what made me unique. I didn't get that one, but I got others. And so, the day came when my parents dropped me off at Connecticut College, a private liberal arts school where the annual tuition was more than my father made in a year.

"Whoa," my twelve-year-old sister said as we pulled up to the dramatic, winding entrance on move-in day. We emptied our family's blue minivan and lugged boxes and plastic storage bins holding hair elastics, sponges that expanded ten times their size in water, dental floss, batteries, SnackWell's cookies, and enough pairs of socks to last me all four years of college, all the way up the four flights, passing three floors of hormone-heavy boy athletes, to the all-girls floor. When it was time for my family to leave, my mother and I cried. She then rubbed my back like I was seasick and kissed my cheek and handed me a Hallmark card and asked if I was hungry because she did have a Snickers in her purse and hugged me like seventeen more times before my father placed his hand on my shoulder and that meant it was time. They wished me well, told me to behave—Pórtate bien—and drove away. This is the exact moment, perhaps, where my map started to look different from theirs.

Put another way, the doors swung open and, just like that, I had entered Camp Conn. Everyone, it seemed, wore Patagonia. Everywhere I looked I caught flashes of Nalgene water bottles, North Face this, L.L.Bean that, tall blonds, short blonds, a view of the actual ocean, a sundial, green grass for days, hacky sacks, sporty backpacks, Phish concert T-shirts, and Volvos, Land Cruisers, SUVs slowing down for the speedbumps on the campus roadways. The SUVs looked so cool, and I wanted to be inside one, to roll down the windows, to turn up the volume, to open the sunroof and feel like I belonged.

The salesman returned with a smile. I stood up immediately.

"So, we can't move on the price," he said.

Blah blah blah blah.

My father shook his head. At the coffee station, my mother reached for sugar packets.

"No seas tonta," she said. *Don't be silly.* That's the direct translation to English, but in my memory it sounds more like *Don't be an idiot.* They explained that they would let me rent their Camry for the year while I saved up more money. The truth was, if they weren't there to stop me, I would have signed any paper that allowed me to drive off the lot in that silver desire.

In college I met friends who liked rock climbing and caving, who had ski houses and trust funds. Yet in all four years of school, I never could get over the fact that the dining hall served frozen yogurt. I always ate it with a teaspoon instead of a regular-sized spoon so that my sundae would last longer. Even though it was all-you-can-eat.

New words I added to my vocabulary: Choate, Milton, Andover, hummus, Netscape, indigenous, Ritalin, hand-me-down Volvo, blue collar, bluer collar. And later: LSAT, GMAT, GRE, TFA, MBA, MFA, PhD, EdD, MA, 401k, 403b, IRA, and MRS.

I made friends easily. One of the first nights in college, a group of us, freshman girls, hung out in my dorm room, two twin beds on opposite sides propped up on cinder blocks, a long-necked desk lamp with a maroon scarf draped over it, and a white mini refrigerator full of Bud Light cans and a Chipwich I'd taken from the dining hall earlier that night. We cracked up over nothing it seemed, dressed in flannel pajamas, using a Swiss Army knife to cut the Chipwich into fourths. One girl with long brown hair had studied Spanish in high school and traveled to the Dominican Republic her senior year. Her Spanish was better than mine. I went to bed that night staring at my Sark poster, *How to be an Artist*, shimmering in the moonlight coming through the curtainless windows. *Swing high on a swing set. Sing out loud. Laugh every day.*

The following morning at breakfast someone said, "I need money."

I perked up.

"Yeah, I do too," another added.

I was about to chime in, mention my drama with work-study, when the first girl said, "Let's stop at the ATM on the way to class."

I drank my orange juice, stayed silent. Of course, this wasn't what I had meant. I needed money as in a j-o-b. It turned out that even with a generous scholarship and "free" meals in the dining hall, there was still a need for money beyond these items—money for booze, makeup, tampons, late-night curly fries at the campus center. Many of my friends had allowances, bank accounts their families dropped money into each semester or for birthdays or end-of-semester encouragement. Not me.

When the car salesman pressed my father and said, "It's *her* decision, though," I wanted to evaporate. Dad had that look on his face like when I got my eyebrow pierced senior year in high school and he threatened to take it out with a pair of pliers. The salesman kept pushing. "I mean, she's the one buying the car, right?"

"We're leaving," Dad said. "Come on, let's go."

"But—" I began, knowing it was no use.

"Sir, I told you. My manager says we can't move on the price, but we can see about getting you your first oil change on us. Free."

Again, that word.

"Nothing is for free," my father said. "Let's go."

"Sir!" A shift in his tone. What was in it? Annoyance? Frustration? Disgust? I'd heard it. I had. We all had.

I wouldn't serve my friends slimy cod or baked lasagna in the hot food line. Not if I could help it. But I still needed money. So instead, I made a flyer with the words:

LOOKING FOR A FUN, RESPONSIBLE,
BILINGUAL BABYSITTER?
LOOK NO MORE!

I cut even strips at the bottom of the flyer and on each one I listed my name and phone number. I pinned the flyer in the faculty mailroom, and within days I had more work than hours in the day.

In college we had something called the Penny Prom, where we dressed up in cheap-looking prom dresses from the thrift store and had messy hair and smudged makeup, cut holes in our nylons, that sort of thing. It was always so fun. People seemed to really let go. At the time, I didn't realize how fucked up it was. At the time, I drank frothy beer and flirted with boys, before settling on one. I asked him questions, responded to his answers, made sarcastic comments, made him laugh, looked at him, looked away, looked back. Later, in my dorm room, with hot, boozy breath in my face, he said, "Wow. Tell me more about your writing and the UN." Then, with the moonlight outside, and the moonlight inside, while hooking up on my futon, the one that my dad helped lift up the stairs and into my dorm room, the futon that my mom bought for me because it was my senior year, the futon that still had plastic on it because I was waiting for my cousin to bring down the frame in his truck before he left for the army, the beer-breath boy touched the plastic and commented, "Just like at home, right, Jenn?"

Thing is, college has many parts. There's the part where my parents visit for Family Weekend and we meet up for dinner with my new friends and their parents, the part where one mom says to my mom, "What's your car phone number in case we lose each other?" We didn't have a car phone. I don't remember what my mother replied, but we laughed about it on the ride to the restaurant and we had a great time at dinner. There's the part where I pulled my first all-nighter during finals week freshman year and I felt so proud in the 5:00 a.m. blue light, before looking out the window and spotting the shadows of the maintenance crew and dining hall cooks clocking into work. There's the part when, senior year, my parents dropped me off on campus for the last time. I sat, squeezed between them, in the front seat of my dad's black pickup truck (not exactly a stand-in for a motorcycle, but close enough). I'll connect this image to the one where they walked me down the aisle at my wedding in Guatemala many years later. But that afternoon, when the earth still burned with the leftover heat of the late August day, we inched our way up the dramatic curved entrance off Route 32, across the bridge. We waved to the guard in a pale blue uniform and smiled.

Then there's the part that spring at the senior scholarship recognition luncheon, when I mistakenly used the dessert spoon for the soup and the soup spoon for the dessert. The mayor of New London sat on my right. To my left another man, maybe eighty years old. He was telling me that he went to Princeton and then Harvard Law School and became an investment-banking lawyer. He wrote a few books. His most successful ones were on Turtle Bay and Greenwich Village. I told him I wanted to be a writer too. On stage, various alumni talked about what their scholarships have meant to them. One woman, a chief of police in New

York City, spoke about how her mother scrounged up enough money to buy her two fancy sweaters so she would fit in with the Connecticut College girls. I thought of my mother. I could practically hear her adjusting hangers as they scraped the sales racks at T.J. Maxx. My mother, who never had the opportunity to attend college. The president then quoted a scholarship donor: "I wanted to send the elevator down to let someone else come up." People applauded. The waiter removed my white plate. After the lunch, a few professors congratulated me on my upcoming job as a congressional aide, saying things like "good entry-level position" and "foundation for your career." I believed them, because why wouldn't I?

Is striving for more as simple as taking two pieces of wood and rubbing them together in hopes of sparking a fire, of making light? To what end? What happens when it burns? My parents moved countries, states, and neighborhoods along the way, never mind language, class, and culture. I know this *now*, but at the time, I was blinded by the flash of the silver. Were we so different? My father came to the United States with a desire for a new motorcycle that he'd ride home to Guatemala. Instead, he stayed in America. My mother, in all her ketchup-packet collecting, yearned for more, more, more. I am their daughter.

I picture them, standing beneath the white tent on campus where the dean hosted a strawberries and champagne reception for parents of graduating seniors. I imagine their side conversations at the event, or perhaps on their drive home (with a stop at Foxwoods Casino, always). What did they say? Look at our daughter, nuestra hija. Or, The champagne was good. I think of how their suggestion for me to rent their Toyota Camry was not a consolation prize, a B side, a second choice, but instead a smart, practical, but still big deal offer in their eyes. Of course, it was. No one had offered *them* such a deal. I was too immature to see it. I want to say sorry to them then, and now. But yeah, in that moment I was blinded by the silver, and it wasn't the car itself but rather the illusion that I would *ever* fit in. Back then

I still thought I could gain a sense of belonging as if reaching for a mug on a shelf. What I didn't yet grasp was the realization that this sense of belonging needed to come from within. And it would take years—and many miles trekked on my own map—for me to believe it.

In the meantime, I did rent their Camry for the year. I paid insurance too. The following June, I bought a green Ford Escape (2002 with a sunroof and tan seats). It was a middle ground, you could say. My father still felt that my car payments were too high, but he agreed to cosign the deal. Maybe it was the part of him that remembered what it was like to want a motorcycle. And maybe it was the part of me that wanted to be like both my parents when I decided to leave everything I knew and move thousands of miles away. That following year, I left my current job (my "good entry-level position"), and drove out west to California to teach. Often, I'd call my mom on my cell phone (silver) while driving on the 101 or 280. My mother who, for years, had secretly collected square napkins imprinted with the college's navy-blue seal and used them to construct table centerpieces at my graduation party that felt more like a wedding. When I called, even though it was three hours later in Boston, she always picked up.

I would own that Ford for ten years and put over one hundred thousand miles on it. Miles spent driving to work as a teacher, to graduate school, on dates, on road trips up and down the West Coast and across the country, to writing colonies, and later, to the hospital to get ultrasounds of my firstborn. I remember the day the speedometer hit the number exactly. I was driving on a country road in northern Vermont in early spring while on my way to a writing residency with my now-husband. We pulled over and I stepped out of the car, circled it a few times, squinted underneath the bright sky, and stared east, then west. Or maybe, it was north, and south. I whispered *thank you* before I climbed back in the car and kept going.

Being a Dad Means Respecting the Yard

Kristen Arnett

I AM AN UNABASHED LOVER OF BACKYARDS.

Getting in some good yard work on a weekend afternoon and then sitting down in that neatly ordered backyard, sipping from a sweaty can of beer, has always been one of my favorite activities.

Part of that love has to do with the fact that I grew up outside. My brother and I were often foisted from the house by our mother during the summer, and when it's hot in Florida, you learn how to entertain yourself or else sweat to death in abject misery. All this to say: we found things to do.

Being in a backyard means discovering the smaller, more intimate parts of your world. There are the plants, sure, but there are also the birds and bugs and furred creatures that live inside that greenery. Discoveries could be painful—wasp stings or fire ant bites or even unknowingly tromping through a bed of nettles—but they could also be awe-inspiring: Holding still long enough to allow a hummingbird sipping delicately from a broken bloom to hover near your face. Pill bugs tucked into palms, unfurling and rolling, the armadillos of the insect world. Squirrels poised midleap on a moss-laden oak branch, cheeks full of pilfered fruit. All this encapsulated in the wild wreck of a backyard afternoon.

But the maintenance of a yard. That's another thing entirely.

Growing up, I wasn't asked to help with any of it. On Saturday afternoons, I was expected to clean. My sister and I had indoor duties. We scrubbed the bathroom and washed the dishes. We dusted the house and swept the terrazzo floors. There was vacuuming. There was laundry. My brother, however, was exempt from these chores—it was his job to help handle the lawn. *Handle* is the critical word here; lawns are managed, organized, subdued. While my sister and I swiped down kitchen counters, my brother was outside in his dirty clothes and yard shoes, helping mow the lawn in careful, precise stripes—"Overlapping," my father would say, "they need to overlap so you don't miss any grass"—while my father went around with the weed whacker and handled any creeping edges.

Living in Florida means that because of the heat and the rain, you need to mow your lawn at least once a week. Wait two weeks and your mower might short out in all the damp from the grass. So on Saturdays, while my sister and I buffed and shined and cleaned inside, they'd be out there, trying to hack the Florida out of the place.

As an adult in Florida, I've cared for many lawns. I've gotten up early on the weekend and yanked out the lawn mower and thrown on my dirtiest pair of sneakers. I've used the leaf blower to get rid of the dead oak leaves and twigs and hunks of Spanish moss that lined my back patio and driveway. I've also hacked away at a spiny bougainvillea with a pair of trimmers, avoiding the thorns as best I could but still coming away with quite a few slices. Part of navigating the backyard is the understanding that plants have defense mechanisms. Sometimes that means bloodshed.

Handling a yard is sweaty, tough business. It's humid and sunburned and thankless. At the end of the day, what you've managed to accomplish doesn't last longer than a week. There is something fascinating about that, I think—yard maintenance is inherently impermanent. Dads who maintain lawns are weekend warriors, brave souls coated in sweat and sprayed by dirt spit up from the back end of a mower. Your clothes are filthy and you stink. Hands calloused from piloting all those bucking, wild tools necessary for cultivation. You yank the pull cord on the mower and pray that the engine turns over. Carefully guide it along the scalloped edges of sod, hoping you got all the debris beforehand so the blades won't shoot a piece of sharpened stick directly at your shin.

There are dozens of ant piles. Hordes of stinging insects ze-roing in on the sunburned skin of your neck. All this at the end of a long afternoon, and you're just going to have to head back out and do it all again the following weekend. But there is some-thing affirming about the exhaustion that comes from hacking a semblance of order into a yard. You treat yourself to an icy-cold beer afterward and survey the damage. You've fought hard and long, and you've fought well. There is a sense of dad-like satisfaction that comes from looking at the work you've done to maintain your household, even knowing those diminished weeds will creep back again after the next summer storm. To be a dad often means contending with nature so your family doesn't have to. Dads are the first line of defense against an encroaching landscape. They are the barrier between wilderness and family.

But, wildness aside, lately I've been more interested in the tenderness of yard care. Part of this has to do with how I want to grow as a person. It's easy enough to hack away at the vul-nerable parts of myself, but it's much harder to treat them with sweetness. I want to explore how being a dad has more to do with thoughtfulness than with severity. As a child, I watched my grandfather care for the flowers that my grandmother loved best. He was painstaking with the rose bushes. Thoughtfully trimmed the crepe myrtle in the winter months so it could grow fuller and lusher in the spring. He hung a swing for us from the branches on an enormous live oak, careful not to mar any part of the beloved tree in the process. He harvested fruit from the loquat out back and showed us how to snag our own without breaking any branches.

In much of Dad Culture, we're sold the notion that dealing with nature requires battle; the yard is portrayed as a nemesis or a foe. But I like to think that with what we know about climate change and invasive species, in order to best execute living in the greenery, dealing with yards requires respect. Not the striking of a tool against the sod in order to break it, but rather offering a gentle hand that attempts to nourish it. Flowering plants and flower beds are traditionally not in the father's purview, unlike how we view cutting grass and weed whacking, but I'd like to reiterate that all these plants grow together in the yard. Everything twines up, tangled in the vinery. If we are protecting our homes by clearing the yard of debris and weeds, then doesn't that act of protection mean we are effectively nurturing and caring for our homes as well?

Though I originally considered mowing as a Saturday chore that engaged my muscles and physical body, as I worked on my first novel I began to view lawn mowing as a meditative process. As I dragged myself out of bed and lumbered outside to yank awake the engine, I let my mind wander. I walked back and forth, carefully lining up the tracks so I didn't miss any spots, and thought about the shape of things other than the grass. It was hot, nasty work, but it was also contemplative. The shriek of children playing in a nearby yard, lizards scurrying to the safety of the trees, ants lazily circling the carcass of a slain beetle. I wondered about myself and my work and how I fit into the world around me. For many dads, lawn care essentially means alone time. It's just you and the mower, moths battering your ankles as you trudge through piles of damp grass.

Over the past year, I moved from my lifelong home in Orlando to a new spot in Miami. The air is swampier here than it would be in Central Florida or the Panhandle or even near the Gulf. The homes are Mediterranean in design instead of one-story stucco ranches. The plants are different too. When my girlfriend and I moved into our apartment, I knew she wanted us to collect some plants for our new home. I agreed; I wanted to live in a place that reflected the wildness of my childhood backyard. We joked that it would be a good time to go to Lowe's, a very lesbian thing to do, but as soon as I got there, I found myself stunned by the variety on display. There were a bevy of plants to choose from: bromeliads and citrus trees and succulents. Tools to collect for the work, like gardening gloves, potting soil, and drainage trays. Though I love the outdoors, I assumed that my girlfriend would wind up caring for this new assortment of greenery. She's always kept plants in pots. That's not the way I've ever experienced vegetation. So much of the Central Florida yard experience is existing in the world that grows around you, despite the way you might try and hack it down.

But once we got those plants potted and set around our new place, I discovered a whole new understanding of care. Unlike the backyards I'd tangled with, opponents I'd battled, these plants required nurturing. They would not grow regardless of my treatment. I had to listen to them. What did they need from me? Water more, water less? More sun or partly shade? I spent weeks struggling to listen when previously so much of my time had been spent fighting. Part of how I think about myself as a dad is how I take care of other people, but it's also in how I care for the living world around me. It requires patience. As a dad who moves through life impulsively, quite often making decisions based on gut instinct, it's a continued struggle to remember that most things in life require time. The world wasn't built in a day, and neither was the potted plant that struggles to find the right amount of sun and shade out on my patio. It doesn't know what it's doing yet, and, frankly, neither do I.

We've been taught that our yards have to look certain ways. They're supposed to be manicured and neat. Trimmed into some semblance of order. Traditional sod lawns require lots of watering and aren't great for the environment. Invasive plants are brought in because people like the way they look. They don't consider the fact that sometimes those beautiful green things kill off the native plants, exterminating populations of bees and birds and butterflies and subsequently devastating entire species of flowers and trees. It's entirely possible that the concept of what makes a "yard" needs its own careful pruning.

The grass will always grow back. The weeds will sprout. The dead tree limbs might need trimming. Plants have belonged in the yard long before we came along with the lawnmower to run them over. I can carve out a space for myself, but there is also room to be respectful of what a lawn needs in order to thrive. Allowing it to grow in the way that works best. To be a good dad, I need to treat it respectfully, not hack it away at the roots.

Not everyone has a lawn or even wants one. What constitutes caring for greenery can be as little as watering a potted succulent. It's all in how you care for things.

We can grow together.

See What You Do to Me

TaraShea Nesbit

SHE HAD BUCK TEETH BUT A LITHE BODY, SMOOTH skin, and I know, from the one glorious time she took her bra off in front of me, breasts as upright and curved as two new bowls. Never did I want to touch something more. She was fourteen and I was twelve. Her hair was the color of a field mouse, cut at her shoulders, shiny and straight, and flipped up naturally at the ends. We lived in the Beaver Ridge Run apartment complex, in a lower-middle-class suburb built in the sixties, before the General Motors plant closed, before the National Cash Register Corporation left.

Sara and I both had younger siblings to watch while our parents worked, both of us responsible daughters. Her parents worked at the factories near our town: a tin factory, a paint factory, then a cannery. Always working and away, it seemed, except on Friday evenings, when they had a large dinner with all the children and a family friend or two. That was the only time I saw her mother, Bernadette, smile, at Richard, her friend, who teased Sara's youngest sibling, still in diapers, and swooped the child in his arms.

Richard was thirty-six and worked at a barbershop in town. His wife was only twenty-one, and together they had two daughters, three-year-old twins. When I met them, they were both wearing immaculate white sundresses. Richard winked to the children, who loved him, or at least loved the attention. He had found himself a perfect family.

My own mother worked twelve-hour shifts as a respiratory therapist in the neonatal intensive-care unit. She was newly divorced from my stepfather. My father lived on the other side of town, a beauty salesman with a budding clandestine side business of which I knew very little, except that he worked nights. Family friends were not part of our meals.

When we were not at the park with our siblings, we were at Sara's house, with its menagerie of animals and children, which gave the house its particular smell of cat, gerbil, and toddler shit. On Sunday mornings Sara would put two quarters in the newspaper dispenser at the 7-Eleven and take all the papers but one, to change the gerbil's cages.

Why leave one? I asked.

So it doesn't look suspicious.

No one ever needed to remind her to do anything, such as chores around the house. She mothered while her mother worked. Both of our mothers would be grandmothers by forty. We played all day during the winter break and weekends and summer, and then we went straight home and called. In our nearly identical homes—same Formica, same dull carpet, same beige walls—I could imagine her, phone cord looping from the bar in the kitchen and back to the bedroom she shared with her sister. I took the phone to my bedroom, and we spoke the inconsequential conversation of girls until one of our mothers yelled for us to get off the phone. Someone important could be trying to call, they would say. We only pushed the limits when we were certain we would not be caught. We were good, responsible daughters. Until that year.

Richard asked Sara to babysit his twin daughters. After she put the girls to bed, Sara always called me. But one night, she didn't.

What happened? I asked the next day, as we walked our siblings to the park, shouting their names, telling them to stop at the end of the sidewalk.

When he dropped me off . . .

Richard returned her to the apartment complex, but he

parked a block away. He cut the lights. He talked to her, told her how much he cared for her. He took her hand. He kissed it. He asked her if she liked it. She smiled. Then he kissed her on the lips. She was fourteen.

I listened to her confession, to what kissing felt like, how he said he could dream in color, how he could make his dreams go where he wanted them to. How she promised she would not tell anyone about them. He'd been in jail in Kentucky, Sara told me, but she did not know why, or didn't want to tell me. He had been married before.

Sara walked with the lightness of a girl in love.

He's married, I said.

But she opposed me so adamantly—as if I did not understand love, as if I were a child—that I knew if I continued criticizing him I would lose her.

We love one another, she said, and I sort of believed her.

With each week's progress, Sara moved further away from me. As Richard inched into Sara's life and body, I shrunk to the size of the sixth grader I was. At the beginning of the summer, Sara's parents moved out of the apartment complex and into a vinyl-sided house on the corner of the main street leading into east Dayton. The streets were narrow and potholed. The schools were ranked low.

I asked to visit her. Both of my parents, separately, said no. It was the only decision I recall that they had agreed on since their separation ten years prior.

I finished elementary school with an honor-roll ribbon and a yearbook with multiple entries of *Keep smiling* or *Smile more*. In the fall I would begin seventh grade, and because of where my father bought a house, I could choose between two junior high schools: the junior high on the wealthier west side of town, where parents, I heard, were mostly doctors and lawyers, or the school on the east side of town, which I knew better, where parents worked the assembly lines, maintenance, medical technicians, and food service.

I kept asking to visit Sara in Dayton. After many nos and much complaining on my part, my parents finally let me go. My mother dropped me off. I wore cut-off jeans and a T-shirt as Sara and I walked the neighborhood. I wasn't wearing anything revealing, but trucks honked at us, men whistled from their porches, and at the post office, one gray-bearded man turned in line to look us up and down. The attention was striking. Men stared directly, gawked.

Where were Sara's parents? Gone. Who knows.

It is violent here, I thought, hearing the car alarms, imagining all the robberies that must be taking place, not realizing how easy it was for an alarm to be triggered.

In the street, wondering which car got robbed, I met a neighbor boy, Jason. He was sweet, but I took my cues about how to talk to members of the opposite sex from what was around me: my mother's self-help books, like *Men Are from Mars, Women Are from Venus*, and the men on the morning talk show on Z-93, who paid a woman five hundred dollars to drive to work topless. I saw a picture of her later in the news from the shoulders up.

I asked Jason about the size of his dick. I had never asked anyone this before, but I was in a new city and trying out boldness.

But how many inches is it?

He demurred.

Go measure.

He demurred. I pressed, I pressed.

His mother's calls for him grew louder and more urgent. *I really have to go*, he said.

Back inside, he called me on the phone.

Soft or hard? he whispered.

I didn't know what he meant so I covered the receiver and said to Sara, *He said, "Soft or hard?"*

Sara just shook her head.

That night at her house, we slept in Sara's twin-sized bed,

but I did not sleep. I do not think we spoke of Richard, not because they were no longer involved, but rather because they were so involved that her alliances had shifted. She was keeping the secret she initially promised she would keep.

I had not been kissed or touched in a sexual way, with only a few exceptions. My stepfather had a swastika tattoo on his right arm and a nose broken so many times—at least once by his own father—that it swooped to the right side when looked at straight on. He used his belt on my toddler brothers' backsides, and once broke the skin until it bled.

When I was nine I kissed him goodbye and slipped my tongue into his mouth like I had seen my mother do.

He stiffened and pulled back. *We don't do that, Sissy.*

This can be our special kiss, he said, and instead rubbed my nose to his.

He nearly drowned my mother once in a river in Kentucky, but he did not want my tongue in his mouth. Sometimes what men did not do was more startling than what they did.

When my mother found out she said, *Who taught you that? Who? Tell me*, the way a mother does when she herself has been molested. But what my mother could not keep me from was my own stubborn wish to have something for myself, my curiosity for knowledge in all forms, for taking whatever was offered, for wanting more.

I turned thirteen in late July. My mother got call waiting. Sara and I spoke less and less. I turned to other friends from the complex, swam at the pool, watched television. But when my mother worked I was not allowed to leave the house, though my brothers, diagnosed as hyperactive, could play outside. My mother was terrified something would happen to me, an unchaperoned girl wearing her first bra.

One afternoon while my brothers were outside and my mother was still at work, I reached Sara on the phone.

What are you doing? I asked.

Douching.

She said it like a secret.

What is that? Why?

I'm babysitting tonight.

She said Richard had a plan to leave his wife out and come back home early. I told her it was unsafe to use her mother's douche.

You could get an infection.

I did not have actual knowledge of this as a fact, it just seemed like it could be true, and something in her voice scared me.

In her silence, I saw a shrug, and I began to worry about Sara.

A few weeks later, Sara was babysitting again. She asked me to call at 8.30 p.m. But this time, Richard answered the phone.

I hung up.

Then my own phone rang.

Hello? I said, scared and thrilled.

Who is this? Richard asked. His voice so deep.

I paused. He asked again. I told him I was Sara's friend.

Is Sara there? I asked.

She is home already. And what are you doing calling my house?

I apologized. I told him sometimes we talked after the girls went to bed.

So when I'm paying her to play with my children she's talking on the phone to you?

I paused and apologized again and said it wasn't like that.

Is anyone at your house? he asked.

My mother had to wake at 5:00 a.m. to have enough time to shower, get the boys ready for day care, drop them off, and drive into Dayton to be at the hospital by the start of her 7:00 a.m. shift.

Asleep, I said.

So, what do Sara and I do together? he asked me.

Oh, how I knew, how I thought I knew everything. And how I had sworn to complete secrecy.

She's your babysitter? I said.

The uptick in my voice, the question, gave him a chuckle.

Hang on a minute, he said. I heard a screen door creak open. He was stepping outside. He wanted to talk to me.

He would call me at ten, after everyone had gone to bed. Since we now had call waiting, I called Time and Temperature at 9:59 p.m. and stayed on the phone, listening to the weather and the time, the forecast and the time, again and again until the phone beeped. Then I settled into my bed and talked about my day. I complained about my mother, my nosy brothers, my homework, my friends. Because he was outside my family and not someone who would gossip about me at school I told him everything I hated and longed for. I told him so much, unconscious of how he would use that information: overworked mother, absent father, lonely thirteen-year-old girl who can't leave the house because of her mother's fear. I was looking for wisdom. He was assessing how much of a risk I was, how likely I was to tell people what we might do, how easily I could become a victim.

After a few evening calls, our conversations veered into all the things he would like to do to me. In response to his questions, I lied and said yes, I was touching my body.

One night he asked, *Could you sneak out?*

Yeah, I said, trying on a casual voice.

Meet me next to the building behind yours.

I checked my hair and clothes. There was nothing to be done. I put a stick of gum in my mouth. I climbed on my bed, slid the window open, and scooted away from the air conditioning and walked out into the warm summer air. Crickets, cicadas, lightning bugs, and the joy of real air, not the closed windows of our apartment.

I turned the corner and there he was, the man I'd been talking to in secret for weeks, reaching into the passenger side of a beat-up blue Honda, opening the door for me. While my mother was asleep and my father was across town arranging business deals, I was getting into a Honda Civic owned by a man older than my father. Richard took my hand. He told me how nice it was to see me, to talk in person. Ten minutes passed this way. He put his lips to mine.

Then he looked over at me with a serious expression and said, *Don't do this with anyone else.*

I laughed.

You could get really hurt. There are bad people out there.

I interpreted this as proof that he was someone who could get jealous, proof that he cared for me. I did not ask him about Sara, but he spoke of her a few times. He felt, I think, a fondness for her that he thought of as love. I hoped she was not still babysitting for him, that she had moved on. When we last spoke she had told me of a new man ten years older than her, who I just had to meet. I did meet him, the one time I skipped school. He took us to the Air Force Museum and fingered her in the stars and planets exhibit. She was kind enough to tell me what fingering was without making it seem like I did not know.

I snuck back into my bedroom. I was freer than before, I thought. I had something that was mine. The luminous idea of a secret.

That night when he got home, he called.

I had such a nice time with you. I hope I dream of you, he said. I fell asleep replaying the sensations his touches gave me.

A week later, I started junior high at the west side, wealthier school. My mother left the house in the dark and dropped my brothers off at day care. I told Richard to look out for her red Buick with the My Child Is an Honor Student at Beaver Ridge Elementary School bumper sticker on it. I'd put that sticker on her car the day it came home from school with me, much to her chagrin. I told him where she parked, her assigned parking spot in front of our house. If her car was gone, so was she. I was doing the one thing my mother had tried to warn me about.

Early on a Friday morning, my first week in seventh grade, Richard knocked on my door, so lightly I thought I might have imagined it. I felt a tingling throughout my body.

I opened the door.

He whispered, *Is anyone here?*

He asked if I was sure. He asked with real fear, as if he had been caught before. I registered this as paranoia and laughed. He stared hard at me.

I answered loudly, *No. Of course not, come in.*

Lock the door, he said.

No one is going to come in. He stared at me.

I locked the door.

He raised his eyebrows at the top lock.

I locked the deadbolt too.

———

He was short, eye-level with me. With the doors locked twice, he kissed me. I smelled coffee, the cheap kind that comes in a can. He kissed my neck, then ran his tongue along it, up to my earlobe, breathing warm air and soft kisses into my ear. I wanted to match his skill, but this was my first real kiss. How should my lips be, my mouth? Where should my hands go? They hung down at my side.

See what you do to me? he said and moved my right hand down past his belt, to the zipper of his soft Dickies work pants. I felt a hard bump.

See what you do to me, he said again.

There was allure, confusion, and fear. I was an irresistible temptation.

But I pulled my hand away. He had crow's feet and a weathered face, which made me feel superior.

Do you know what this is? he asked and put my hand back to his cock. *It's how much you excite me.*

He kissed me urgently again and led me toward the couch, then asked, *Where is your bedroom?*

I walked backward, kissing him, leading him to my bedroom.

Gone was the brass daybed my mother bought me one summer when I was six and we lived in Florida. On my last birthday, I got a full-size mattress and box spring on the floor, and on it was my first bedspread, reversible: one side was navy, one side was white with navy stripes.

He moved his hands up my shirt and with one motion unhooked my first bra. He asked, afterward, if this was okay. I nodded.

He said, *Say it.*

I said, *This is okay.*

We kissed. He cupped my breasts and I touched the outside of his pants until seven fifteen. At seven fifteen he drove me to school in a rusted ivory pickup. He parked a block away. We must have looked like father and child. He was twenty-four years older than me.

Then he drove himself to the barbershop where he worked, three blocks from the school.

By day, Richard cut hair. In the evening, he drove his rusted truck to a wooden house in south Dayton. In the morning, before work, he came to my apartment.

He told me about his disgust at the women who walked by the barbershop in heels and wearing lipstick on their way to the bagel shop.

What's wrong with heels? I asked.

That clackety-clack-clack, he said. In winter it was not practical.

I did not like it when he spoke of adult women this way,

even though I liked that he didn't admire them. But what would he think of me when I had grown up?

I changed the subject and asked what his favorite music was.

Traditional country, he said, *like Lee Greenwood*, so I ordered Lee Greenwood's greatest hits from the BMG Music Club.

On his second visit, he put his finger in my vagina. I held my breath and stiffened, preparing for more pain.

Is this okay? he said and put my hand on his cock. *See what you do to me.*

It was a molehill, but I was doing something to him, so I focused there instead, on my ability to create excitement in him rather than the monotonous in and out of his finger.

You are so tight, he said, and I apologized. He smiled and kissed me more urgently.

We heard a sound from the apartment upstairs. He stopped, shifted, looked toward the door.

What was that? he asked.

I told him it was the neighbor. I told him to relax. I reminded him it was a garden-level apartment, easy to climb out if my mother came home.

Had someone else invited me to sneak out of my house and meet them, had they been vetted by a friend, as Sara had vetted Richard, I would have met them too. I had a boyfriend now, a sweet boy who was in eighth grade, nicknamed Oregano Joe because he once tried to sell oregano as marijuana. I spoke to him on the phone briefly most evenings, but inwardly I groaned each time he called—how unwise and infantile peer conversations seemed. Twice we had gone to the movies. His affable stepfather picked me up in a conversion van with airbrushed beach scenes on the side panels and drove us, as we held hands secretly in the back seat, to the Dollar Movie Theater. I mentioned the boyfriend to Richard, hoping he would be jealous. He said it was good for me to be with boys my age, which made me feel like a baby.

When, on the next visit, Richard slipped a second finger into my vagina I thought, *I do not like this*. I thought, *This is what he did with her*, and I felt closer to my friend, Sara, in one way, and further away from her than ever.

The clitoris was a discovery I had already made. Richard moved one finger, and then two, in and out of my vagina as if his fingers were a toilet brush. In the background, Lee Greenwood sang how proud he was to be American.

Richard would have been a better pedophile had he known how to warm a female body up.

And yet, I was lured by my desire for knowledge. What were the bounds of physical sensation? What could another person do to me? I had a school boyfriend, but I knew that I could not explore these things with a school boyfriend. A school boyfriend would tell people. Going beyond kissing with a school boyfriend would get you labeled a slut.

One morning when Richard was over, the phone rang. We were in my bedroom. Richard made for the window.

Just wait, I said, coolly.

Hello?

What's wrong with you? my mother said.

Nothing, I said, trying to readjust my voice.

Richard moved in to me and kissed my neck. So close to my mother's voice. I pushed him away.

She reminded me to unload the dishwasher and turn down the Crockpot before I left for school.

I said okay. She was my mother then. Perhaps sensing something was off, that afternoon she surprised me by coming home early. I was drinking hot chocolate and doing homework when she came in with my brothers.

On his next visit, he led me back to my bedroom and lay me down on the striped side of my reversible bedspread. We kissed until the sun made a harsh morning light that showed his wrinkles and his buck teeth. Richard pulled down his pants. He pulled down his white underwear. I saw his scarred, crooked, thick penis, the first one I had ever seen. He pulled the skin back to appear larger but came across instead as insecure.

Look what you do to me.

I smiled. This was supposed to be empowerment. But empowerment was telling him no again and again, empowerment— as I thought of it then, though I did not know the word—was the books I read and the movies I watched: Maya Angelou's "Phenomenal Woman" read by Janet Jackson in *Poetic Justice*. Empowerment was a man looking at you—every curve—and you declining.

He approached my face with his cock.

I turned my head away.

Let me lay it next to you, he said.

He put his upright cock against my cotton panties, the tip lying on my stomach, and looked at me as if I would not be able to resist this alluring thing so close to my body.

He asked me to take off my panties.

I just want to lay it next to you, he said.

I squeaked out a no.

Instead, he slid his cock through the leg hole of my panties. I could feel it up my leg and between the lips of my vagina. I'd been warned in health class of how easily one could get pregnant. Our bodies were constricted by my underwear. He moved in a bobbing motion, the shaft of his penis rubbing against my skin. My mother birthed me at seventeen. I was panicky with thoughts of pregnancy. He leaned in and kissed me with his stubbly face.

His body held no allure. The only desire he offered was being desired.

He slid his cock out of my panties and climbed off me, his pants around his ankles. He got on his knees and pulled me to him. My bra was askew. One breast flopped out and the other was beneath the thinly padded lace and polyester.

Just kiss it, he said, and moved my shoulders downward.

I turned my mouth away.

No, thank you, I said, as if he were a friend's grandmother offering candies.

Don't you want to? he said. And then that refrain, *See what you do to me?*

Yes, I thought, this attracts you. Now tease me to the point of extreme anticipation, give my body warmth and tingling, show me what it feels like with another person. But he never did.

Come here, he said.

When I did, he pushed my head downward.

Try it, he said, the most forceful he had been. He shoved my mouth onto his cock.

His cock was in my mouth and because of his force, I gagged.

I lifted my head up.

He apologized, but with happiness.

I sat away from him and fixed my bra.

Have you had your period yet?

I had, two years prior, at Sara's house. She had shown me how to insert a tampon. I confirmed I had started my period but left out the other details.

He frowned. Then he sighed.

We should get you to school, he said.

That was the last time I saw Richard in my mother's apartment. We both knew this was not leading anywhere. I would never consent to *Just kiss it* or *Let me lay it next to you*. None of it was interesting beyond what I had gleaned in those few months of heavy petting. He stopped calling. So did I.

Why didn't I tell anyone? And why did I pursue my best friend's pedophile? The lure of knowledge was greater than loyalty. I did not feel powerless, but powerful. It was I who was desired. I did not speak because I did not want to see the disappointment on my parents' faces. Richard told me he could read people's thoughts and visit their dreams. He told me this, obviously, to try to contain me, to ensure our secret was not out. I let him believe that I believed him.

But I tested him. *Oh yeah? What am I thinking right now?* I said. He said something about fear and excitement and that I desired him.

Nope, I said.

What then?

I was thinking about an elephant.

I was thinking about an elephant. I already knew it as a thing one can't not imagine when asked to, something I'd learned in health class.

But he just said, *Huh?*

He never said he loved me. Confessing love would be the strongest tool for girls like us. I hoped for it, not because I loved him, but because I always wanted the ultimate.

A year later Richard and Sara were distant childhood memories. But then, Sara called.

For you, my father said. I picked up my bedroom phone.

How could you? she said.

I said nothing.

Why did you do it? she asked. *Why did you?*

In her voice were rage and betrayal, but not disbelief. She saw my disloyalty—to my social class, to my neighborhood, to my family, to my friends. The disloyalty that would later enable me to separate emotionally from them, leave them, leave Ohio.

I did not speak. She hung up.

When I called her back to apologize, her younger sister answered. She said Sara was not there. *She says never call her again.*

Soon after, my father suspected I was getting into trouble, so he read my diary. In it, I had written down everything I had done with Richard. He called the police. They photocopied every page and called me in.

A white man of about forty-five asked the questions. *What did you do with Richard?*

We sat on a bench, I said.

Where? he asked.

The park. The park by my house.

What did you do together? he asked again.

Talked.

He gave me a skeptical look.

Had he been a woman, I might have said more. A woman would have seen through me in a way that would compel me to want to explain.

I saw I would have to confess something, to give him something. But I'd watched detective shows. I knew it was quite possible that my father was behind those mirrored walls. I thought of him, his disappointment and his belief in my ability to, as he said, *achieve anything you want.* How he wanted me to finish college, as he had not. How he wanted me to make money, legally. I thought of how I had disappointed him in wanting something so lascivious, so base, so vile, with someone so ordinary, or, rather, so perverse.

We kissed, I said to the investigator.

You kissed?

Yes.

How often?

Once.

Once? he said, eyebrows arched.

Once. I repeated, and repeated, *We sat on a bench and kissed once.*

What else?

Nothing.

This went on for several minutes.

When I started to cry, he pressed me more. I stuck to my story.

He stepped out of the room, came back, and said, *Okay. You can go.*

I was protecting Richard, saving him from jail time, but that was not my intention. My intention was to protect myself, to not to have to go back on my word. If I told a lie, I stuck to it. I thought it was the only way.

For months, my father called the police again and again to check the status of the case. I listened in on the other phone. The detective said, *She says it was a single kiss. I can't make a case on that.*

Another year or two went by. I was nearing the end of high school. I got a job at Discovery Zone, an indoor playground at the mall, as a birthday-party hostess. When there weren't birthdays, I ran concession. One quiet Wednesday afternoon they came in. Richard ordered pizza and soda from another person working concession. Sara held the hands of his two children. I did not look at her directly. I had a blue Discovery Zone baseball cap on and imagined that from this "disguise" she would not recognize me. *Should I say hello?* I wondered. I felt dread, and the recognition of what I had done came back as shame. We acted like we did not know one another. Did I think she would not remember me? I wondered if she was pregnant. To speak to her would be to acknowledge what I had done, when all I wanted was for the action to go away. I hid in the kitchen, dunking dirty plates into the sink. I hid until it was time to host another party, and when I emerged, Sara, Richard and the two daughters were gone.

Recently, I took a job at a university an hour from the apartment complex I grew up in. Now that I am a mother and professor, sometimes working with young women from the neighborhoods I know from childhood, Richard's story is acutely on my mind. How many threats are out there for my daughter and for my students? I visit the Ohio legislature website to learn the statute of limitations. Could I help stop one pedophile?

The Ohio Special Statute of Limitations for Childhood Sexual Abuse, effective August 3, 2006, limits survivors' ability to report and prosecute a perpetrator to twelve years. I am thirty-six. Richard entered my mother's apartment twenty-three years ago. It took me twenty-three years to understand I was not culpable for opening the door to my mother's house, to see beyond myself to what a threat he posed to others. When the Ohio statute had run out, I was in Denver, getting a PhD, at ease with my queerness, writing stories, hiking mountains with friends, mourning aspects of my family and relationships, but not thinking about Richard. All that time, he was in Ohio, raising daughters. Did Richard note the passing years and breathe more easily? Or was there always a twelve-year clock, always a girl or two? Is there now? I can drive by the barber shop and still see Richard standing there, cutting hair, and this enrages me. I do not remember Sara's last name. Though I look for her, wondering if I'll see her when I visit Dayton, the friend I desired and the friend I betrayed is lost to me. What happened to *her* is what I want to know most.

My partner and I read picture books to our three-year-old daughter about winter approaching. In one, the female narrator says that the rabbits in the forest are alert because danger is out there everywhere.

What is danger? our daughter asks.

We fumble to find the words to describe this to her without scaring her so much that she will not sleep through the night.

Recently, before she began preschool, I talked to her of consent. I told her that her body is hers alone, that nobody can touch it unless she says so. But it is difficult to do this and not evoke too much fear.

Why do people need to ask? she wondered.

So far, the only way I've seen consent materialize is that

now if I kiss my daughter's forehead she says, with a mischie-
vous smile and a low voice, *You have to ask.* Then she puts her
lips on mine. When I return the kiss she smiles and says again,
Mommy, you have to ask.

Desire in the City of Subdued Excitement

Rena Priest

THE TOWN I GREW UP IN IS CALLED BELLINGHAM. We call ourselves Bellinghamsters, and we have an official slogan, "A refreshing change," but our unofficial slogan is much more fitting. We are the City of Subdued Excitement. Desire is a type of excitement! Here in Bellingham, we subdue all that.

I recently watched an SNL skit where two middle-aged mothers were asked what they wanted for Christmas. They let loose their hearts' truest desires: grandchildren. The joke being that it's refreshing for a middle-aged woman to be asked, for once, what she truly wished for.

A Christmas wish list can reveal much about a person's desires. My husband wants a featherweight tent and other odds and ends for motorcycle camping. He desires to ride his bike off into the sunset to camp and do man stuff alone in the wilderness. My daughter, who is working on becoming a chef and recently severed the tip of her thumb while chopping chives, has three different types of sharpening stones on her list for Santa. She assures me that the sharper the knife, the less likely you are to slip and cut yourself.

A pair of black cowboy boots are at the top of my Christmas list, followed by new blush, beaded earrings, a kettlebell, and cute workout clothes. I desire to be a blushing and physically fit cowgirl.

The boots: my intense desire to own these boots is entirely irrational. That I should want something so extravagant and frivolous surprises even me. I will wear them with my bar-star Stetson and pretend that I am from a place with sunshine and tacos, a place where cowgirls go two-stepping to three-chord songs about heartbreak and ruin in honky-tonks with handsome, good-timing cowboys.

The opposite of a cowboy is an Indian woman. I exist in the aftermath and ruin wrought by cowboys.

Call it cultural appropriation. I want to dress up and play at cowboy culture. I desire the power available to the self-assured cowboys of the American West. The kind of arrogance required to swagger in, take what I want from this world, and feel 100 percent entitled to it. Entitled to do genocide. Entitled to cause the extinction of people, their customs, cultures, food sources, extinction of lifeways, extinction of entire populations of fish, animals . . . fuck 'em all. If I want it, I'm takin it. If you're in my way, you can get the fuck out or die. Howdy, y'all. Yeehaw!

That's what these boots represent to me. Do you think I'm terrible for wanting that? Are you white? Do you live on stolen land? I'll send back the gently used boots if you give back the maimed and battered Western hemisphere, taken and passed down by way of the attitudes and activities described above.

I live on stolen land. But the stolen land I live on was stolen directly from underneath my ancestors 167 years ago. I pay a mortgage on a house built over the top of a village site that I'm told was burned to the ground after the Treaty of Point Elliott was signed in 1855 and my ancestors were forced to move to the reservation.

That was eleven generations ago. My mother has a photo of herself with her great-great-grandparents; five generations in one photo. My daughter can sit in my mother's living room and see back seven generations through that photograph. The great-great-grandparents in that photo were the great-grandchildren of the first people to live within the confines of the Lummi reservation.

When I share the untold history of this region, the response from individuals of European descent is often a history lesson of how the Romans colonized the English or the English colonized the Welch, Irish, Scottish, etc. They want me to relate to their suffering. They seem to say, *It's just the way of the world. Oh well, too bad, better luck next time.*

I see this type of response as a resistance to the fact of the continued oppression of Indigenous peoples by the dominant culture of which the lesson giver is a part. Don't resist. I know it's hard. Try not to be agitated by what I'm saying. Agitation is a form of excitement. We subdue that. Just sit with it. See if it changes you inside. See if it changes what you desire.

In the Treaty of Point Elliott, the reservation is identified as being located on the island of Chah-choo-sen. Diverting of rivers turned it from an island into a peninsula, but it becomes an island again during floods.

There is an actual island nearby called Lummi Island on which only two Lummi tribal members reside. The rest of the 903 inhabitants are rich white people and hippies. Every day, between 6:00 a.m. and midnight, they speed through the reservation to the ferry. The road to the ferry cuts a straight line through the middle of my family's land, which was done without my grandfather's consent. We've lost many family pets to ferry traffic. Other families have lost daughters and sons.

As a child, I lived on the eastern shore of the reservation. Our house sat atop a hill overlooking the bay. Across the bay sits the town of Bellingham and the "usual and accustomed" fishing, hunting, and harvesting grounds of the L'haq'temish people. That's the real name of our people, *the people of the sea.* We are called Lummi because that's easier for white people to say.

I always felt some deep, inexplicable desire to be on the other side of the bay. I thought then that the desire grew out of boredom from the emptiness that filled my days. I think now that I wasn't bored. I know how to entertain myself, and did then. I think my DNA was restless and lonesome for the days when Lummi people roamed freely throughout the region and Bellingham was only *one* of our many village sites.

We traveled to different sites throughout the spring, summer, and fall. We followed fish runs and staple crops on a tour through the straits. In the winter, we hunted game and fowl and hunkered down in the longhouses to enjoy the bounty of our harvests. I think I would have liked that life. Going with the flow, always feeling part of it. Instead, I have drifted from job to job, apartment to apartment, working hard to keep my head above water. Trying not to drown.

For many years my heart's truest desire was to be able to one day buy a house in the lettered streets of our town, a little house for my daughter and me. A place to be safe and cozy—a house she could grow up in and have fond memories, maybe even a rope swing. Until her junior year in high school, we lived in a studio apartment downtown, and she had to walk to school past encampments of the unhoused. She walked alongside a creek where her friend's dad found a dead body while jogging.

That creek is the creek for which the county is named: Whatcom. Xwot kwem: xwo = water, kwem = strong. It is the place of strong water. It is where my ancestors brought the first white men who arrived in their shores. The ancestors thought they were going to carry out a great endeavor with these men. They likely didn't realize that these people didn't see them as people, let alone partners. They couldn't have known what plans those white men had for the future.

Before that moment in history, my ancestors fished, lived, and were happy along that creek in their village for thousands of years. I live five blocks away from that creek now. There very well may have been a little summer shack belonging to a Lummi family here on this plot at some point in the past.

When I married my husband, we went shopping for houses in the lettered streets. The first house we looked at was on B Street. It was built in 1910, only fifty-five years after the signing of the treaty. The house had been in the owner's family for several generations and had only ever been sold one other time, in the 1930s at a very cheap price.

This means that if we'd purchased that house, the generational wealth attained by the owner who benefited from my ancestors' displacement would be paid out again by me. Because my ancestors were Indians and not cowboys, I pay double, plus inflation, plus the pain caused by knowing the manner in which it was all stolen. White people inherit houses and stolen land. I inherit heartbreak and intergenerational struggle.

This is not an essay about struggle. This is an essay about desire. I harbor an aching and persistent desire to write without all this baggage. I really wish I could write love poems and things to make people feel nice so they'd love me. But people are always asking me how my heritage influences my work, and I have eleven generations of paradise lost to contend with. It makes writing kinda suck a little bit. It's not pleasant material to work with and it's nothing anyone really wants to hear. Nobody likes to bear bad news, but bearing it alone is even worse.

If you stop reading, you leave me here alone with the baggage of our shared history, just like white people have been doing to Natives for five hundred years, abandoning their own story—turning away and disclaiming responsibility when asked to make things right. You're better than that. Stay. Listen.

I desire to be treated and thought of in a dignified way without having to overcome stereotypes in people's minds. I desire not to have to work twice as hard to be seen as half as worthy. I desire not to have to worry about any of this.

When I was a child, the first boy I ever kissed broke up with me suddenly for no given reason. Years later I learned that when we were kids, his father coached basketball and would drive the Native players home to the rez after practice. The boy would ride along, no doubt noticing how the reservation was different from where he lived. Having seen the conditions of some of our homes, did he think of himself as a greater and I as a lesser? My brand-name clothes, bought from the rez "shopper" who acquired them with a five-finger discount, they couldn't fool anyone who'd actually been to the rez.

We keep boats in our yards and in some places let the grass and blackberries grow wild along driveways and ditches. But zoom out. We are fisher people. We have been harmoniously fishing these waters for millennia. We have boats, and nature is a fine landscape artist. We have no historic obsession with making fools of ourselves by trying to imitate aristocracy. Perfect green lawns and trimmed hedges are a fashion that was established by lords and ladies in England in the seventeenth century—and at the cost of the land.

Wealthy landowners relied on servants to tend their lawns. At some point, the servants acted on their desires to keep tiny lawns for themselves. Today, Americans waste a ton of water and effort to maintain their little green patches. That saying "the grass is always greener . . ." establishes the green lawn as the pinnacle of happiness for which one should strive.

One should always desire to have the absolute greenest grass so that anyone looking over the fence will be covetous. We should desire to have others desire what we have.

Everyone in my family is colonized by the lawn concept. They all tend a lawn. The massive environmental destruction wrought by lawns began with someone's desire for a vast expanse of green grass. What if we desired something that costs less and doesn't take any work? The lawn seems to be something from which there is no going back. It's the same way with many things. Plastic shopping bags and landfills for instance.

I remember a time in school when a conversation about the rez came up at the lunch table.

"I hear they dump their trash in the street," said a little white girl, who was Jehovah's Witness.

"Is it true? Does your family dump their trash all over the road?" the other girl asked.

"Heck no!" I said. "We burn our trash." I said it with pride, as though we were doing our part to keep things tidy. Both girls giggled.

"You burn your trash!" the Jehovah's Witness asked with disgust. As if her people didn't believe that human beings should burn in hell, like trash, for all eternity if they dared to celebrate a birthday.

We didn't always burn our trash. We only did that if we had more than a trash bag full before we could make a run to the dump. Why hadn't I just said we take our trash to the dump? Because I thought of the dump as a shameful and disgusting place, while a fire was just a fire? She'd made me feel so small and ashamed, thinking of all the times that I'd stood over the burn pile, making sure that nothing blew away to catch anything else alight.

I didn't elaborate on any of this. I realized I'd made a terrible social misstep. It was a feeling I had become familiar with in my dealings with the white kids. These kinds of experiences had led me to believe that I'm a socially inept person.

"Why don't you just pay the trash man to pick it up?"

I shrugged my shoulders and kept silent.

"Don't you know that there's a hole in the ozone layer?"

I'd heard this but didn't really know what it meant. I just knew that they said my stepsister's Aqua Net was having a bad effect. For the rest of that recess, I sat quietly as the other girls talked, and this became the pattern of my life. Later that night I asked my mother when I got home, "Mom, why do we burn our trash? Why don't we pay the trash man to come pick it up?"

She was making dinner and she laughed at me and said, "Don't be dense. The trash man won't come out to the rez. They don't come here because they say Indians won't pay. I don't know how they know that since they've never tried, and we pay them enough to drop our trash at the dump." She sounded bitter and then finally she asked sharply, "Why?"

"Because the girls at school say there's a hole in the ozone layer and we shouldn't burn our trash."

My mom smiled and said, "Well those girls are dense if they think that just because someone comes and picks up their trash it magically disappears. Listen to me now. This world and all the pollution—*we don't make it.* The fish don't make it, the clams don't make it, the berries don't make it, and nothing we were doing here before they got here was putting a hole in the ozone layer. We just use their trash along with everyone else because they took away our ability to live in a balanced way. Now don't worry about what those ugly girls say. Just focus on getting good grades."

To be ugly meant to have bad feelings and behaviors toward other people. My schoolmates often revealed their ugliness, and I grew up to understand that if I desired not to be ugly myself, I would always be on the outside looking in. It's a painful kind of isolation. Since leaving the rez I've been to plenty of ugly places and survived. These days I'm okay with being a little bit ugly; just enough to fit in and enjoy a pair of sexy cowgirl boots. It's an *adapt-or-die* situation.

People who spend their lives on the outside looking in die of demoralization. My brother died of grief over the lost salmon fishery that was tied up so tightly with his identity. He'd been fishing with my dad since he was seven. I think he believed that he would always be a fisherman and when he saw the fishery dwindling away, he dwindled away with it. I remember at his funeral hearing his friend Clara say, "Some people have too soft a heart for this wicked, wicked world."

My stepsister died of grief over her murdered mother. They think they caught the killer (a white guy), but not until my sister was forty. A motherless child is vulnerable and people can sense it. I remember how she would tell me about how the boys at school would stick their hands in her pants or up her shirt while she stood at her locker. She was upset one day because a boy actually put his fingers all the way inside her. She told an adult. Nothing was done.

She was very pretty and had developed young. She was in C cups by the time she got to middle school. She had a best friend named Patsy. Patsy and Tess. The boys called them Pussy and Tits. Tess tried to giggle about it. I know how it made her feel. Both my brother and sister died trying to make their pain stop. Brother of an overdose, sister's body just surrendered. This is a hard thing to know. I myself have tried suicide; once by taking a cupboard full of pills, and indirectly many times by disappearing into the oblivion of drink to see if I would emerge sober or vanish to the other side. I don't do that anymore. I desire to live. Maybe this is the afterlife.

Why tell you all this? Here you thought you were going to read an essay about desire. But if you ever ask an Indian about what they desire, don't be surprised if they say something about *Land Back—land back the way it was*; the way it was before the white people came with their Jesus and boarding schools and plastics and *the Great White Father in Washington*. This type of answer is probably why everyone takes such care not to ask us.

Before the colonizers came here, the weavers kept adorable white wooly dogs. Their fur was soft and was spun together with goat's wool to make blankets. The Hudson Bay company exterminated the breed in order to sell blankets to the Indians.

Before the colonizers came, there were staggeringly abundant salmon runs and herring spawns. Between 1882 and 1973 the canneries harvested the fishery to near extinction. Tribes were forced to watch in horror from the shoreline as our fishing villages and reef net sites that we had been promised in the treaty were crowded out and replaced by fish traps and canneries.

Prior to the Boldt decision in 1973, tribal fishers were not allowed to participate in the fishery in their own territories. When the treaty fishers were allowed back out on the water, they were given separate openings from the nontreaty fishers, *the cowboys*. Tribal fishers call them cowboys because during those early days after the Boldt decision they behaved with hostility toward the tribal fishers, like they were playing the role of cowboys in the old cowboy and Indian movies. They were angry about having to share with people who weren't white.

Tribal fishermen recall the violence and tension at the harbor in those days. They recall being shot at from houses along the shore while they set their nets. After a verbal altercation on the docks, someone set my dad's boat on fire. Another time, someone slaughtered a pig and hung it from the boom of a tribal fisher's boat, insinuating that he was being piggy after making a big catch.

The fishermen knew this was coming when they fought for their right to fish. Previous generations had fished in protest of the unfair laws that kept them off the water. Their nets and canoes were confiscated by the Washington Fish and Game Department. In 1882 a canoe would have been the equivalent of a car or a horse to a tribal family. A canoe was also more than that. Canoes were living beings.

They were thought of as the continuation of a tree's life, having moved from the land to the water, the way a caterpillar moves from the land to the air when it becomes a butterfly. The tree retains its spirit. To have it confiscated meant losing someone who was close to you, someone who chose you as the being they would carry on their existence with. I desire to live in a world that honors that relationship.

I know a white poet who shares a poem about his great-grandmother, who was an early colonizer in Montana. He calls her a pioneer and talks about her bravery in settling a hostile and unknown landscape—about how she had to be self-reliant in order to survive.

It takes everything in me not to call bullshit and tell him that she wasn't self-reliant, she was relying on the bounty and abundance of the earth. She wasn't alone in a hostile landscape. There were Indigenous peoples living there for thousands of years before she arrived. Perhaps she didn't know though, because they lived there in a low-impact kind of way. Would it have killed her to learn those ways instead of insisting on her own—a way that responded to the world as one responds to hostility, by stamping it the fuck down?

No. The settlers didn't settle anything. They unsettled it. Before they came there were abundant forests and berry patches; there were lots of fish, and animals, and the animals had autonomy. They lived out their lives according to their own aims and purposes, and people lived in a respectful, reciprocal way with the beings with whom they shared the earth. I desire to have it be this way again. It would be a refreshing change.

That's all the desire I've subdued for now, and now that it's written, perhaps one day it will be so. Perhaps this desire will take on a life of its own, become even more powerful than a green, green lawn and a pair of star-spangled cowgirl boots. Skoden. Stoodis.

The Good Girl

Sonora Jha

WHEN I WAS FOURTEEN, I WAS ONE OF THE GOOD girls, but I did a dangerous thing. I went on a walk with a boy.

I did it because he wasn't just any boy. He was Aman, the most handsome boy on my side of Bombay, the boy who made my heart skip a beat anytime I saw him come around the corner of the street on which I lived. He was how I found out I had a heart and that it could skip a beat and leave me still living.

In 1982, my country was thirty-five years into its glorious independence from British rule. The blush had worn off to be replaced by the ruddiness of hard work and virtue. The pythons of economic liberalization lay coiled around the corner, but in 1982, our parents raised us to be diligent, to obey their elders, to let in Pink Floyd and Michael Jackson, but to marry young.

Aman was a boy from another school. Boys from another school were not to be trusted. They didn't have the same teachers and they wouldn't be beholden to the same rules. They could not be given the same punishments. They could take what they wanted and disappear.

And yet when he walked up to me one day and casually asked if I'd meet him at the gates of the United Services Club the next day for a walk, I had said yes. I had only ever seen Aman walking by with other boys in the neighborhood, teenaged boys with their doubled-over cackles and their violent jostles and their whoops that almost certainly came in the wake of dirty jokes about us girls. Aman always seemed on the periphery of these packs, with them but also elsewhere.

The United Services Club was a country club for the officers from the Indian army, navy, and air force. It still sits at the tip of the best sweep of the city now known as Mumbai (but forever Bombay on my diasporic tongue). The club had facilities and activities for the families of the men who put their lives on the line for their young nation. We had a library, tennis and badminton courts, lush green lawns, and liveried waiters serving cutlets and finger-chips to women in sarees and bell bottoms playing Tambola. Friday night English movies on a big screen, moonlight picnics, and dance nights for teens. Boys would seek my brother's permission to ask me to dance.

I never saw Aman at the dances. All the girls had crushes on him, but he didn't come to the dances.

On the day of our walk, I was worried he would not like me because I walked with a limp, from childhood polio. He didn't seem to notice.

Aman led me down Golf Course Road, which, as the name suggests, bordered a golf course, also a part of our club. Luxuriant, undulating greens stretched out to our right, and to our left stretched the Arabian Sea. We walked on the edge of the sea, turning our faces to it every time a wave crested in warning and then, perhaps startled by our wanting, crashed and offered us disappearing beds of lace.

Aman and I didn't speak much on that walk. He walked a few feet away from me. He kicked stones in his path. He broke twigs off trees and gently chewed on their edges. He couldn't stop smiling.

We couldn't bear to look at one another. I'd sense his eyes on me, and when I'd look, he'd quickly look away.

There's nothing more enticing to a good girl than a bad boy turned shy in her presence.

We sat on a bench and watched the sun give itself to the sea. The glow it left behind filled me with shame. I felt the warmth coming from the body of a boy I liked just sitting there next to me. I wondered what would happen if I reached out and held his hand. I tried not to breathe, so I could imagine what hell would break loose if I turned my face to kiss him. I was gripped by an ache that threatened to carry me away in its emerald undertow.

The officers were not too far off on the golf course, our friends perhaps likely to come upon us at any moment. Everyone knew everyone. I was Major Jha's daughter walking with Lieutenant Colonel Lall's son. My father was away, stationed in a small town in the Himalayas. My brother, no more than a year older than me, was in charge of my protection and the preservation of the family reputation. My mother and us three children—my older brother and baby sister—lived in what the army called Separated Family Accommodations. For all the sadness in the name, the eleven-story flat was clean and airy and had a balcony with one of the most coveted views in Bombay—up close and wide, the Arabian Sea. We were fortunate to have this life.

Aman and I walked home within the echoes of guns shooting in a target practice range nearby, reminding us of who we were. I wondered who we were at war with.

I never saw Aman again, or if I did, he became just one of the boys in those packs. Later that year, my father returned and we moved to the other side of Bombay. Someone told me Aman had moved, too, to another city.

In all the years after, I wish I'd kissed that boy. I wish I had pulled his beautiful face to mine and kissed the corner of his crooked smile, then the salt on his jaw jutting toward the angles of adulthood, then an eyelid, until he grew impatient and pushed his lips on mine.

All this without ever having read one of the Mills and Boons romance paperbacks my girlfriends passed around under the wooden desks of our classrooms.

In all the years after, I can't recall things I should have been able to easily recall. What did we talk about that day? Why did he never ask me to walk with him again? Wait, maybe he did? A memory would surface of another plan to walk again the next day, but I think I didn't show up. Maybe I'd left him waiting.

In all the years after, I try to imagine what I was wearing that day. I imagine myself in my school uniform—white blouse, beige pinafore, green tie, a metal badge pinned on my left chest with my Catholic school insignia and the words *Truth Shall Prevail*. My pinafore reaches down to my knees, or a teacher would be right to whack a foot-ruler against my thighs and leave a red welt. You could tell when a girl in our school had been chastened for hemming her skirt up. The lines of a hem reopened never flatten enough to disappear.

My breasts had only just started to grow and I had only recently started to wear a bra. My mother was thirty-three years old and, like many terribly young mothers, was unprepared for her daughter to turn into a woman. Whatever I knew about the secrets of my changing body were learned through the giggles of older girls, the sneers of Catholic school teachers, and the warnings of Bollywood films, in which women were coy or they were vamps, and the coy ones were sometimes raped or became pregnant because the men they fell in love with became too aroused. Rape and/or unwed pregnancy required that the woman kill herself—by hanging, or leaping from a building, or poison, or laying herself on train tracks. I promised myself a gentle hanging.

In all the years after, I grasp at the disappearing lace of memories, but the only thing I can recall is that I had never felt safer with a man than I did in the company of that boy that day.

Forty years later, when the thought comes up again and I have to know why, I find him the way anyone can find anyone these days.

Then, the name I had once carved into a cactus along with mine with a heart in between flashes on my phone and the view of Lake Union from where I sit in my condo in Seattle turns blurry from the rush of memories of other waterscapes. He lives in Hong Kong now. He moved there for work. He was married once. He is single now.

I was married twice. I make a weak joke about my two divorces. We talk about our children, his daughter and my son.

I ask if he remembers a walk.

I fall silent as he speaks. He remembers every little detail. His voice carries the same accent as mine, a 1980s Bombay accent, British English enriched with an Indian heft. His voice is deep, commanding, sexy. I should have kissed him again and again.

There were two walks, he says.

Huh.

Why didn't we hold hands, I say.

"Have you forgotten we held hands on the second walk?" His voice rises an octave, with laughter.

And suddenly, I remember we held hands.

I imagine the hands he just spoke of, my girlhood hands. The year before, at thirteen, they had reached between my legs and discovered the love only I could unfailingly give to my body. In the decades since, my hands would steward my body and soul to the prevailing truth of masturbatory pleasure. Those girlhood hands in the hands of a worldly-wise sixteen-year-old boy were already capable of so much more than he and she asked of them on that walk by the sea.

Of course, I don't tell him this.

Then he tells me we didn't just hold hands. We kissed.

I tell him he is lying. I keep my voice playful, the way you must when you speak to someone after forty years. I tell him the first time I kissed someone was when I was twenty-two. I change the subject and we talk about old friends. One of them is dead now. Not dead, *passed away* is the term Aman uses. His voice and his stories are clear, honest, steeped in detail.

He tries again. He asks me to recall the shed at the entrance to the golf course. That's where we kissed, he says. He wants me to remember.

I can't recall it, I say.

He asks me to recall the intersection of Robert Road and Magdala Road. He says we held hands until we came to that fork in the road. "You asked me to let go of your hand at that spot."

He says I had pointed to my building—Menaka Building—in the distance. "You said that from the spot where we stood, we had come into view of anyone watching from the eleventh-floor flat where you lived. You were afraid that someone from your family or your neighbors would see us. So, I let go of your hand."

I am silent on the phone, and then I tell him I have to go, that we can talk again soon. I spend the day unmoored from the dry ground of my own memory.

"Wake up, wake up," I text him the next day. "I have questions."

"Awake, awake," he texts right back. "It's 11:00 a.m. here."

Was the walk a bet with the other boys? That the good girl would do as you asked?

No.

Was it to lure me into sex?

No. "But in all honesty, of course I would want more than a kiss. I was a sixteen-year-old boy! But I knew you were younger, and I wouldn't have. I liked your sweet, happy smile. I wanted you to be my girlfriend."

He used to watch me walk past his house on Magdala Road, he says.

"Was your house near the jamun tree?" I ask him.

"Yes!" He is pleased I remember something.

He goes on talking, but I am assailed by another memory. I used to slow down and pick up the jamuns that fell from the tree—plump purple berries that would fall to the charcoal asphalt that often bubbled over in the summer heat. The jamuns that burst open on impact would show their pink-veined insides that quickly stained my fingers. Those ones were not to be eaten. The birds could peck on them later. The jamun that stayed intact, unbroken, the ones that had had a soft landing, were to be rubbed clean in your palms and tucked carefully into your pocket or bitten into if you couldn't resist. The juice was tart and sweet and its tannins would coat my tongue and pucker them dry, tight. They would turn my lips a florid purple.

One day, a man walked by as I picked the fruit off the ground. He slowed down and watched me. He showed me his penis. I turned my head away and spat out the berry in my mouth. A woman who was walking by saw him. She worked as a maid in my building. She yelled at the man and scared him away. I never lingered at the tree again.

I ask Aman why he recalls everything so clearly. He says he doesn't know why, but perhaps it was because of how sad he felt as I started to cry and walk away.

Why did I cry?

I don't remember crying, I say.

It's true. What's even truer is that I misremember.

I pause in my thought. Am I letting a man gaslight me? Why should I believe his version over mine?

I should, because this is what he says next—

He says when I took my hand from his, I suddenly accused him of liking another girl from the neighborhood, a girl I was friends with. I told him I saw him walking with her two days ago on the same road we were just on.

"I never went on a walk with that girl," he says now into the phone. He sounds like a sixteen-year-old and I want to laugh.

He rushes to explain. "She had come over to get a puppy from my dog's litter and you had walked past my house and seen us together and came up to talk to her. She was mean to you, she ignored you. I think that hurt your feelings and so you mixed it up somehow with me taking her on a walk?"

My breath catches in my throat, and it's not because of these new truths. This man on the phone is fifty-six. He's talking about something that happened when we were in our teens. Not just talking; he is *asking* about it. He had spent some time thinking of all this. He had questions in all his years after.

I had hurt that boy. I know now what I didn't know then—that boys hurt too. I am the mother of a boy, now a young man.

At fourteen, I had made up a story in which a boy broke my heart so I could walk away. I took step after judicious step toward the rules of good girlhood.

I loved the rules. I looked down on the bad girls, the sluts. Their tattered reputations would lead them to doom. Girls who lied to their parents about late-night parties in which they would let boys touch them down there, girls who ran away with their driving instructors to never be heard from again, girls who had secret abortions, girls who were abandoned by boys who they thought loved them, girls whose families would marry off their damaged daughters then to lesser men. Girls who only *thought* they were having fun.

In the years after, my body had remembered the trauma of my childhood and youth. It had forgotten the pleasure. I remembered clearly the sexual assaults of all the years. I forgot the time I had owned—and used—my sexual agency.

When we hang up the phone, I enter "Golf Course Road" and "Mumbai" in a search and am suddenly suspended in space, diving down from Google Earth onto a map of lanes where my feet had once danced and limped. I see the dark gray of the Arabian Sea, I see Menaka Building, I see my high school. I see the street corner Aman spoke of, where I had asked him to let go of my hand.

I swoop down some more, into a bird's eye view of my longing. I squint and I see that girl and that boy on that street corner.

I see the just-kissed slutty girl. She looks happy. I see her pause, hesitate, and then turn to the boy and lie her way out of her own desire. I see her walk away.

Yes, the girl is watched, but not by a young mother or watchful brother or a nosy neighbor on the sky-scraping balconies of her childhood home. She is watched by a fifty-three-year-old woman half a lifetime away on another continent. The woman sees the girl walk shakily away with all she was allowed to know and have. A few years later, the girl would be drawn to a line from an Urdu poem in which a lover's wisdom is to leave a story at a gentle twist of plot when it wasn't possible to bring it to a denouement. A few more years later, she would name her newborn after this poet.

She will follow a life of rules until the rules turn on her.

The woman looking from the sky turns her gaze now to see, for the first time, the boy. Not just a forbidden boy, not just a handsome boy, not just the object of muffled desires, but a boy whose father had passed away from heart failure the year before. The boy is watching the girl with the sweet smile walk away and he is hollowed out with a grief from here and there. He will remember.

The fifty-three-year-old woman shuts her laptop, closes her eyes, and steadies herself from the vertigo of time, the precarity of satellites taking pictures from the sky.

She writes a message and taps on an arrow.

Does your work ever bring you from Hong Kong to Seattle?

Yes, it does. I will be in Seattle next month.

Bodies of Water

Karen Russell

IN MIAMI, THE SKY IS ALSO A BODY OF WATER. LAKES of rain fell on my best friends and me during the summer of 1995. That July and August we were always wet, pedaling through spectacular afternoon thundershowers along Biscayne Bay, the thirty-five-mile inlet of the Atlantic that indents the southeast coastline of Florida. We rode our bikes everywhere, which felt to us, at that time, like a superpower. For a trio of thirteen-year-old girls, this was a wild and unprecedented autonomy. Nobody had cell phones then. None of us wore helmets (a memory that horrifies me now, watching my own kids wobbling down the sidewalk on their tricycles). We made landline plans to meet, then set out from our respective homes, promising our parents we'd stay on the bike path. The speed at which our promise became a lie: mere seconds, as we went bumping off the curb toward U.S. 1. Nobody knew where we were for hours at a stretch—our location was a secret that traveled with us.

In my memory, the thrill of disappearing in tandem is inseparable from the sudden flashes of salt water behind the mangroves, the heat pulling at our spines. We rode through neighborhoods we'd known since birth but had never seen alone, unchaperoned and unsurveilled. What watched us, instead, was the ocean. A great, lidless eye, inhumanly blue, following us along Main Highway through Coconut Grove toward Miami Beach; waiting for us also if we chose to pedal in the opposite direction, down Old Cutler Road to Matheson Hammock, a manmade coral atoll pool bordering the real bay. In sunny weather, you could see the chrome stalagmites of downtown Miami; on a gray day, you could believe the land had been erased entirely.

The ocean haunted us even when we could not see it. Infiltrating our senses as a warm tarry pungency at low tide, or a ticklish, ionic charge gathering under the banyan leaves before a 3:00 p.m. storm. Private estates barricaded their property lines, and yet we could turn down any cul-de-sac and find Biscayne Bay waiting for us.

We hugged its rocky coastline, waiting for it to soften into sand. Pumping our legs, gasping for air, scaling bridges. We wore our bathing suits under our clothes so that we could strip and swim. One afternoon, we ate soggy KFC biscuits in the rain on a wealthy, empty private beach just off the Richenbacher Causeway, skipping the toll booths and pushing our bikes through the sea grapes, our leg muscles still spasming from climbing the steep bridge that connects mainland Miami with the island of Key Biscayne. This was our longest ride; we had traveled, at most, eleven miles from our homes. I'm not sure why buying fried chicken with our parents' money and eating it on the damp sand felt like the epitome of freedom, but it did. We knew better, by age thirteen, than to trust the sun. In Miami, a storm can blow up in minutes. The dry thunder used to make me itchy with a wish for the sky to erupt. I had already learned, earlier in childhood, that you can begin to desire the very thing you fear. A release from the agonizing vigil, the end of dread that comes with your fear's dark fulfillment. Pour down on me, I remember goading the sky.

Manatees in Dinner Key Marina. BEWARE OF ALLIGATORS signs at Matheson Hammock. The stink of low tide, the tiny crabs waving their pitchfork arms at us from the exposed rocks like a mob of irate villagers. Deep in the back of our brains, we could hear our parents yelling, "Slow down! Slow down!" Instead we let our arms extend into a fixed-wing soar over the handlebars, echoing the gulls that wheeled above us.

Sometimes our parents' flickery omniscience detected a breach in the system, and they'd notice, for example, that we'd returned home penniless with soaking hair. But "riding bikes" sounds so innocent, and we still had the round eyes of children. We had the bodies of women, which meant that men had begun to holler at us from passing cars, words that drew butcher-shop lines around us and made us consider ourselves as an assemblage of parts: breasts, asses, thighs, faces. During rush-hour traffic, we had to pedal through this uglier sort of thundershower, our faces burning. At certain intersections we knew to sit and hunch over the handlebars, our eyes on the pavement.

But once we made it over the bridge, the huge, blue solvent of the bay erased whatever hideous self-consciousness we'd felt while riding along the highway. To get to the beach, we had to stand to pedal, and then the fire left our faces and came from inside us, from our lungs and calves—I discovered how strong my body was on those rides, pushing uphill. We went shrieking downhill toward the wavy tarpaulin of the bay. At last, we could relax into the sea, with its beautiful elasticity, its deep and generous amnesia. Like us, Biscayne Bay could forget a violent storm in an instant. We swam through smooth water, hidden up to our necks, buoyed inside the happy silence that follows great physical exertion.

Under that moody, aqueous sky, my two best friends and I turned fourteen. I didn't know then that I was coasting through the best summer of my life. In my memory, that summer is a suspension bridge over the water, connecting the worlds of childhood and adulthood. Fall came and we started high school, a violent eviction from the freedom of those afternoons.

There are plenty of places that you can get to by bicycle, even in a city as vast as Miami. The vaquita that sells to minors. Tattoo parlors with a financial stake in believing that you are eighteen, despite the evidence presented by your body and face. The houses of male strangers willing to extend to you this same line of credit. The Planned Parenthood. When I think

about the dark straits that young women have to travel, I remember racing the waves on either side of a winnowing road.
The Biscayne Bay I've written about here is not a place to which
I can return; in the past decade, eighty percent of its seagrass
meadows—more than 25,000 acres—have died, and its famous
aquamarine color belies the devastation of raw sewage, chemical
runoff, global warming and acidification, toxic blooms of algae.
We girls were not amnesiacs, as it turns out, and neither is the
ocean; the damage we sustain lives on inside us. So does this
memory: the bridge to a blue expanse of dreaming time that
girls deserve, and not only for a summer.

Last Supper

Torrey Peters

THE LAST THING I ATE AS A HUSBAND—AND, arguably, as a man—was a fried tilapia. The fish had been caught from a skiff on the shore of Lake Victoria and only an hour or two later dredged in flour, fried to a golden crisp in a vat of vegetable oil over a wood fire, and served to me with lime and piri-piri sauce. I could still taste the green flavor of algae in the flaky white flesh. My senses all registered that I had before me a truly excellent meal, but I ate it glumly across from my then-wife, Olive, who picked at a matching fish.

We sat on plastic chairs at a wood table banged together with pegs. It was the rainy season: low skies reflected in the puddles that pooled in the ruts of red dirt roads leading up to the shore. Huge marabou storks—known as the undertaker bird on account of their haunted movements, leprous pink skin, and dark wings that hang like cloaks—slipped and flapped through the grasses around us, contributing to the funereal mood of our meal.

Olive and I had lived in Kampala for almost a year by then. She was a graduate student and had received a National Science Foundation grant to write an ethnography of Uganda's only lesbian bar. From appearances, a lesbian bar was an odd choice of study for an American woman in a heterosexual marriage. But it had happened organically. Three years before I'd come out to Olive as transgender but told her—or, rather, told myself and her by extension—that I'd never transition. My mind turned constantly, thrillingly, to the idea of myself as a woman, but I loved Olive and didn't want to mess up our relationship by transitioning. I assured her that I could manage as a man just fine.

The summer I came out to Olive, she traveled to Uganda as a doctoral student to work with an NGO. But newly curious about trans people, she ended up meeting and befriending members of a nascent trans movement in Kampala.

In 2009, urged on by members of the American evangelical movement, the Ugandan government considered a bill to strengthen laws against homosexuality (making no distinction between it and trans identities). Proposed punishments included imprisonment or possibly even death. And yet, in the midst of this, a group of trans men and lesbians kept the bar open—packing it every night of the week despite harassment, police raids, and daily hateful screeds in the local tabloids. Olive had returned that summer, and there, under the shadow of the anti-homosexuality bill, she and her friends came up with the idea: she'd write a yearlong ethnography of the bar and its patrons. As her husband and a nominal trans person, I went with her.

In the U.S. I'd been experimenting with gender presentation: pierced ears, eyeliner, tighter shirts. I'd watch RuPaul and be inspired to try out a full drag look—which led to a desperate euphoria for days after, a wild-eyed happiness that I've since encountered in other trans people and understand can be both annoying and alarming. I reasoned that it worked like a safety valve—give me a day of gender obsession every few months and I'd be a good husband the rest of the time.

I put my gender on hold in Uganda. In truth, because I'm white and American, it's not like I was risking arrest or the death penalty like queer Ugandans were. Two Ugandan trans women I knew there had each been arrested multiple times. What they suffered in an Idi Amin–era bunker isn't mine to recount, but suffice to say it was horrific. By contrast I couldn't even be honest with my wife about my own gender. I might've been ashamed of this, but that's the whole point of repression: to remain unconscious of one's own cowardice.

In high school my friend's dad caught him smoking and did that legendary dad thing where he then made my friend smoke an entire pack of Marlboro Reds. My time in Uganda was the masculinity equivalent of smoking an entire pack of cigarettes. I bought a four-by-four truck and drove it around dusty roads. Hot water was unreliable, so I rarely shaved and grew constant stubble. People told me T-shirts were disrespectful and slovenly, so I took to wearing button-down shirts and ties. I spent evenings grilling steaks in a simple pizza oven I'd made of mud and straw like some wayward suburban dad. The cows of Uganda grazed on anything green so that grass and floral flavors marbled the meat and only the simplest marinade was needed.

I learned a few phrases of Luganda, but, generally, I couldn't follow conversations. So I came to speak even English in a terse, clipped manner—to avoid letting my confusion or helplessness show. It was effective. I made friends easily. People thought I was competent. But the more I leaned into masculinity, the more opaque I became to myself. My internal landscape desaturated. Sussing my own emotions was like feeling for lost objects on the bottom of a murky pond. Affection withered before I could express it. I stopped touching Olive. Couldn't express any kind of sexual desire. At night I'd catch her watching me, the brief gleam of her sad eyes in the dark as she contemplated why this man she married no longer wanted her. Rather than face those eyes, I'd roll over and away. In the morning neither of us could talk about it.

All day long Olive spoke with queer activists—everyone wanted to tell the American ethnographer of furtive hookups made hotter by danger, of the dish-shattering drama of breakups and cheating, of clothing and bodies pressed close to late-night beats, of slipping away with your crush to the back of a broken-down 1980s Corolla imported from Dubai. Olive and I would laugh along and perform that same open exuberance—but alone, under the mosquito net in our rented room, we suffocated on humid air and unsaid words.

By the winter of 2010, it became clear that a proxy culture war was being waged by the West in Uganda. The religious right—especially the Americans—were losing the battle of gay marriage at home, so they turned to the global South in search of new fronts and alit on Uganda, a country with policies unusually open to foreign organizations. Money from U.S. churches was pouring into the accounts of right-wing politicians, and European NGOs and LGBTQ+ organizations were funding counteractions.

The atmosphere grew increasingly hostile. Olive's friends found their pictures printed daily in the tabloids along with unfounded accusations. Long nights of flirting over roasted maize, sambusa, and Nile brand beers turned into survival-strategy sessions.

I awoke one morning to Olive crying. A friend of hers, prominent LGBTQ activist David Kato, had been killed with a hammer. Within hours Hillary Clinton had denounced the murder and the anti-homosexuality bill. Later that day Barack Obama. Right-wing politicians saw this as foreign intervention in Ugandan affairs. They turned Kato's death into a political flashpoint to rile up followers and defended his killer, who in court employed "gay panic" as a justification for the murder. Olive spent a month helping out during the funeral and its aftermath: a descent into fear and paranoia that swept over Uganda's queer and trans activists; the sudden hunt for asylum applications, safe houses, European sponsors.

While she worked, I stayed home, read novels, failed to write my own novel, worried about my truck, and occasionally drove it out to the countryside. I bought enough 3G internet credit to browse faraway trans websites—extremely slowly—on my third-generation iPhone. Olive and I went days without seeing each other.

It was during this era that we sat down to that dinner of

fried fish at a place we'd been to a few times before—a grassy field that ran into a muddy shore north of Ggaba Beach. On weekends people rented it out for weddings, but on weeknights a group of women brought tilapia and lake perch to fry in open vats for passersby picnicking on the grass. That night, because of the intermittent rain, we were the only customers.

Tilapia can be a maligned fish—freezer-bitten, bland, often ending up breaded in tacos. But fresh from the water of its native lake, it rivals red snapper for flavor. And I wanted to eat something worthy of a last meal because I knew something Olive didn't: I was leaving.

Maybe I wanted her to plead with me to stay. But she didn't. She just asked me if I would please sell the truck because she didn't want to deal with it.

I gazed out at Lake Victoria. A few men were casting nets into an algae bloom offshore. The evening was so still that the sound of their grunts carried over the water. "When you finish here, will you come home to me?"

She didn't respond. After a while she picked off the tail fin of her fish, sucked at it, and threw the bones to one of the marabou storks that peered at us from a dead tree. It did a macabre dance of delight, opened its cloak, and descended upon us.

How I Got Over

Amanda Petrusich

1.

WE DON'T GATHER OURSELVES AND WALK AWAY FROM certain kinds of pain the way we instinctively retreat from other dangers. We nurture some agonies, exaggerate them, let them fester and rot and worsen: "The insatiable wound inside me bled and grew, and I was doing everything I could to make it bleed more," poet and Trappist monk Thomas Merton wrote in 1948. Merton was talking about first love, but I'm not sure that impulse lessens over time or via repetition, or that it's exclusive to romantic devastation. Sometimes you are doing something that feels terrible, and you recognize it, maybe even lament it, but nonetheless proceed apace with the thing. Suffering helps quantify the depth and purity of certain feelings, making real what would otherwise be too ephemeral to register. We cling to pain not because good feelings create an inverse or a shadow, but because without it they are too invisible. We can't see them.

2.

Merton was born in Prades, France, in the eastern Pyrenees, on January 31, 1915. His parents were both artists; he and his brother, John Paul, were baptized in the Church of England. The family moved frequently and took off for New York City when Merton was just eight months old. Merton's mother, Ruth, would die there six years later, in Bellevue Hospital, of stomach cancer. Many of Merton's biographers consider Ruth's death not just fundamental but inescapable for Merton—because his first formative relationship with a woman ended prematurely, in tragedy, he spent the rest of his life attempting, in one way or another, to resolve it.

About a year after Ruth's death, on a trip to Bermuda, Merton's father, Owen, fell in love with a married novelist named Evelyn Smith. He began traveling around Europe with Smith and her husband. I can't quite discern the logistics of their arrangement. At some point, Owen and Smith discussed marriage themselves, but Smith wasn't especially kind to Thomas, and Owen ended the affair, choosing, instead, to protect his first son from further heartache. I sometimes try to imagine what that experience might have been like for a very young boy: the worry that your recently deceased mother could be replaced, imminently and with scandal, by someone who doesn't like you very much.

In 1926, Merton's father enrolled him in an all-boys boarding school in Montauban, France, the Lycée Ingres. In *The Seven Storey Mountain*, the autobiography Merton published in 1948, he writes of his classmates' "fierce, cat-like little faces, dark and morose . . . [with] glittering and hostile eyes." He was kicked and insulted and tormented. The language he uses to describe the experience is animalistic: he was "swarmed," "stung." Eventually, his father sent for him to come back to America. He had a new suit made. In 1931, at age sixteen, Merton boarded a boat to New York. The journey took ten days. On the second day, he met a girl.

Merton learned a lot about love just then: how good it feels, how bad it feels, how irresistible its pain can be. "I made a declaration of my undying love," he writes. "I would not, could not, ever love anyone else but her. It was impossible, unthinkable . . . Love like this was immortal." And yet, at the end of their voyage, they say a gentle goodbye. In *The Seven Storey Mountain*, Merton looks back on his fixation with a mix of bemusement and total, abject terror. "I would rather spend two years in a hospital than go through that anguish again!"

He spent the summer roaming the city, alternately lovesick and liberated, looking at the crowds of people, eating hot dogs and drinking orange juice, "smoking cigarettes and hugging my own sweet sense of independence," relishing in the particular liberation of New York—the way it both exaggerates lonesomeness and, on occasion, relieves it.

Then, in 1933, at age eighteen, Merton ended up in Rome. He was recovering, again, from a failed courtship, this time with a young woman he'd met in Bournemouth, England. It is tempting, now, to imbue that visit with portents—it was his first sustained exposure to Catholicism—but he had not yet been called toward the church. ("My first preoccupation in Rome was to find a dentist," he writes.) Still, after several weeks of exploring various houses of worship—he was enticed by the art on the walls—he began to understand something about God, to develop what he later called "true knowledge." He would look back upon that visit as paramount. It changed him, although he didn't know it yet.

3.

The only Bible I've ever owned belonged to my aunt Joyce, a woman I never met because she died in a car accident several decades before I was born. She was just a teenager. It's inscribed: "Presented to Joyce Touchton from Calvary Presbyterian Church, November 5, 1961." I tug it from my bookshelf from time to time. I never quite find what I'm after in there. On the first page of Genesis, someone—my grandmother, probably—handwrote "In the beginning . . ." in watery blue ink. The script slopes downhill. There is something nearly ominous about the particular angle of the words.

As a child, I was enrolled, briefly, in a Catholic school, where I wore a plaid skirt and ran from the nuns and said all

my prayers at the appointed hour. We were taught the literature. Back then, I thought the Book of Genesis was the most
riveting and dramatic bit of the Christian origin story. After the
flood, Noah's sons went forth and multiplied, they built cities
and towers and fell in love and helped each other out and got
into trouble and did unkind things. Man was still man, still vile.
That couldn't be rewritten or washed away.

Sometimes our mistakes recur like a record stuck in groove:
the same mistake, reiterated endlessly. But God made a cov-
enant with Noah and his seed and every living creature, "all
that went out of the ark." No more floods, no more destruction
of flesh. We are the generations of the sons of Noah; we falter.
Sometimes change is the thing we give up on.

4.

In October 1933, Merton enrolled in Clare College at Cambridge. His personal recollections of this period are deeply
strange. He seems convinced there was something dark and
sinister embedded in the atmosphere there, an evil inherent in
the "damp and fetid mists," some pox upon the place, and it got
him: "For me, with my blind appetites, it was impossible that I
should not rush in and take a huge bite of this rotten fruit." He
was subsumed by a lust to "grab at life," but not in a hopeful,
carpe-diem sort of way—the sanguine, go-get-it ethos many of
us internalize as coddled children—but a desperate, starved, av-
aricious way. Real disgust is palpable in his prose regarding this
time. He describes his classmates as morally dead. He describes
himself as stupid, bitter, selfish, miserable, hungover, dissolute,
sensual, proud, undisciplined, weak, vain, and obscene.

The Seven Storey Mountain is scant on specifics, likely due
to the Trappist censors who dug through Merton's manuscript
before it went to press. He speaks about his sins in a general and
melodramatic way. But I get the impression Merton was hurting women. Not that he was physically abusive, but that he was

psychologically and sexually manipulative, a serial emotional predator. He booked it every time someone got too close. Most scholars agree he fathered a child while at Cambridge, likely with a local shop girl, although his son or daughter has never been identified. A financial settlement of some sort was negotiated. There is speculation that both mother and child were later killed during World War II air raids, but I still wonder if he or she survived, and knows—has read the passages that pertain, even obliquely, to the moment of conception. They're not kind.

"Urge and urge and urge / Always the procreant urge of the world," Walt Whitman wrote in 1855. Merton was less forgiving of desire. In January 1935, after consulting with his guardian and godfather—he hadn't been attending his lectures, and a career in the British Diplomatic Service, once an aspiration, was becoming increasingly unlikely—he transferred to Columbia University in New York City. He credits the mercy and love of God for releasing him from Cambridge.

In New York, Merton became interested in Communism (he assumed the party name Frank Swift) and was pleased by his classmates' apparent unpretentiousness ("You got the impression that all these people were at once more earnest and more humble, poorer, smarter perhaps, certainly more diligent than those I had known at Cambridge."). He took a formative class in eighteenth-century English literature from the poet Mark Van Doren and began a lifelong friendship with the minimalist painter Ad Reinhardt. He joined a fraternity and frequented jazz clubs. There is a funny passage in *The Seven Storey Mountain* in which he recounts getting rebuffed by a woman he was pursuing ("I was at last treated in the way I had treated not a few people in these last years") and soothed himself, *Cathy*-cartoon style, by eating "quarts and quarts" of ice cream (he had also come down with gastritis).

During his tenure at Columbia, Merton read two books he would later cite as pivotal to his spiritual journey: *The Spirit of Medieval Philosophy* by Etienne Gilson and *Ends and Means* by Aldous Huxley. The latter was a particularly transformative text, as it contained evidence of what Merton understood as a conversion—a disavowal of want in favor of prayer, asceticism, and mindfulness. Huxley had been grasping for (and achieved) freedom from "a servitude to flesh that must ultimately destroy our whole nature and society and the world as well"—the same impulses and longings Merton had been tussling with for years.

It's clear to me, reading his recollections of this era, that Merton had begun to understand the abandonment or foiling of certain desires as a kind of completion of self—that by communing with God in a sacrificial way, man becomes whole. It's the central and animating tension of *The Seven Storey Mountain*: 461 pages on the practiced denial of desire. Over and over and over again, Merton writes about the misery of being held in thrall to want, and the transcendence of refusing it. It still strikes me as a fundamentally antagonistic and binary notion: that we are born containing some unresolved circuit, and that our life's work is to overcome the imperatives of our bodies and souls, to nullify and conquer them. That we are born struggling against ourselves.

In 1938, Merton graduated from Columbia and enrolled in the university's graduate program in English. He began writing his master's thesis on themes of art and nature in William Blake. That same year, he visited Corpus Christi Catholic Church on 121st Street in Morningside Heights, just a few blocks from campus. Something had been stirred up in him that couldn't be easily sated or ignored. He'd been spending most of his weekends out on Long Island with a girlfriend but soon heeded "a growing desire to stay in the city and go to some kind of a church."

One Sunday, Merton attended an 11:00 a.m. low mass, finding an "obscure" spot in the back to observe, get a sense of things. The first person he noticed was a "very pretty" girl on her knees, praying. He was moved by her focus, and the sermon that followed. By the time mass was over, he had undergone an epiphany, changed: "All I know is that I walked in a new world."

He begins the practical process of conversion: baptism, confirmation, communion. One morning, following an especially rambunctious night at a jazz club with his buddies, Merton ventures out to fetch breakfast, returning with cardboard containers of scrambled eggs and toast and coffee, a fresh pack of cigarettes jammed in his pocket. "But I did not feel like smoking," he writes. "While we were sitting there on the floor playing records and eating this breakfast, the idea came to me: 'I am going to be a priest.'"

Merton considered various orders but felt a palpable kinship with the Franciscans. He set up a meeting with Father Edmund at the Monastery of St. Francis of Assisi on Thirty-First Street in Manhattan, where he was told he could apply to enter the novitiate the following August. That summer Merton had a crisis of confidence: "I suddenly remembered who I was, who I had been." He met with Father Edmund and related his past sins in some detail. The next day Father Edmund told him he should write to the provincial and tell him he had reconsidered his application. He was not who they were looking for. "There seemed to me to be no question that I was now excluded from the priesthood forever," Merton writes.

Instead, he took a job teaching English at St. Bonaventure's, a Franciscan university in upstate New York. He recalls packing up a trunkful of books, a typewriter, and a portable phonograph machine and moving into a little room on the second floor of a red brick building, with a window overlooking the chapel. He started abandoning indulgences, like smoking ("My mouth was at last clean of the yellow, parching salt of nicotine") and the cinema ("I had rinsed my eyes of the grey slops of movies"), entering a kind of quiet, Spartan cloister ("and my ears, too, had been cleansed of all wild and fierce noises").

In April 1941, he attended a Holy Week retreat at the Abbey of Our Lady of Gethsemani, a Trappist monastery near

Bardstown, Kentucky. He had been spending his free time in New York reading Lorca, fasting, and writing poems. When Merton arrived at Gethsemani, he was enthralled by the solitude and gravity of the Trappists: "After Communion I thought my heart was going to explode." In December 1941, after leaving his job at St. Bonaventure's and giving away most of his things (according to a biography by Jim Forest, Merton retained only a Bible, his breviary, a copy of *The Imitation of Christ*, a volume of Saint John of the Cross, a collection of Gerald Manley Hopkins's poems, an anthology of William Blake, Dante's *Vita Nuova*, *Canzoniere*, and *The Divine Comedy*, an edition of Italian poems, the clothing needed for a one-day trip, and his rosary), Merton was accepted into the monastery as a postulant by Dom Frederic Dunne, Gethsemani's Father Abbot.

Daily life at Gethsemani was austere. Even more so, I'd imagine for a recovering sensualist like Merton. The Trappists are a penitential order (the urge toward practiced self-flagellation was, in part, what drew Merton toward them), and the monks slept on pallets of straw laid across wooden boards in dormitories that were ice-cold in the wintertime and sweltering come July. They fasted for half the year and ate sparsely at other times (according to Forest, a typical meal from that time included bread, potatoes, an apple, and a cup of barley coffee). They performed physical labor—maintaining the grounds, weeding the potatoes, hoeing corn, tending the rectory—and prayed, communally, for nearly eight hours every day. On Fridays, monks sat on their cots and flogged their bare backs with small whips while reciting the Our Father. They communicated with each other mainly via sign language, and only when necessary. Four times a year (Easter, Assumption, All Saints, and Christmas) the monks were allowed to mail four half-page letters to friends and relatives. Merton took to it, even thrived. He wrote his dear friend Robert Lax in 1941: "What surprises me is not that I am happy here, but that I ever tried to fool myself I was happy anywhere else."

5.

There's a passage toward the end of *The Seven Storey Mountain* in which Merton begins referring, in a dissociative way, to the part of him that wants to produce literature—the part that finds writing to be a liberating and sense-making process, a salve. He couldn't shake that other self upon entering the monastery, the way we sometimes successfully disavow whole versions of ourselves, shedding them easily, like a jacket in the sun. "But then there was this shadow, this double, this writer who had followed me into the cloister. He is still on my track. He rides my shoulders, sometimes, like the old man of the sea. He still wears the name of Thomas Merton. Is it the name of an enemy?"

Merton considers his writing-self vampiric, hysterical, traitorous. There is a sense, reading these sections, that he wants to vanquish it, like an evil twin. He is nearly conspiratorial. "Nobody seems to understand that one of us has got to die."

And: "Sometimes I am mortally afraid."

Writing compromises the contemplative vocation, distracts the mind from God. Historically, the Trappists have been wary of intellectualism, and monks read only scripture or recountings of the lives of saints. But Merton must have believed there was something mystical and necessary about the creative experience. He couldn't give it up. Serendipitously, Dom Frederic Dunne was the child of a bookbinder and publisher; he held the literary arts in an unusually high regard. Merton was encouraged to continue making poems. In 1942, he placed a poem in *The New Yorker*. In 1944, New Directions published his first collection, *Thirty Poems*. Eight more collections would follow.

In *The Hudson Review*, the critic Robert McDowell called Merton "a first-rate poet . . . one of the great poetic talents of the twentieth century." There are moments in his pieces that recall Whitman—Merton becomes ecstatic on the page, electric, so satisfied in his relationship with God, so moved by the tenderness of the landscape it feels as it whole passages simply willed themselves into being, as if Merton were merely a conduit, held in rapture for the rest of us. While he wrote frequently about magnificence, he also explored its antagonists (pain, decay, anguish). But for Merton, there were few things prayer couldn't nullify or ease.

There is also a compulsive quality to many of his best pieces. I understand how denying the urge to witness, parse, and record—to write—might've felt impossible to him, exhausting, like trying to hold a balloon under water forever. I also understand the mortal fear: the sense that a person could write or not write himself into oblivion. Sometimes there are things you need to excise in order to go on living.

6.

The greatest sacrifice of monastic life—the detail that chokes the secular world—is the deliberate renouncement of certain carnal intimacies. Practically speaking, that's the primary thing separating a proper monkhood from a subdued, God-fearing life in the hills. Without underselling the physical ramifications of sexual denunciation, deliberately forgoing the closeness that comes with sex (the way it feels to be undressed, to have someone's hands move over you and pull you nearer) seems so nonnegotiable to our psychic well-being that to deny it feels like a particular kind of suicide.

Merton's more official biographies tend to make quick work of his unholy early years: "After a rambunctious youth and adolescence, Merton converted to Roman Catholicism" is how it usually goes. It seems obvious to me, reading his journals and poems, that love and sex were a very big deal to him. Eating potatoes and staying quiet is one thing, but successfully shutting down the part of you that requires another person? That feels impossible.

"Human nature has a way of making very specious arguments to suit its own cowardice and lack of generosity" is what Merton would have told me.

7.

In Merton's most recent Selected Poems—*In the Dark Before Dawn*, published posthumously in 2005—there is a section called "On Being Human." The pieces included there are mostly about love. Some are about writing.

In March 1966, when he was fifty-one years old, Merton received back surgery at St. Joseph's Hospital in Louisville. In his recovery, he was tended to by a student nurse, a dark-haired twenty-five-year-old with gray eyes named Margie. She gave him a sponge bath. They made some dopey jokes about Snoopy. Merton fell hopelessly, urgently in love with her and began thwarting all kinds of monastery rules in order to nurture and satisfy his feelings.

Aside from the complications of their particular circumstance—*The Seven Storey Mountain* had been a colossal global success upon publication, meaning Merton had by then become one of the most famous living Catholic monks in the world—he was also contending with the doubt and anxiety that all love kicks up. "I have got to dare to love, and to bear the anxiety of self-questioning that love arouses in me," he wrote in his journal.

That May, James Laughlin, Merton's publisher at New Directions, and the Chilean poet Nicanor Parra visited Merton in Kentucky. Borrowing some coins from Laughlin, Merton stopped the car and telephoned Margie from a roadside pay phone, convincing her to join them for a meal in the Luau Room at the Louisville airport. There is a mania to these events. It's as if something inside him opened up—a need so clawing and severe he had no choice but to attempt to satiate it. People talk about the ecstasy of this kind of thing—of knowing, suddenly and for certain, that you've found the best person for you to love—but there is panic in the experience too. Love razes a body: you crack, reform. Afterward, you are somehow both exactly the same and fundamentally different. Merton must have been terrified.

On May 5, he wrote a poem called "Louisville Airport." He describes "four wet eyes and cool lips." He says, "There is only this one love / Which is now our world." Later, in his journal, Merton talked of how his feelings for Margie were unprecedented and unreplicable. It was revelatory—not like with other women he'd known. Merton understood, for the first time, that "the deepest capacities for human love in me have never been tapped, that I too can love with an awful completeness."

I wonder, sometimes, about the modifier he uses there: *awful*. Is that love, that awfulness? They saw each other whenever they could. They may or may not have had sex. They shared a bag of cherries in Cherokee Park, tossing the stones in the grass. They discussed marriage—Merton leaving Gethsemani, giving up his vocation for her. They devised a plan to each listen to Joan Baez's wary version of the folk ballad "Silver Dagger" precisely at 1:30 a.m., right when Margie's shift at the hospital ended. Reading Merton's poetry from this time, you can feel his desperation on the page, like another layer of ink. Frantically wanting and not wanting the same thing at the same time—it bends a person at the knees.

8.

"I have always tended to resist any kind of a possessive affection on the part of any other human being—there has always been this profound instinct to keep clear, to keep free," Merton writes in *The Seven Storey Mountain*. He wasn't talking about Margie— he didn't know about her yet—but I still think he was trying to confess something. That he didn't want to be counted on.

Merton had read John Donne—the sermons, the love poems, the elegies. Of all the great metaphysical poets, Donne had a singular knack for acknowledging truths most people edge away from. He was a womanizer and a cleric. He fathered twelve children in a secret marriage. In 1615, he became an Anglican priest. The critic Andrew Motion once wrote of

Donne's particular genius, "it finds its energy in exhaustion and its spiritual hope in bodily defeat." But Donne wrote beautifully about need. In his famous "No man is an island" devotion, he asks, rhetorically, "How little and how impotent a piece of the world is any man alone?" Then, and even more strikingly: "Any man's death diminishes me, because I am involved in mankind."

"Involved in mankind"—there is an elegance and nobility to Donne's engagement with the world. Had Merton read Tocqueville? An historian, Tocqueville fretted endlessly over the toxicity of individualism: "it throws him back forever upon himself alone and threatens in the end to confine him entirely within the solitude of his own heart."

The implication is that to live in cloister is selfish, self-serving, cruel, and cowardly. Choosing to join a monastery is not the same as simply choosing to live alone; for the faithful, God is omnipresent, everywhere. But those men still knew something about interconnectedness—about what we need to survive.

9.

Even though there are whole institutions in place to support these feelings, it's still easy to experience something akin to shame when certain longings manifest, become imperative: Merton's "possessive affection." That dumb, gaping maw—the desire to have someone call you their own, to be worthy of ownership. It's irrational, maybe, but it imparts vital stakes to the entire venture, reflecting both the idiocy and the drama of love. "Be mine." *Yes.*

It becomes hard not to think of everything else as middling, perilous, approximate. Timid. "Should we have stayed at home and thought of here?" is how Elizabeth Bishop puts it. I like to think there is real vitriol in her poem.

Perhaps the greatest boon of monastic life is that it clarifies the tension between what we think might make us happy—the systems of being and interacting our civilization has created and nurtured, all the things we're socialized to want—and what does. Maybe that's how Merton got around to beating it.

I envy whatever pushed him over. He and Margie gave up on their love. I don't know how mutual it was, which one of them said goodbye first or meant it the most. Those who knew Merton have intimated that he never really stopped loving her. There's a letter he wrote that summer—it's unclear whether he sent it—in which he seems to ask for her utter submission: "There is something deep, deep down inside us, darling, that tells us to let go completely," he writes. "Not just the letting go when the dress drops to the floor and bodies press together with nothing in between, but the far more thrilling surrender when our very being surrenders itself to the nakedness of love and to a union where there is no veil of illusion between us." He wanted all of her. I don't know if he asked for it. I don't know if he let her give it to him.

10.

"The intellect is only theoretically independent of desire and appetite in ordinary, actual practice," Merton posits in *The Seven Storey Mountain*. For Merton, the answer—the only way to reconcile all those selves—was "grace, grace, docility to grace." In late October 1966, he and Margie saw each other for the last time. Maybe she was the one to finally balk. He couldn't give her what she wanted. She made plans to split town, took a job in a different city. He recommitted himself to the monastery. He had his own unburdening to do. He even made a signed oath. On September 8, with abbot Dom James as a witness, he promised "to spend the rest of my life in solitude in so far as my health may permit." I wonder if he had to take a breath before putting pen to paper. If his hand twitched a little.

In 1967, Merton wrote in his journal: "What is 'wrong' in

my life is not so much a matter of 'sin' (though it is sin too), but of unawareness, lostness, slackness, relaxation, dissipation of desire, lack of courage and of decision, so that I let myself be carried along and dictated to by an alien movement. The current of 'the world,' which I know is not mine. I am always getting diverted to a way that is not my way and is not going where I am called to go." His life had become unrecognizable to him. It felt false. Somebody else's choices mapped onto him; his own lack of choices, compounded.

I can't tell if Merton was speaking specifically here about Margie distracting him from his faith, the Abbey distracting him from Margie, or both—woman and God distracting him from the business of being alive on earth. Or maybe he wasn't talking about any of those things. "Dissipation of desire." Losing the thing that made you feel awake. Whatever form it took, Merton hated himself for not fighting harder in its honor.

A year later, he was dead. In 1968, while visiting Thailand, Merton was electrocuted in a freak accident. He put his hands on a badly wired fan and collapsed on the terrazzo floor. A third-degree burn, six inches wide, ran down the right side of his body. Earlier that day, he'd given a lecture titled "Marxism and Monastic Perspectives." In it, he'd said monasticism is imperishable. "It represents an instinct of the human heart, and it represents a charism given by God to man. It cannot be rooted out, because it does not depend on man." Faith, like love, is not something we can monkey with. It is not something we choose.

11.

I started reading Merton in a serious way sometime around the start of my thirty-fifth year. I'd recently found myself seized by two dueling impulses: to be alone all the time and to never be alone. I recognized this need as semireligious, or at least monastic: a desire to gently withdraw from the culture and to find intimate, constant communion with God. I'm not sure whom or what

I thought "God" was. I'm not sure if this was a calling, in the traditional sense, or just a moment of deep psychic exhaustion. Regardless, I spent several months subsumed by an odd, dull sadness, an ache so banal and nonspecific it hardly feels worth describing. I loved and valued the life I had in New York City—a partner, an apartment, a good job—but I had become frightened of it.

When I wasn't reading compulsively, I was writing compulsively. Not researched, realized pieces for publication, but endless, unrelated scenes. There was something about this process that helped me feel in control, something about it that felt like a kind of cleaving: if it was on the page, it wasn't in me anymore. I thought I recognized a similar impulse in Merton's journals from Gethsemeni: an urgent need to chronicle, to exorcise, to transmute the chaos and ambiguity and boredom of life into clean, ordered sentences. To harness and then to make sense of the dizzying whims of the human heart. To turn desire—which is so inherently nonsensical—into a logical process, a wish and its fulfillment. And then to be done with it entirely.

That fall, I had been accepted into a writer's residency program, and in early June, I moved into a tiny stonemason's cottage in a clearing in a tall pine forest in New Hampshire. The program was prestigious enough that it felt like a kind of excuse—institutional validation of an otherwise shameful need to briefly disappear. The cottage had been built around 1926; it had a slate roof and a big brick fireplace and a screened-in porch with a rocking chair and tall, diamond-paned picture windows that I kept open almost all the time. I arrived with a trunkful of books, a laptop, and a portable record player. There were major thunderstorms that June, and runoff from the roof gouged a little moat around the place. For part of the first half of the century, you could see the pale, quartzite summit of Mount Monadnock—beloved peak of Emerson and Thoreau—from the eastern facade, but the forest had filled back in, puffed up, obscured the vista. Mostly, I saw trees.

I wanted to live as a monk for a while, or at least some

approximation of it. I wanted to outrun my need for either more freedom or less freedom—I couldn't really tell which—or at least find some way to vanquish it. I read and wrote and drank and listened to records. I went on long walks through pine forests. I felt guilty all the time—what an indulgence, to drop out! What an odd and unsociable wish, to want to be alone! I had been driven there by some foggy, unarticulated failure, and I felt constantly haunted by it.

Shortly before he died, Merton became interested in the Buddhist idea of desire as the source of all human suffering. It's a brutal cycle—we want things, we get things, we want more things, we get them, we want more. Merton wanted and didn't want in equal measure. So did I. I had so much, yet I still felt empty and scared.

I'd gone to New Hampshire thinking that it would be a chance to be alone and sit around and feel terrible about the circumstances of being alive in the second millennium. I thought I would feel sorry for myself and cry a lot. Instead, I read poems and wrote sentences and listened to records and drank cups of rye whiskey until, slowly, I started to feel better. I fell asleep to the ululating hoots of barred owls. In solitude, with study—I was unburdened.

I imagine Merton's later years in Kentucky were spent something like this: reading, feeling cowed by the nightly appearance of constellations, thinking of what we can ask of others and ourselves, contemplating our missteps, reassembling a self. Finding a way back from some unforeseen break. I didn't want to become stuck, as Merton was, between two magnitudes decreed mutually exclusive—to be coerced into shutting down the processes that make us permeable to each other and to the world.

12.

Merton wrote often about Margie in the last few years of his life, both during their relationship and after. He didn't try to hide those poems. He gave copies to Laughlin for posthumous publication. In "For M. On A Cold Grey Morning," he writes:

> A grey good morning and rain
> And melting snow
> Far from any help
> Or love, I am warmer
> At least wanting you.

"Cherokee Park," which wasn't released until 1985, contains one of my favorite stanzas:

> Love on this silent
> Hillside
> Wars with need aim and time
> And with humane summer
> With both images of
> Heaven and Hell and high-low
> Belief and the incredible
> Yes and No

I sometimes think everything Merton worked on after that was for her: "For I am without you / And unable to forget it." Merton knew that his journals—including the pages detailing their affair—would become part of the Merton Literary Trust and therefore end up in his archive at Bellarmine College in Louisville. I suspect he had reached a kind of détente with his own humanity. It didn't shame him anymore. All the fierceness of *The Seven Storey Mountain*, those violent, screaming renouncements: he saw them, now, as folly.

There Is a Name for This

Joanna Rakoff

ONE NIGHT, NOT SO VERY LONG AGO, I WALKED INTO a bar and found, as if he had been placed there just for me, the most handsome man in the world. He sat on a low couch, surrounded by women, not in the style of a cinematic playboy holding court over his admirers but in the manner of a very different sort of handsome man: The man whose attraction lies, in part, in his absolute and complete inner peace, in his lack of insecurities and anxieties, in his ego's egglike self-sufficiency. The man in utter control of himself, his thoughts, his mind. His body. This man—the most handsome man in the world—did not need the attention of the women surrounding him and, thus, he possessed every iota of it.

But in truth I barely noticed the women. All I saw, all I could see, was him. His slender legs bent upward in a V, too long for the trendily low sofa, and his mouth, which was full, turned upward, just slightly, in a smile. What did he look like? Does it matter? I suppose it does. A stranger might have presumed him foreign—Italian, perhaps, or Spanish or from some unspecified corner of South Asia or the Middle East—due as much to his close-cut, dark, elegant garments as his olive skin and hooded eyes and curling black hair, rapidly fading to white at the temples. And his hands. His fingers. Long, elegant, expressive. He held a glass of clear liquid that I suspected—no, I knew—to be pure water. Water unadulterated even with ice.

I spotted him, at first, out of the corner of my eye, as I

walked from the entrance of the bar to its rear, looking for the friend I'd planned to meet for a drink before heading out to a party. I wore a new dress, two layers of black silk, high-necked, long-sleeved, cut close through the shoulders and waist, a dress I'd bought with this evening, this party, in mind, for I had long been looking forward to this night, on which I'd see friends from all over the country, friends I loved and missed.

"You look like Monica Bellucci in that dress," my friend Ashley had told me, weeks before, when I tried it on at a local shop, the only dress shop in my barren Lower East Side neighborhood. "Like a bombshell." But I did not want to look like a bombshell. I wanted to look like a nun. I had long ago given up on the idea of romantic love, as least as it pertained to me.

I entered the bar filled with excitement purely at the prospect of the party I'd be attending, at which I'd talk frantically with those friends about books, about dresses, about the weather, about anything other than my life itself. But now, in the face of this man, the importance of the party, of my new dress, of my friends, fell away. The entire world fell away. Except for him.

For a moment, I stared at him, my hands shaking, heart hammering—those sound like clichés, I know, but please understand that I'm merely reporting what transpired. Though icy water had soaked through my boots, stiffening my feet with cold, and the wind had numbed my cheeks, the rest of my body had grown hot. Uncomfortably, horrendously hot. Under my arms, my silk dress clung damp with sweat. So much sweat that I feared wet circles had soaked through the soft wool of my coat. For a moment, the room spun, in a sickening way, and I braced myself on the arm of a nearby sofa so as not to fall down. I had, I realized, been holding my breath for a murderous amount of time. As if possessed, I turned my face back toward the man, twenty feet away, who was now laughing at something uttered by the woman to his left, his face glowing with delight. And as I shifted my eyes in his direction, the word for what was transpiring in my body, in my mind, came to me: desire.

The bar, I should explain, comprised the lower lobby of a large hotel, the Sheraton, in downtown Boston, adjacent to a sprawling convention center. Fourteen thousand writers had now converged on this small, elegant city, this city about which I knew nothing, despite its proximity to my own, not even that the neighborhood in which sat this bar, this hotel, possessed the graceful name of Back Bay.

Outside, a terrible storm sent wind across Boylston Street in painful, swirling gusts, a lethal mix of sleet and snow coating the dark streets with a strange, slippery crust. Across a narrow side street, in another large hotel, my children sat with their father in a dim, anonymous room, propped against the headboard of a plush queen bed, eating room service chicken fingers and watching an animated movie.

That afternoon, my husband and I had taken turns registering for the conference—he was attending not as a writer but as the staff member of a literary trade magazine—and looking after the children. For this was how we lived our life: separately. This was the only way we could have a life together. Separately. I had, over the course of our marriage, contemplated a life apart. Of course I had. For years, it was all I contemplated. The day after our wedding, I called my mother, in tears, and whispered, "I've made a mistake." She sighed, as if she had expected this call, though perhaps not so soon, and said, "Well, you've made your bed. Now you have to lie in it."

Fifteen years later, in Boston, as winds battered the windows of the Hilton and my children changed into their soft, cotton pajamas, I washed my face, swiped on mascara and lip gloss, and slipped my new dress over my head, reaching around awkwardly to pull the zipper from my spine to my neck, for I did not, not ever, ask my husband for help with anything, certainly not something as intimate as zipping up a dress. Quickly, quickly, I kissed my children goodbye, filled, for a moment, with an intense, animalistic desire to sink into bed with them, to fall asleep with their soft, curling hair on my shoulders, their warm faces buried in my neck. "Are you sure I should go?" I asked my husband. "You should go," he said. For tonight was my night. Tomorrow would be his night to venture out into the cold to see his own friends. Separately, we would have fun on this trip. Separately.

In the cold, overbright lobby, my reticence slipped away and I felt almost giddy—elated—with excitement. I was alone. Obligated to take care of no one but myself for the evening. In a new, beautiful dress. I pressed open the heavy door of my hotel, fighting a huge gale, and made my way through the snow and sleet, slipping in my kidskin boots, across the street to the Sheraton. The wind, this time, helped me with the heavy glass door, almost pushing me into the hotel's lower lobby, dimly lit and lined with low sofas.

But on one of them, of course, was him.

Across that alleyway, my children sat, warm and fragrant from their bath, and for a moment I wanted nothing more than to venture back out into the storm, to tap my plastic key against the door and sink into bed with them, to close my eyes and go to sleep. My life was not a terrible one. I had learned, by willing myself to learn, how to comfortably lie in the bed I'd made.

In a moment, I thought. In a moment, I'll go to the bar. Or I'll go back to the room. In a moment.

Instead, I turned my eyes back toward the man, the handsome man. And as I did so, he turned his eyes from his rapt companions and saw me, across the room, my dark hair, he would tell me later, crusted white with ice, and stood up, turning his body full in my direction. For a moment he stared at me, his mouth open, his eyes wide with shock, then he shook his head, as if clearing the remnants of a bad dream, and in a clear, deep voice—a voice choked with emotion—called out my name.

Twenty-three years earlier, on a scorching August morning, my parents pulled up in front of a small brick box, ferried my various bags to the second floor, hugged me fiercely, and began the long drive north and east, back to New York. Alone, I placed my new plant on the windowsill, smoothed maroon sheets on my bed, and pinned to the cinderblock wall the one poster I'd brought with me, advertising Elvis Costello's *Trust*.

I had, of course, been looking forward to this moment for the past six months—perhaps the past six years—but now that it was upon me, I felt sick with terror. The dorm in which I sat, paralyzed, stood on the eastern edge of Oberlin College, the school that has now come to signify a very specific sort of preciousness and privilege but then was regarded as a sanctuary for refugees from the tyranny of the Reagan-and-Bush United States. "People who were outcasts in high school can be cool at Oberlin," *Sassy* magazine had explained, the year prior, when they'd deemed it "the coolest college in America," confirming what I already knew; I'd had my heart set on Oberlin for years. For I, of course, had been an outcast, not just in high school but from the moment my mother dropped me at kindergarten. For as long as I could remember, I had been anticipating this exact moment, when I could say goodbye to my anonymous, conservative suburb—a town straight out of a John Hughes movie—and start anew. At Oberlin, I would be among my own kind, those inclined toward music and theater and novels, partaking of movies with subtitles, opposed to the impending war, and uninterested in sports.

In my cinderblock room that stifling August day, I connected the wires of my complicated stereo, then wandered out into the dank, carpeted hallway, unsure of where I might go. Was I allowed to leave my dorm? To walk around on my own? I did not know. Before I could figure out the answers to these questions, a boy emerged from a room down the hall and began walking toward me. Tall and long-limbed, so thin that his jeans, a faded blue, threatened to fall off his frame, he smiled and raised his hand in greeting. Awkwardly, I returned the gesture.

"Hi," he said, as we met in the middle, outside our RA's door.

"Hi," I said back, tamping down my confusion, for he was

not, not at all, the person I'd expected to meet at this college. He looked, as my high school friends would have said, *normal*. Sort of. His hair, a depthless black, lay close to his head, but I could see that it was as curly as mine, that it would grow wild and enormous if not tightly shorn. A neatly trimmed beard lined his wide jaw, and round wire-rimmed glasses—the sort ubiquitous at the time—covered his eyes, which were large and dark, with the heavy eyelids ascribed to the saints in Cyrillic paintings, which gave him a sleepy, bemused affect. He wore a loose T-shirt, almost ostentatiously plain; it bore no band name, no team logo, no political slogan, only the signs of many washings. Normal.

And yet.

I felt a strange, unprecedented desire to rest my head on this shirt, on his chest, on *him*, and close my eyes. This boy, for reasons I couldn't understand, felt—in the instant we met—more familiar, somehow, than the people who had raised me, than my friends from home, than anyone I had ever known. When he smiled at me, I felt something shift inside me, as if I were letting out a breath I'd been holding for my whole life, taking in an entirely new genus of air, air that made my whole body vibrate with excitement, with possibility.

It would be years, decades, before I realized that there is a name for this phenomenon: love at first sight.

His name was Keeril and he was from a town analogous to mine, a manicured New Jersey suburb, though he had not—like me—wasted time bristling at its cliques or closed-mindedness. He did not care, in the least, what anyone thought of him. Nor did he care about what constituted "cool" in 1990. He was a composer. This was how he introduced himself, casually, as a composer, as if it were perfectly normal for eighteen-year-olds to already possess a vocation. He was enrolled in both Oberlin College, like me, and Oberlin Conservatory, a course of study known as double degree. He had promised his father, an engineer, that he would major in math at the college, but he cared, purely, about writing music. His name derived not from the common Russian name Kiril—derived from the Greek Kirillos, meaning lord—but was invented by his parents, who took three letters from each of their names, Franklin and Renee, to form a new one. Its singularity seemed, somehow, a metonym for Keeril's person. For there was, it seemed, no one even remotely like him in the world.

From that moment, in the hallway, we became fast friends, a mirthful unit during the absurd icebreakers of orientation and a subject of intense speculation among our hallmates. Over the years that followed, I called him, to anyone who asked, "one of my best friends," though we saw each other largely when, for one reason or another, our paths crossed in the mailroom or the quad or a dining hall. Each time we met, it felt as if we were picking up a conversation we'd left off five minutes before, as if our whole friendship were one long-running, endless discussion. I found myself, always, telling him things I'd told no one else and laughing with him over things that had previously plagued me. He had, somehow, the ability to make me see—in an instant—the absurdity of, well, everything, including myself. Each time I saw his tall, slender figure coming toward me on the path that ran from the student union to the library, or crossing Tappan Square, my entire body quivered, as it had that first time, on the second floor of Fairchild.

Each time, I wanted to rest my head on his shoulder and never pick it up.

But I also wanted—though I could not admit this to myself, or to anyone—to tilt my head up toward his and place my mouth on his full lips, which seemed to radiate a heat of their own, as if they were calling to me. I wanted to press my face to the tender skin of his neck, especially the place where it met the muscle of his shoulder. I wanted to wrench the clothing from his slender body and take him to bed and stay there forever.

Spring semester of my junior year I studied in London. The following fall, I dropped my bags at my house on North Professor Street and walked across campus to the defunct gym that served as an ad hoc registration center. As I left the building, flipping through paperwork, I ran directly into Keeril. The relief I felt on seeing his face felt akin to nothing I'd experienced in my life so far. He'd changed, a bit, in the last nine months. His voice, always low, had sunk into an even deeper grumble. His shoulders had broadened. My mother, I suppose, would say he'd "filled out." He was no longer the skinny kid I'd met in the hallway of Fairchild.

"What are you doing now?" he asked.

"I was heading into town to buy a new bike," I told him, my commitment to this plan fading even as the words left my mouth. "Mine was stolen while I was away."

"Actually," he said, "I have a bike for you. The old tenants left a bike in my house. I think it should fit you. Do you want to come see it?"

The bike fit.

In his room, on the second floor, I said, "I missed you," my voice breaking, and he put his arms around me, after all those years, and kissed me, and the world suddenly shifted into perspective, as if everything that came before this moment had been a mere blur. This, I realized, was what a kiss was supposed to feel like. This was why people liked kissing. A moment later, we were in his bed, and I had the same thought about sex. Our bodies seemed, somehow, to already know each other, like they had been designed to fit together. I felt none of the awkwardness, the self-consciousness, the confusion, the irritation I'd felt with the others—there hadn't been many—before him. But also—decades later, this is still hard for me to say—I wanted him, in a way I had never, not ever, wanted anyone before. Every encounter that preceded it had stemmed from some boy's desire for me, rather than mine for him. I'd felt, purely, grateful to be wanted. My own desire had never even factored into the equation.

From that first day on—the day of registration, the day of the bike—we were inseparable, as if to make up for lost time, for all those years in which we could have been together but somehow could not allow ourselves to be. When we parted, for class, or to see friends, I didn't consciously long for him, but the minute we returned to each other—his long arms wrapped around me; my face burrowed into his neck—the world made sense again. I wanted him every second, inside me, all over me, his mouth, his beautiful hands, the bristle of his jaw.

After graduation, I returned to London—I'd been accepted into a one-year master's program in literature—while Keeril stayed on for another semester to complete his double degree and finish up his own applications to doctoral programs in composition. In January, he would join me for six months until we returned to the States for him to begin graduate school.

Though I believed myself to be having a grand time— seeing plays every night, eating jacket potatoes in pubs with classmates, wandering through the Tate alone—when Keeril showed up on the doorstep of the shabby house I shared with some classmates, I collapsed into his arms, sobbing, and buried my head in his chest until he gently untangled my arms from his waist and guided me upstairs to my room, where we went immediately to bed.

The next day, Keeril set about making us a new life in London, together. While I went to my seminars and tutorials, he found us an absurdly beautiful apartment in Belsize Park, with double-height ceilings and wedding cake moldings, and he landed a job at my favorite bookstore, where the largely female staff doted on him. With Keeril, London felt less like an adventure and more like a home.

Together, we taught ourselves to cook, in our miniscule

kitchen, by working our way through Nigel Slater's *Real Fast Food*, a recommendation from one of his coworkers, and took long walks through every corner of the city, stopping in the National Gallery, when the mood struck us. We attended operas and plays and concerts and ate dim sum and got lost on Hampstead Heath.

But there was one catch, about which I tried not to think: I could no longer write. The deadlines for my seminar papers came and went as I stared at the cursor on my laptop, huddled in our apartment's sleeping loft. I couldn't think either. In the fall, I had bubbled over with ideas, my heart racing with the thrill of making connections between, say, Dickens and Washington Irving. Now, as London sloughed off the gray haze of winter, as the trees on our street broke into blossom, I sat in silence, listening to my classmates argue. I told myself that this was, perhaps, a sign that I was burned out on academia, that I should have taken a year off, as my Oberlin advisor suggested, and worked in publishing or at a magazine or traveled. Perhaps graduate school had been an enormous, expensive mistake, for I seemed to have lost all desire to write esoteric papers on Sylvia Plath's English landscape poems or the Jamesian roots of Lynne Tillman's *Motion Sickness*.

I had also, perhaps even more troublingly, lost all desire to compose poems and stories—as I had since childhood—or even to write in the journal I'd scrupulously kept since first grade. I even had trouble *reading* in our stunning apartment. My mind no longer seemed my own. Sometimes, at night, I'd sit at our lovely dining room table, my notes spread out in front of me, the little radio on the mantle tuned to the shipping news, and listen, transfixed, as the announcer softly intoned the names of mysterious cities. Maybe, I thought, the problem was London. Maybe, if I traveled to Lundy or the Faroes I would be able to think again, I would be able to form sentences, like my former self.

In March, Keeril got the news that he'd gotten into Berkeley.

Which was not a surprise. I've not yet mentioned, I suppose, that Keeril was a star. A genius, in the literal sense of the term. Regarded as such by his mentors and peers at Oberlin. And while I knew nothing about classical music—despite having played violin from age three on—it was clear even to me that his pieces were brilliant and bombastic and life-changing. Keeril's music was broad and emotional but not sentimental; it incorporated themes and ideas from the traditions he'd inherited—classical Indian on his father's side; klezmer on his mother's—and created something entirely singular and gorgeous, but also provocative and somehow physical. You could feel his music resonate in your body.

But his genius lay, I suppose, not just in his considerable, terrifying talent but in his singularity of purpose. Keeril did not fuck around. There had been no question that he would get into Berkeley—his program of choice—and, now, there was no question that I would join him once I finished my studies that fall. Midway through one of the hottest summers in London's history, Keeril flew home to get things ready for his move, *our* move, to California. I would remain in London until September, when I would sit for my exams, and then fly back to America. I could not afford our apartment on my own, so I moved into a Hampstead dorm to finish out my time alone.

At the tiny desk in my tiny room, I researched my master's thesis—on those dull Plath landscape poems, after all—reading and rereading Plath's letters and journals, and took punishing runs up and down the hills of Hampstead, Plath's thoughts weaving in and out of my own. Plath was afraid "that the physical sensuousness of marriage will lull and soothe to inactive lethargy," obliterating her "need to write." Was that what happened to me, when I was with Keeril? I suspected so. Because now that I was alone, I had resumed writing—and thinking— again. My papers, my thesis, came easily to me. I filled the pages of my journal with thoughts and ideas and observations. And as I ran up and down the cracked sidewalks, stories began to unfold in my mind, stories I wrote down with an almost cine-matic urgency.

When my mind went in this dangerous direction—as I sat at my built-in desk, studying—I began to feel vaguely ill, and pulled on my running shoes and ran out the door, racing un-safely down the dorm's narrow staircase, then taking off down the hill. As the summer wore on, I found myself going to the movies, endlessly, in an attempt to shut off my mind, to stop this unnerving question from surfacing again and again.

Why? Why couldn't I write, why couldn't I think, when I was with Keeril? What did this mean about him? Or about me? Or about us together?

I did not go to Berkeley.

I went home. To New York.

At first, I told Keeril—and myself—that I would be heading out there soon. I just wanted to visit with my friends, who were all teaching dance at Brooklyn Friends or starting film school at Columbia or assisting editors at Random House. I went to their parties, at tenements in the East Village and rambling lofts in Williamsburg and found reason after reason to delay heading west: I'd fallen into a job as a PA on a Barbra Streisand film! And then another, as the assistant to a legendary literary agent! It will just be a month, maybe two!

And then, somehow, a year had passed, and then another. And, somehow, I had a boyfriend, and then another, and then several at once, all of them Keeril's inverse and opposite, riddled with insecurities, ruled by ego, vaguely macho, all of them vocal about their outsized love for me, their desire for me, their cer-tainty that I was the most beautiful woman in the world, their perfect mate, sentiments Keeril had never expressed, because he did not need to; his every glance, his every gesture, told me all I needed to know. From Berkeley, he wrote to me, first on paper, then over email, about his frustrations with academia and the rarified world of classical music, and I wrote back, about my job in publishing and the column I began writing for a magazine and my first poem accepted by a literary magazine. At night, sometimes, I came home from a party, or a date, or a reading, and sat down at my desk, hoping to find a note from him, longing for his singular take on the world. I missed him, dreadfully; missed him in all ways; sometimes, as I lay in bed at night—in the various apartments I inhabited in those first years apart—I found myself quivering with longing for him, burning for his touch, for the sound of his voice in my ear, the specific warmth of his head resting on mine, his arms around me.

Why did I not return to him? Why did I not, like a Nora Ephron heroine, race to the airport, buy a ticket at the counter, fly out to Berkeley, and show up at his door?

At the time, I believed that I had lost him, that I had hurt him so badly he could never forgive me; I believed, too, that this—my abandonment of Keeril—was the greatest mistake, misstep, of my life, a tragic error, the unhappy outcome of which—a life without true love, unconditional love, without happiness, without desire—I deserved, in full, in perpetuity. Three years, nearly to the day, after I failed to arrive in Berkeley, I married the man who shouted the loudest, who desired me the most, or so he said, so he believed. Perhaps because he—a would-be poet himself—saw me, first and foremost, as a writer, and a talented one, and I could envision a life with him, with my work at its center, a life in which I woke up and wrote, and fell asleep with my head on the page, my hand gripping the pen. Perhaps because I didn't love him, didn't desire him, in the way I did Keeril and there was no danger of losing myself.

Years passed. A decade. Then half of another. Keeril won fellowships and awards and commissions that took him all over the world. I stayed in New York and wrote and wrote, struggling to lie in the bed I'd made, intent—for reasons that now elude me—on presenting my marriage, myself, to friends, to the world, as perfect, as normal, as happy. Keeril married, too, eventually, and moved to Paris, then Illinois, then Cambridge to teach.

Years passed. Sometimes, he'd come to New York, repeatedly, for a commission or a performance and its associated rehearsals, and we'd see each other every day, taking long walks through Central Park on his breaks from Carnegie Hall, eating afternoon-long lunches at quiet restaurants, my body slowly igniting with desire. Sometimes, on the bench of a subway car or seated next to each other on a friend's couch, I let my head rest on his shoulder and cried, quietly, overcome with longing and loss. Sometimes, he read an essay of mine in the *Times* and called, overcome—I see now—with longing and loss. Sometimes, we went months, years, without speaking to each other, terrified of the feelings that would arise at the sound of the other's voice. Sometimes, we spent hours on the phone, day after day, talking about everything, every single thing, in our lives, a practice that alarmed and enraged our spouses. Understandably, I suppose. They knew we were not having an affair, virtual or otherwise. The truth, I suppose, was more frightening—to them and to us—that as the years went by, we grew closer rather than apart, we moved in the same direction, as artists, as people, and we somehow understood each other more, and more, with each passing year. Sometimes, they asked, separately, for us to break off contact—my husband more forcefully, more ragefully—and we complied. Until the next essay, the next trip of his to New York or mine to Boston. Until a cold afternoon in the fall of 2010, Keeril in town for a series of rehearsals, when we lingered over lunch for hours, then walked and walked around the West Village, not wanting to part ways, until we arrived at the borrowed apartment at which he was staying, and I followed him upstairs, where our conversation suddenly ceased. We sat, stiffly, on the couch, avoiding each other's gaze. We had not, I realized, been alone with each other in fifteen years. "I want you," he said, raising his eyes to meet mine, "but I don't want to have an affair with you and I don't want to destroy your family." I nodded, unable to speak, for I knew if I opened my mouth, no comprehensible words would emerge—no "I agree" or "I feel the same," though I did—but simply cries of rage and frustration.

And pure, unmitigated desire.

Two years later, give or take a month, I walked into a bar in Boston, a city about which I knew nothing—never guessing that a few months later, it would be my home, that I would write my next book from a desk two miles west of this hotel—and found myself in front of the most handsome, most attractive man I'd ever seen. Every night, since we'd parted, I'd dreamed of him—his arms around me, his cheek against mine, his long body next to mine—and yet, for an instant, I still thought him a stranger, the most handsome stranger in the world. When I realized he was he, I nearly collapsed with terror and grief and pain and desire.

Across that room, he saw me and stood, shocked, and stared in my direction, shaking his head in disbelief. "Jo," he called, in his low, quiet voice. It occurs to me, only now, that I could not have heard him, as the bar thrummed with voices and music and the clanking of glasses, but that I merely saw his lips move in the shape of my name. And I found the courage to move toward him, rather than run away, run back to my children and husband, as he unfolded himself from the couch, stepping away from his companions as if they were strangers, moving toward me, until, as in a dream, I was in his arms. The world, as it had twenty years earlier, fell away. Did we stand there, amid the jubilant crowds, for a minute, an hour? Eventually, he looked down at me and said, "How are you?"

How was I?

I truly did not know. I thought of my children, across the narrow, curving alleyway, snuggled together under the heavy duvet, and the afternoons we spent wandering through museums or turning cartwheels in the park. I thought, for a moment, of my tiny office in my apartment four hours south, a closet I'd converted, and the happy hours I spent there, lost in the worlds of my characters or teasing out the thread of an argument. I thought, too, of the panel on which I was scheduled to appear the next day, which had seemed exciting and important an hour earlier and now struck me as absurd and trivial and devoid of meaning in the face of Keeril, as did everything, everything. I wanted to lay my head on his chest and never pick it up again. I wanted to press my lips to the warm skin of his neck. I wanted to take his hand and go wherever he took me. I wanted him.

"How are *you*?" I asked, with a shrug. His full mouth grew slack with pain.

"I'm not good, Jo," he said. "I can live without you. But I can't be happy without you."

I don't need to explain, I suppose, that the same was true for me.

My Dick, Your Dick, Our Dick

Amy Gall

THE WOMAN BEHIND THE CASH REGISTER LOOKED UP as we opened the door, the breeze lifting the wings of her salt-and-pepper mullet.

"Do you need any help?" she said.

I looked down and assured her we did not.

"Actually," Stephanie said, squeezing my hand. "We want to get a strap-on."

"Well," the woman smiled. "Seems like you came to the right place."

Surrounding us on all sides, like a genital amphitheater, were shelf upon shelf of dildos. There were dildos made of silicone, dildos made of blown glass, dildos made of a new hyper-realistic material that felt so much like touching human skin it made me wonder if there was a different kind of underground organ market I didn't know about. Dildos complete with balls and scrotums, dildos that bore only the most abstract expressionist resemblance to a penis. There were dildos in every skin tone and dildos the color of unicorn princess parties and dildos that looked like a dynamic suspension of fire and water and earth, such that if you were penetrated with one, Captain Planet might emerge from your pussy.

I was thrilled by this bounty. I also had no idea what to do with it. In 2005, the lesbian internet consisted mainly of a handful of badly designed Angelfire websites filled with *Xena* and *Star Trek Voyager* fan fiction. Facebook and YouTube were only a few months old, *Autostraddle* did not exist, even the *L-Word* cast wasn't doing anything more penetratively complicated than banging their hands into each other's crotches at Dinah Shore parties. There was nowhere private to go to find out from other queer women how queer sex with strap-ons actually worked.

I was nineteen and in my second year at a liberal arts college. I had heard talk of these mythical instruments from older dykes, and I could have asked them for more information, but that would have been too public a reveal of how little I knew, and, up until that point, I firmly believed my survival as a lesbian meant always appearing to be a seasoned pro.

I held several dildos up to the light and turned them like an expert sommelier selecting a bottle of wine.

Stephanie rolled her eyes.

"How do you know if it's the right fit?" I asked.

The cashier came out from behind the register, revealing acid-washed jeans and a pair of steel-toed leather boots. As she walked over to us, her hips shifted back and forth in a way that let me know the answers to our questions lived inside her body.

She explained that if we wanted to figure out if the circumference of a dildo was right for us, we should do the finger test. "That is," she said, holding up her thick, calloused hands, "if you like two fingers inside yourself, you lay those fingers against the shaft of a dildo until you find a thickness that matches up."

I stared at the lineup, my hands clenched at my sides. I had come out six years earlier and quickly learned that my feelings for and the things that I wanted to do with other girls in school were not reciprocated. When I did start dating, what seemed to make me sexually desirable was not my body but what I could do to my girlfriends' bodies. Once, after trying, unsuccessfully, to make me cum, my high school girlfriend even said, "Your body just doesn't want this and I'm not going to try again."

Rather than being heartbroken by this, I inverted the pain and wrapped it around my body like a protective cloak. I wasn't being touched because I didn't want to be touched. I wasn't being pleasured because pleasuring my girlfriend was more satisfying. I wasn't broken, I was potent.

I reached for a dildo that was about five inches long. It was the color of a fire engine and had an ovular head slightly thicker than the shaft. I turned my back to Stephanie and the woman and laid two fingers against it; the outline of the shaft aligned perfectly with the edges of my skin. I felt hopeful and nauseous. Was there actually a formula for my own body's pleasure?

"Yeah, this one's okay," I said, clearing my throat.

"Then," the woman said pointing to another wall, "you'll need a harness."

A harness, it turned out, was like a really confusing seatbelt for your pussy. It attached to your legs and around your waist with a complicated series of straps, and in the center was a hole you threaded the dildo through. Some of the harnesses had a nonadjustable hole, but the better ones had even more snaps where you could attach a rubber circle, called an o-ring, which kept the dildo flush against your pelvis and—because there were different sized o-rings—allowed for a greater level of versatility in the size of the dildo you could use. Like dildos, harnesses could be made of all sorts of materials. At the woman's behest, I rubbed my hands across the buttery expanse of a leather one that was mounted on the wall—the smell of animal blooming in my nose. Since there were no changing rooms, I slipped the harness on in the middle of the store, which was, thankfully, empty. Stephanie adjusted the straps, like a mother helping a toddler find the correct pair of pants. It fit.

Stephanie chose her own dildo: three fingers thick and about nine inches long, with a head that puckered and veins that snaked down the sides. I anxiously noted how much larger and closer to the real thing hers looked in comparison to mine.

Stephanie had slept with women before, but until we got together, she had only been in serious relationships with men. Stephanie was studying feminist psychoanalysis and I was friends with lesbians who were reading Judith Butler, so there were some hazy conversations about how maybe phalluses were just social constructs, and something something Law of the Father something something hegemony, but Stephanie had selected a dildo that looked like the real thing and this, to me, indicated her desire *for* the real thing. And while the guys she'd been with had decades to get used to the swinging appendages between their legs, I would have all of thirty seconds. Stephanie assured me she wouldn't be comparing, but, as we took our purchases back to campus, I worried I wouldn't measure up.

Though I didn't know it at the time, the dildo has always been attached, so to speak, to men and their dicks. Of course, when men are the interpreters and recorders of history, how could it be otherwise?

In the Ancient Greek comedy *Lysistrata*, one of the earliest appearances of the dildo in written form, the title character tries to get the women of the surrounding Greek cities to withhold sex from their husbands as a way to end the Peloponnesian War and at one point laments:

"As for old flames and lovers—they're none left.

And since Milesians went against us,

I've not seen a decent eight-inch dildo.

Yes, it's just leather, but it helps us out."

Here as in other fictional accounts written by men at the time, the dildo is at its most palatable because it most directly represents the male body and women's dependence on it for sexual satisfaction. In more recent times, eighteenth- and nineteenth-century Nantucket whalers even brought back dildos from China, which they termed "he's-at-home" as a way to prevent their wives from cheating on them on their long trips at sea.

However, when a dildo was uncoupled from the dick it practically became a terrorist threat. In "Dildos and Accessories: The Functions of Early Modern Strap-Ons," Liza Blake found that the earliest documentation of strap-ons in the real world came from court cases brought against women who dared use them. "In sixteenth-century Spain," she writes, "the legal theorist Antonio Gomez declared that 'if a woman has relations with another woman by means of any material instrument' she must be burned, and says that two Spanish nuns suffered precisely this punishment. In France in 1533 two women were put on trial and tortured because they were accused of having sex using a dildo . . . and around 1535 a woman was burned for the 'wickedness which she used to counterfeit the office of a husband.'"

Strap-ons and masculine dress also allowed women to "pass" as men—regardless of what their actual gender or sexual identity might have been—and gain access to the privileges afforded to men, which included free public movement, jobs, and with that financial independence, land-ownership, and even marriage. These cases not only served as a deadly form of punishment for women who attempted to free themselves from male control; they also reasserted the idea that even when women have sex with each other, they are doing so only in a misguided attempt at replicating heterosexual sex.

Nowhere is this truer than in the eighteenth-century Prussian court case brought against Catharina Margaretha Linck, who dressed in men's clothing most of her life and married a woman. She and her wife remained married for four years, at which point the wife's mother, according to court records, "charged the defendant with being a woman and not a man . . . ripped open her pants, examined her, and . . . found not the slightest sign of anything masculine" and, along with a neighbor, beat Linck up. When the case was brought to trial, Linck's wife claimed that she had no idea Linck was a woman since Linck only had sex with her with what turned out to be a dildo made of stuffed leather and that as soon as she found out about Linck's "deception" she refused to have sex. Linck was charged with sodomy and beheaded. Link's wife was imprisoned and later released when she "admitted" that the sex they had was forced on her by Linck.

There have been other cases similar to Linck's, even in more recent times, in which one woman wearing masculine dress and a dildo "tricked" another femme woman into having sex. Regardless of what was happening behind closed doors, in the public theater of the court the roles of the two women were inflexible—there was always a more masculine woman and a more feminine woman. The masculine woman always strapped the dildo on, the woman who was more feminine was always penetrated. When faced with the horror of her own impending death, it is no wonder that the feminine woman would rush to claim that she had been tricked, that only by believing she was having sex with a man would she dare have sex with a woman. But it is telling that the "masculine" woman was so threatening to male power and control that, even if she renounced her actions, she had to be destroyed.

In the darkness of my dorm room, Stephanie and I slipped off our clothes. I held the harness against my pelvis with one hand and tried to tighten one leg strap with the other, which caused the buckle of the other leg strap to pop open. Reflexively, I moved my hand to hold that strap together, which opened both straps. The dildo slipped backward out of the o-ring, bounced on its head, and rolled under the bed. As I crouched down, feeling around for my dick, I could hear Stephanie's low, soft laughter.

"Let me do it," she said.

When the dildo was finally snug against my body, I knelt next to Stephanie and she wrapped her fingers around the shaft. I felt the pressure travel from the tip of the head to the buzzing core of my pussy.

"You're so beautiful," Stephanie said, which felt both emasculating and like I was receiving the highest compliment in the world.

There are times when having no history or language for what you want can feel like disappearing, and there are times when the unspeakable boundarylessness of queer sex nails you to the floor with pleasure. I thrust into Stephanie. Her legs wrapped around my hips. Her fingers held and then dug. We groaned into one another's mouths. It felt tender and brutal and like we were creating an entirely new person between us and falling together into their depths.

After Stephanie came, I held her steaming body against mine. "I didn't know you could do that," I whispered.

"Take it off," she said and as I did, tears pearled at the edges of her eyes.

For Stephanie, this was the first time she'd experienced a dick as a tool solely for her own orgasm that she could then make disappear. She both loved and was overwhelmed by this. I wanted Stephanie to feel good, but I also wanted the dildo to be real, for me to be able to feel the very deepest parts of Stephanie as I ejaculated inside of her. And after, I wanted it to remain on me in a softer, smaller version, until *I* decided I wanted to have a pussy again. But I thought that desire made me the same as the selfish men Stephanie had felt so used by, so I simply held her until she stopped crying and we fell asleep.

When Stephanie penetrated me, the process was far less transportative. The smallest o-ring we had was still too wide for my dildo, so we resorted to padding it with wads of toilet paper to keep it from falling out of the harness. Even then, Stephanie often had to hold the base of the dildo steady with her hand, which meant she couldn't go deep enough for me to feel much of anything other than embarrassment.

What I didn't know then was that the dildo I had chosen for my vaginal penetration was a buttplug. Most dildos below a certain circumference or height are, in fact, marketed for anal use. This detail may seem, well, small, but it is another way of dictating to women and their vaginas what they should want. And while the sex toy industry has recently begun to make harnesses for smaller dildos, this seems to largely be a response to the popularity of pegging, as these strap-ons are explicitly marketed to straight women and their male partners. Of course, not knowing this, instead of being angry at the sex toy industry I was angry at myself. Here was further proof that I wasn't meant to be an object of desire, that fluidity was not something to be celebrated but a problem to be fixed.

Many of the women I was closest to seemed to confirm my fears. When I showed one friend the dildos, she nodded in approval at the large, realistic looking one I used on Stephanie, but upon seeing the one I chose for myself, she burst out laughing.

"Amy," she said. "Do you want to get fucked by a fourth-grade boy?"

Another group of friends bought me a butt plug for my birthday for me to use on Stephanie. The next morning they crowded around me at breakfast to ask how she liked it. When I told them that Stephanie had used it on me, they fell silent.

"Whoa," one of them said, her chin dipping into her neck. Usually, we would gossip for hours about the things I did to other women in bed. But when I was the one getting fucked it was somehow embarrassing to all of us, to the point of being unspeakable.

To make matters worse, about two years into our relationship, I found out Stephanie had been secretly and consistently sleeping with men. I was no innocent myself; I'd been carrying on flirtatious, emotional affairs with other women for almost as long and even broke up with Stephanie at one point to be with someone else. Still, this new information destroyed any remaining interest I had in my own penetration. Men, after all, didn't get penetrated with dicks in their vaginas, so maybe if I didn't get penetrated by Stephanie, *my* dick would be enough for her.

By the end of our relationship, penetrating Stephanie with a strap-on was the only way we had sex. Instead of a bridge between us it became a barrier, a way for us to touch less, to avoid skin-to-skin contact with our softest, open parts. And instead of making me feel potent, it made me feel like I was disappearing, becoming the performance of the men she actually wanted to be with and would, eventually, leave me for.

———

As history has shown, and as I was at the time experiencing, a strap-on can be sexy, but it can also be a failure and a threat. It draws attention to how contradictory and fragile our definitions of male and female are, and how tightly we cling to them, even in relationships between women, where gender and sexuality are more flexible.

I think it's important to look at how this played out, not just in the history of straight men policing lesbians but in the lesbian community policing itself. In the 1940s and 50s a bar scene began to develop in cities across the country, marking the first time when lesbians, particularly working-class ones, gathered publicly and in large numbers. During this time a butch/femme culture developed that included strict codes of dress and behavior both in and outside the bedroom. Butch women slicked back their hair, wore suits and jeans, and were, generally, the "givers" of sexual pleasure. Femme women wore dresses and makeup and were the "receivers" of sexual pleasure. In some ways, this culture was liberating, as it represented a powerful, cohesive group aesthetic and safety in numbers. Especially for women who actually identified as butch, it was also a chance to finally adopt masculine dress without being seen as failed or dangerous but rather as sexy and loveable. For others this culture was a trap, pushing women into restrictive sex and gender roles in the same ways heterosexuality had. It is by no means the only lesbian aesthetic, but I think part of the reason it has stuck around for so long in the popular imagination as *the* way lesbians are is because it allows straight people to again see themselves as the center of the sexual world.

In either case, strap-ons were not widely used, or at least not talked about. In *Boots of Leather, Slippers of Gold*, a book that documents the lives of Black and white lesbians in Buffalo, there is a pretty exhaustive set of interviews about sex acts and terminology, but no one mentions owning, liking, or even trying sex with a strap-on. Indeed, the one mention of a dildo is one of bewilderment as Vic, a self-identified butch, talks about her friend pulling her into the bathroom to show her the new strap-on she got. "Jesus, she whipped this thing out . . . I'm supposed to be butch and my face felt like a neon sign. I could feel the embarrassment. How do you admire a dildo? No seriously, what do you say?"

Butches in the book took great pride "in their own hands and their ability to please," which "did not dispose them to think that a dildo would improve their lovemaking." It's interesting that they considered the dildo less potent and successful than hands. This could be read as displacing the power of the dick, but, coupled with the silence surrounding strap-on use, it also points to a greater fear about the lesbian body. How regulated and small it had to be to exist. How easily it could be diminished by something outside itself, or destroyed altogether.

In the lesbian radical feminist movement of the 1960s and 70s, there was also a great deal of attention focused on creating distance from dicks. Jill Johnston argued in *A Lesbian Nation* that the only true road to female liberation was the conscious "withdrawal at every level from the man to develop woman supremacy." This meant that not only butch/femme dynamics but also penetrative sex were out. Anne Koedt developed the theory that the vaginal orgasm was a myth perpetrated by Freud in order to center male sexual desire for penetration, though her evidence for this was a study done by Kinsey—a man—that found the vagina was not particularly sensitive to touch. True orgasms, Koedt argued, only came from the clitoris—even though she interestingly also called the clit "the female equivalent of the penis"—so if women wanted to have enjoyable sex there was no need for penetration, only clitoral stimulation. Andrea Dworkin went so far as to call the penis "a hidden symbol of terror" and argued that "violence is male, the male is the penis."

Dorothy Allison writes about the effects this had on herself and other lesbians at the time. "No one admitted to using dildos, wanting to be tied up, wanting to be penetrated, or talking dirty—all that male stuff . . . my lover wanted us to perform tribadism, stare into each other's eyes, and orgasm simultaneously. Egalitarian, female, feminist, revolutionary." In attempting to free themselves from the penis, in many ways radical lesbians ended up reinscribing the power of the dick and sacrificing the range of sexual pleasure they could experience in the process.

In a counter to this, the lesbian sexual outlaws of the 1970s, 80s, and 90s argued that dildos were actually great, not problematic, but primarily because they didn't reference the penis at all. Some even argued that wearing a dildo turns a woman into a cyborg, not woman, man, or even human, just a body involved in the mechanistic movements of giving and receiving pleasure. While there is something freeing about this argument, as it gets us out from under the idea that we can't talk about strap-ons and that a woman wearing a strap-on is only trying to make up for a never-ending lack, it still bypasses the sticky, complicated reality of the gendered/human world we live in and the simple fact that sometimes lesbians want strap-ons to look like penises.

All of this begs the question: can a dyke wear a dick and just have some damn fun?

I got a text from Jane. "Can we go on a date-date?"

"Yeah," I wrote back. "Want to go to Babeland and buy a strap-on?"

I met Jane in a fiction workshop my second year of grad school. When we both handed in short stories about lesbians, Jane asked for my number and we made plans to get together at her place and "write." After many beers and zero writing, Jane and I had sex. Lying in bed afterward, I surveyed her studio apartment: the giant flat screen TV on her dresser, the sheets from Anthropologie, the view from her window of Sixth Avenue.

"I can't believe you live alone in Chelsea," I said.

She ducked her head into the crook of my neck. "My father helps me out."

The fact that Jane could commit her every waking moment for the next two years to writing, and would leave grad school debt-free, made me jealous. But her father's "generosity" was not without its own limitations.

That summer, Jane had dated a woman for the first time; when she told her parents, they told her not to tell anyone or talk to them about it again. Jane scurried back into the closet, claiming it was just a phase she needed to get out of her system. Her father now prefaced his monthly deposits in her bank account with "until you get a husband" and threatened at different times to summon her back to the West Coast if "things didn't go well" in New York. The fact that Jane's father used his money in an attempt to enforce Jane's heterosexuality made us both want to use it to enact a very gay vengeance upon him.

While Jane perused Babeland's selections and talked to staff, I hung back, nodding like the sage dildo professional I was. I spotted a large, thickly veined dildo that looked exactly like the one I'd used with Stephanie.

"Let's get that one," I said.

We didn't buy a separate one for me because I had already decided I was not going to be penetrated by Jane. Rather, I was going to use the same dick that had failed me with Stephanie to regain my lost sense of control.

Back at Jane's place, I put the dildo on alone in the bathroom, avoiding the vulnerability of an audience, and when I came out we proceeded to fuck our way through the West Elm catalog of her apartment. It was fun, but it was also awkward. I couldn't read what Jane wanted, and I was so caught up in the performance of my own cocksureness that I also couldn't tell what I wanted. Eventually we stopped.

"Your turn," Jane said.

I laughed. It was most certainly not my turn.

"We'll use the lube," she said. "It'll feel good, I promise."

It was scary to hear my words in someone else's mouth, scary and kind of hot.

"Ready?" she said

I felt myself parted, stretched, and then ripped. A burning wicked my insides and climbed into my stomach and chest. Aside from one night, when I was fourteen and accidentally popped my own cherry with a vibrator, I had never hurt from penetration before. I had always avoided being the recipient of sexual pain because of how much it disrupted my sense of control. And yet, here I was, allowing a near stranger to tear my pussy open with a giant, undeniably phallic stick. I was frightened of this vulnerability, this blind dependence on someone else to determine what I would feel next, but when Jane asked if she could go deeper, I said yes, without hesitation.

When Jane eventually pulled the dildo out, there was blood on the shaft. I stared at the red liquid, trying to understand why I felt ashamed and blank and thrilled at the same time, why it felt like I had just pushed my body off a cliff with no idea if I would survive the fall.

There is this idea that turning points are clean and complete, but while my body seemed to want more of these experiences with Jane, my mind remained wary and confused. It was like a tug of war: one minute, I would buck against the dildo Jane held in her hand and the next I would push it out of me. I'd hover above Jane, careful to keep from resting even an ounce of my weight on her and then I'd suddenly plop down on her lap and grind down on her like a pestle. I'd thrill as Jane's eyes roamed across my body and then I'd hear myself say, "Stop looking at me."

For so long, I had dismissed the parts of me that wanted to be an object of desire, telling myself that my worth lay in the pleasure I gave to other women. And while I had squirmed against the butch label, that was perhaps because I also saw how I much I hid behind the swaggery, masculine aspects of it to keep myself safe from rejection. When I was suddenly faced with a person who actually wanted the soft, vulnerable—dare I say feminine—parts of me, who made me feel fuckable, it took time for the old stories to sieve their way out of me. And they never did completely. But as we kept having sex I began to feel relief instead of fear in giving up control. I began to appreciate the space it afforded me to start paying attention to what made *my* body feel good and not just my partner's. I also began to see how femininity and objectification held their own power. There is something so emboldening about holding a lover's gaze, about allowing them inside the deepest parts of you. And even when you are "the bottom" there is a constant dance of consent and choice being navigated between you and your partner. Understanding this made me a better lover when I was topping too.

It is not as if being fucked with one big dick a few times made me comfortable with the fluidity of my gender and of my sexual desires, but as Jane and I continued to stretch each other's boundaries inside of a monogamous, trusting relationship, and my adult friends embraced the sex we were having, I started to experiment with my body in other ways. I asked Jane to show me how to apply my own lipstick and eyeliner. I started wearing dresses and heels, first to fancy occasions and then, sometimes, just because. I stopped pretending I always knew what people were talking about and discovered the joy of learning what was on the other side of an admission of not knowing. Jane changed too. She bought ripped jeans and T-shirts. She cut her hair short. She became more assertive and direct, eventually coming out to her parents. Once Jane and I realized we could actually inhabit the things we were attracted to in the other person, that it wouldn't compromise what was already there, we also became kinder to each other because we stopped needing the other person to be a certain way in order to feel complete.

After two years, Jane and I broke up. It was painful, not

devastating. We hadn't hidden or twisted our desires with each other, so when we couldn't meet them, it didn't feel like a rejection of who I was but rather an indication that we had simply changed as much as we could together, and whatever else we were changing into, we had to change with other people, and perhaps, more importantly, on our own.

A few years ago, I went back to the same sex shop Stephanie and I had visited nearly a decade before, although now it was on the main street of town instead of relegated to a back parking lot. It was bigger and snazzier too, with sleek metal shelves and changing rooms, all of which I decided to take as a tidy metaphor for my own personal growth.

When the woman at the counter, her mullet now completely white, looked up, I recognized her immediately.

"Do you remember me?" I said.

"Sure I do, darling,"

I stayed for two hours, touching every make and model that caught my eye. I didn't need to be told to consider my needs or masquerade as someone who already knew it all. When I had questions, I simply asked them.

In the changing room, I adjusted the straps on the carbon copy of the dildo I'd bought with Stephanie and again with Jane. It was like a line connecting my present body to all my past penetrations. But this time, the pleasure wouldn't be attached to one partner or set of dynamics. This time my body was the only constant.

I chose two other dildos, each for a different sensation in my body, and took my haul back to the place I was staying for a self-imposed writing retreat. By day I drank coffee and listened to my mind; by night, I listened to my body.

I set a dildo on the nightstand next to me and I rubbed my clit. I gulped in breath, closed my eyes, and when I came, I screamed as loud as I could, reveling in the sound my voice made in an empty room. Then I covered the dildo in my favorite lube and fucked myself. I fucked myself slowly, quickly, in my pussy, in my ass, in both holes at the same time. I fucked myself on the bed, standing up, kneeling on the floor. I stopped to watch several episodes of *Law & Order SVU*—nothing like watching Stabler's neck muscles bulge as he screams at a sex offender to get one going—and fucked myself again. In the morning, the fog hovered like a ghost over the field outside my window, and I fucked myself until the sun edged over the clouds and spilled its buttery light onto the grass.

It was scary at times, how ravenous my desire for myself was. But there was also a tremendous release and permissiveness in sexual solitude, especially since penetration is something that is always imagined as an act that needs a partner to be successful. I got to be curious about my body, what felt good and what didn't, without worrying about having to ask or explain or attend to someone else. Time, which when I had sex often felt like a reminder of my failure to not do something quickly enough, came to feel in that week of self-intimacy like a gift.

Sex with strap-ons continues to be contradictory, but as I become more able to accept the shifting desires inside myself, it has also become more fun. Strap-ons allow me to be both the possessor and the possessed, intimate and disconnected, satisfied and wanting and satisfied in wanting. At times I feel that having sex with a strap-on makes me hover completely outside of any concepts of male or female; at times I feel like I'm taking them both inside me and feeling the tickle of their hands as they swing from my pelvic bones. Given what normative society values about dicks, a dildo is actually more of a dick than a dick is: it never gets soft, it feels no pain, it cannot be castrated, it has no orifice through which it can be penetrated. I now enjoy the fact that strap-ons can tap into a very patriarchal, heteronormative form of sex and womanhood. It feels great to slip into a performance of invulnerability, to feel my body becoming a hard line. Or conversely, to become nothing but a hole, an opening whose pleasure is dependent on something outside of myself. But while dildos, on some level, still draw comparisons to dicks, their ability to be shared and shed keeps those feelings, and everything in between them, in the realm of choice, which queers everything up very nicely.

Now when I reach into my drawer, I am greeted with a long, hard reminder that power does not have to be fearful and possessive. It can be elastic, expansive, slipping endlessly from one state into another.

The Broken Country

Molly McCully Brown

THE FALL I WAS NINETEEN, I CAME INTO MY COL-
lege dining hall in California just in time to overhear a boy telling a table of mutual acquaintances that he thought I was very
nice, but he felt terribly sorry for me because I was going to die a
virgin. This was already impossible, but in that moment all that
mattered was the blunt force of the boy's certainty. He hadn't
said, *I could never. . .* or *She might be pretty but. . .* or *Can she even
have sex?* or even *I'd never fuck a cripple*, all sentences I'd heard
or overheard by then. What he had done was, firmly, with some
weird, wrong breed of kindness in his voice, drawn a border
between my body and the country of desire.

It didn't matter that, by then, I'd already done my share of
heated fumbling in narrow dorm-room beds, that more than
one person had already looked at me and said *I'm in love with
you*, and I had said it back. It didn't matter that I'd boldly kissed
a boy on his back porch in sixth grade, surprising him so much
that the BB gun he was holding went off, sending a squadron
of brown squirrels skittering up into the trees. Most of me was
certain that the boy in the dining hall was right in all the ways
that really mattered. He knew I'd never be the kind of woman
anyone could really want, and I knew that even my body's own
wanting was suspect and tainted by flaw. My body was a country of error and pain. It was a doctor's best attempt, a thing to
manage and make up for. It was a place to leave if I was hunting
goodness, happiness, or release.

I have the strongest startle reflex in the world. Call my name in the quiet, make a loud noise, introduce something sudden into my field of vision, and every time I'll jump like there's been a clap of thunder. It's worst, though, if you touch me when I'm not expecting it. I startle the way a wild animal does. For years I thought only the bad wiring in my brain was to blame, the same warped signals that throw off my balance and make my muscles tighten, keeping me permanently on tenterhooks. Then I met Susannah, whose first memories are also of a gas mask and a surgeon's hands, of being picked up, held down, put under. She too jumps at the smallest surprise, the slightest unanticipated touch. Now I think that feral reflex also arises from something in that early trauma: all those years of being touched without permission, having your body talked about over your head, being forced under sedation, made to leave your body and come back to a version that hurts more but is supposedly better—the blank stretch of time when something happened you can't name. I think it matters that the first touch I remember is someone readying to cut me open, that when I woke I was crying, and there was a sutured wound.

For the better part of my childhood, I was part of a study on gait development in children with cerebral palsy. At least once a year—and sometimes more frequently if I'd recently had surgery—I spent an afternoon in a research lab, walking up and down a narrow strip of carpet, with sensors and wires attached to my body so doctors could chart the way I moved. The digital sensors composed a computer model of my staggering shape, each one a little point of light, and when I peeled them off they left behind burning red squares like perfect territories. But the doctors also shot the whole thing on a video camera mounted on a tripod and gave us the raw footage to take home. The early films are cute; I'm curly haired and chatty. The bathing suit I wear so that my legs and arms are bare is always either a little too small or a little too big, a hand-me-down from my older sister. I trundle happily down the carpet. As I get older, though, the tapes become more complicated. By the time I get to footage where I look anything like myself, I can't bear to watch it anymore. I'm a teenage girl in bike shorts or a bathing suit, being watched by a collection of men, walking what's essentially a runway like some kind of wounded animal.

Even today, I can't quite tell: Do I hope that when they looked at me back then, mostly undressed, they saw only a crop of defects that needed fixing, a collection of their best repairs? Or do I hope that one of them—maybe the redhead, not yet thirty—felt some small press of desire, knew I was a girl on the edge of womanhood and not a half-lame horse or subject Number Fifty-Three? I know I hated being watched. I also know it never occurred to me that anyone watching would see something worth wanting. They took those videos throughout most of my adolescence. Do you know I still can't stand to watch myself walk? I put my eyes on the floor when I pass department store mirrors or a window's reflective glass. I catch a glimpse of myself and my stomach turns. When I asked the first man I loved about the way I moved, he said, *It's nothing. It doesn't matter*—he meant it as a comfort—but I thought, *You're wrong. It makes me what I am.*

Chronic pain makes you good at abandoning yourself. It teaches you to ignore your body until it insists on being noticed, until your joints ache too badly to stand, until something buckles, until you fall and then you're bleeding hard enough to ruin your clothes. There's a certain low thrum of hurt I don't notice; it's just the frequency at the bottom of everything. A good day is one when I hardly think about my body, when I adjust for its flaws by instinct, when there isn't any sudden spike in that low pulse of pain.

On a good day, my body doesn't embarrass me. It does what I ask it, lets me walk short distances and do my job. I don't notice people staring, don't trip on my way in to teach a class, sending thirty-five student papers flying everywhere. I don't have to pause at a threshold and ask a stranger to help me lift my wheelchair up and through a door. No one I don't really know needs to put their hands on me. No one in the grocery store asks, *What happened, sweetie? You're so pretty to be in a wheelchair!* On a good day, my body pulls hard at the hem of my dress, and I hiss back, *You don't exist*, and it goes somewhere else, or I do.

In bed, a man pauses, puts a wide, gentle hand on my face and asks, *Honey, where are you? Come back here.* I want to, and also I don't.

Just as I hit adolescence, my body abruptly began to break down. I grew, and so did my physical instability. My tendons tightened, and my pain increased. The doctors scheduled another set of medical procedures: a surgery, a summer in a set of full-leg plaster casts and then a pair of heavy, bulky metal braces. Just as I began to learn I could feel sexual desire, I was splintered and in pain again, and the fact of it demanded most of my attention. My earliest experiences with lust feel shrunken by the trauma, vague and distanced, as if I watched through a scratched viewfinder while they happened to someone else. I can't identify them for you except as strange, dark shapes at an unreachable horizon line.

Those years I had to wear parachute pants—specially made by a tailor who regularly asked my mother to remind her what was wrong with me—and giant sneakers to accommodate the braces. Besides all that, I had the usual adolescent problems. I hadn't learned that you really shouldn't brush curly hair, or that if you have hips and spend most of your time sitting or bent over, low-rise jeans are a terrible idea. Not only was I far from resembling the kind of girl I could imagine anyone finding desirable, I was so occupied with pain and with being a patient, perpetually hamstrung between taken-apart and put-back-together, that it would take me years to really look at myself and realize I was also a person. A woman. That there was a whole other way I could want to be touched.

I belonged to an adaptive skiing association and spent most of the time I wasn't in the hospital or physical therapy learning to hurl myself down snow-covered mountains with men who'd been paralyzed in car wrecks. But I didn't know a single adult woman with a disability comparable to mine. Nowhere on television, or in any magazine, did I see any portrayals of disabled women as sexual and desirable (let alone as partners or as parents), and most of the solace that the early 2000s internet had to offer was in the form of assurances that I might one day be the object of some very particular fetish. It matters that when any adult spoke to me about my body, they did so in purely utilitarian terms, said that I should want the best range of motion, the least pain, the highest level of mobility, so that I could one day buy groceries, live independently, hold a job. Of course, nobody warned, *You'll want your hamstrings to be loose enough that it doesn't hurt when your muscles tense before you have an orgasm.* They also didn't say, *We want to do all this to you so that one day your body can be a thing that brings you pleasure, a thing that you don't hate.*

The truth is, my first real flushes of lust happened when my own body was a dangerous thing I couldn't trust not to fall to pieces or to lunge at the rest of me with its teeth bared, out for blood. So much of my somatic experience was agonizing and frightening. I had no idea what my body would look, move, or feel like five years down the line. Desire wasn't entirely crowded out by pain, but I distrusted it the same way I did everything that felt born in my body, as if it were an instant away from morphing into suffering, waiting only until I attended to it to become a thing that hurt me. I playacted at desire often—mimicking the adolescents around me when they traded gossip about crushes, had first kisses, held hands furtively underneath their desks in social-studies class—but I couldn't afford to get to know its real contours in my life, to attend to my own sensations, or to believe in a future with real space for that kind of pleasure or intimacy, that kind of love. To survive, I had to stay unfamiliar to myself: neutralized, at arm's length. Sometimes, I think, all these years later, I'm still hunting the part of myself I exiled.

When I was newly seventeen, one of my closest friends put her head in my lap, said, *You're so gorgeous*, and then leaned up and kissed me. I would spend the better part of the next year alternately pushing her away and pulling her close, trying to figure out whether I wanted her, too, or only the plain, un-apologetic fact of her desire for me. Her gentleness, her confi-dence in her own body and its hunger, the fact that when she watched me move, I felt like a painting come to life and not a patient or a busted windup toy. A decade later, I still feel guilty for all the secretive back-and-forth I put her through because I was unwilling to be open about our romantic relationship, and the answer to the question of my own desire still feels fraught and muddy.

A handful of years after that, I was in a coffee shop with a man I half-thought I'd marry, in a youthful, abstract way, and someone in line assumed he was my brother, though we couldn't have looked less alike. When we corrected her, she looked over my head at him and said, gently and admiringly, *She's so lucky to have found you.* He bit his tongue when I squeezed his hand. I didn't want to think about it anymore. We turned away.

We started dating after he attended a reading I gave. When it was over, he came up and kissed my cheek, said, *That was so incredible that I forgot to breathe while you were talking.* Then he turned on his heel and walked away. I rolled my eyes but couldn't get him out of my head. The way I moved was nothing. He was proof it didn't matter.

At a taffy shop on the boardwalk in San Francisco, the weekend we first say *I love you*, a middle-aged man is pushing a woman, clearly his wife, in a wheelchair. They are laughing, and his head is bent so that their faces are close together as he walks, intimate and tender. We bump into one another in the aisle and pause—two couples exchanging smiles—while we make room for her wheelchair to get past mine. They walk on, and then we kiss, fierce and happy there. We're young and don't know anything. We both think *maybe*.

Later, we're in Florida at the beach, and I've been stiff and hurting for weeks from a summer of travel. In the bathroom, while we're changing into bathing suits, he looks me up and down. I'm prepared for him to try something—to kiss me—and I'm prepared to put him off, we don't have time; we have to meet my family by the water. Instead, he asks me tenderly, *Do you want help clipping your toenails, baby? They're getting kind of long.* That night, in bed, I roll away when he reaches for me. My body is no country for desire.

A couple of years later still, another man—charming, boy-next-door-beautiful, and quarterback-confident—has started spending evenings in my bed, or with me pinned to his couch. He tells me I'm sexy, asks to read what I'm writing, then asks quiet questions about poetry and movies that I love. But he won't be seen dating me in public. When I tell him I'm more than happy to be fooling around, but that I won't sleep with somebody I hardly know, he puts all his weight on top of me, says, *Oh, if I wanted to have sex with you, you'd know.* Then flips me over. Pushes my head down hard enough that it hurts. I think, *He's embarrassed to be seen with me. He gets off on how fragile I am. I'm too old to put up with this.* But I let him. I let it go on for weeks and weeks like that before I stop returning his late-night texts.

I want him to want me, and though I can't quite admit it to myself, I am also a little afraid. Always, I'm aware that I'm particularly vulnerable: I couldn't run if you came at me. I'd fall to the ground if you touched me even slightly roughly. I will always startle at an unexpected hand.

But because some of you are wondering (I see you leering at me, stranger at the bank. I see you, terrible internet date); because we live in a world that often assumes disabled people are sexless or infantile; because I wish I had heard anyone who looked or moved like me say it when I was fourteen, I want to be very clear: I can, in fact, have sex. I am a woman who wants in ways that are both abstract and concrete. I have turned down advances from people I wasn't attracted to, and said yes to a few advances I'm sorry about now, and more that have been lovely, surprising, and good. I've had a date who didn't realize I was in a wheelchair turn and walk out of a restaurant when he saw me, and I've watched the light behind men's eyes turn from desire to curiosity to something else when they realize something's wrong with me. I've been hit on while on barstools by people who disappear once they've watched me get up and shuffle slowly to the bathroom. I've used that trick to my advantage. I've spent a summer weekend taking baths and eating overripe peaches in a seedy motel with someone I loved, and another getting lusty-whiskey-drunk with someone I didn't but whom I was still perfectly happy to have unbutton my shirt. The explicit details I'll keep to myself, except to say that my familiarity with how to jump-rope the line between pleasure and pain has done me some favors. If you're listening, younger self, some of what you're learning will, I swear, eventually have uses no one's naming for you, uses that no one orbiting around you can locate, name, or even imagine.

In another kind of story, I would leave it there. Or I would say that I've arrived at a reconciled point, that no part of me ever still believes that the boy in the dining hall, who was certain I would die a virgin, hit on some real truth about the ways my body is defective and repellent; that, now, I can watch myself move without feeling some small wave of shame; that I've completely stopped abandoning my body out of instinct, or habit, or what feels like necessity, in moments when it should bring me pleasure and intimacy and joy. I'd have fully worked out how to be with a partner who I know really sees my body, its contours, its scars, and its pain, who I can let give me the kinds of help I need and still trust to see me as sexual and desirable. But that isn't where I find myself. I don't know exactly where the reconciled point is, or even what it looks like. Instead, things just get more complicated. I really want children, and in the last few years that prospect has collided with questions of intimacy and desire. I worry about finding a partner truly willing to parent with me in the ways I know my disability will necessitate, and to sign up for the medical uncertainties I know are around the bend in my own life. I worry about the toll pregnancy might take on my body, and about being physically capable of being a good parent once my children are born. I worry that my clock is ticking faster than most people's, my body wearing down and wearing out. And, in the hardest moments, that whatever small kind of beauty and desirability I might, in fact, possess is wearing away with it. I'm still surprised by my own limits, still frustrated and exhausted by pain. Sometimes I still feel suspicious of all my body's sensations, the good ones tangled too tightly with the bad. But not all moments are the hardest ones, and maybe the point is simply this: that I am still alive, still in the business of heading somewhere, still a woman who can stumble, hurt, and want, and—yes—be wanted. That there is no perfect reconciliation, only the way I hold it all suspended: wonderful, and hugely difficult, and true.

Allergic

Tara Conklin

ABOUT TEN YEARS INTO MY MARRIAGE, I DEVELOPED an allergy to my wedding rings. I wore three: a plain platinum wedding band; a modest one-carat engagement ring; a narrow infinity band of tiny sparkling diamonds that my husband gave me after the birth of our first child. A push present, we called it, only half-joking. My reward for delivering our daughter out into the world.

These rings formed a brilliant trio that I often admired as my hand gripped the steering wheel of our family car. They weren't ostentatious or grand, but they were pretty and charming, I thought, a solid, unique stack of stone and precious metal that reflected my status as wife and mother. This woman is loved by another, the little stack proclaimed. She will be loved forever.

When the skin beneath those rings turned a bright, hot pink, I attributed the problem at first to dish soap. Or maybe chlorine. Recently I'd been jumping into a public pool with our middle son during his swim lessons. He was afraid of the water and needed me to coax him in. You can do it, I would say again and again as he stood trembling at the edge of the pool. I'm right here.

The irritated area beneath my rings swelled like a bite from a mosquito or spider. What I had once so valued and admired now became the source of discomfort and pain. I began to remove them every night before bed. Brush teeth, take out contact lenses, set the alarm, slip off my rings. Some mornings, I forgot to put them on again, and I would go about my day with an alarming red welt around my left ring finger. "Isn't this weird?" I would tell anyone who asked. Eight years of marriage and now, all of a sudden, *look*.

This was in 2013. The #MeToo movement was still years away; Harvey Weinstein remained entrenched as the king of Hollywood; Chanel Miller had not gone to that ill-fated party on Stanford's campus. I identified as a feminist, had outearned my husband for years, but now found myself in a marriage that looked increasingly like those I saw in TV shows about 1950s suburbia. The husbands went off to work while their wives, sleep-deprived and puffy, overworked and alarmingly bored, remained at home with the kids. I was ostensibly writing my second novel, but sometimes the hours of my day flew by in such a storm of dirty dishes, piano lessons, art projects, playground visits, grocery shopping, doctors' appointments, book reading, hair braiding that I realized only later in bed in the dark that I hadn't written a word.

It was about this time when my marriage began to falter. Or rather: I acknowledged that my marriage was faltering. There was the disproportionate childcare and domestic responsibilities, yes, but deeper tensions too that I found difficult to name precisely. Changing priorities, diverging interests. My generalized dissatisfaction. My feelings of restlessness and impatience. A pervasive lack of joy.

My husband and I signed up for counseling sessions. Every week we met with a tall, impeccably dressed woman with long, elegant fingers and talked about our problems. We met in the woman's home office, a side entrance flanked by two large hydrangeas, as the dull thumps of her own family's movements filtered down from the floors above. At her suggestion, my husband and I initiated a date night. I promised to be less critical. He agreed to help out more around the house.

The problem with my rings worsened. The skin began to crack and flake like a burn or burst blister. I decided to stop wearing my rings for a spell. The skin just needs to breathe, I told myself. It needs time to repair and heal. It was not lost on me that my wedding ring problem coincided with my marital malaise, but it seemed a too-pat metaphor. This was my life, after all, not a novel. I wanted my marriage to succeed. I wanted to love my husband.

In our counseling sessions, we discussed our childhoods, our relationship history, how we met, how and when we fell in love, how we envisioned an intimate partnership. We listed all the things we liked to do for fun. We looked at each other and talked about the last fight we'd had or the last time we'd felt unfairly dismissed by the other. We did not discuss our sex life, at least not at first, not that I can remember. At that point, it seemed largely irrelevant. Of the myriad issues I faced in my marriage, bad sex seemed the least of them.

All things considered, I am one of the lucky ones. I married for love. My sexual self had the time and space to develop naturally, with a relatively low level of fear, shame, or embarrassment. I've never been raped or seriously sexually assaulted. There were incidents, of course. A first date pushed my head toward his crotch and held my wrist hard—too hard—when I pulled away; a man shoved his hand under my skirt on a bus so crowded that I could not move away even as his fingers pushed inside of me; one night I was mugged violently on an empty sidewalk. These and other episodes left me shaken and fearful for weeks, even months, but they didn't fundamentally change my appetite for sex. I loved sex with men. I pursued it, sometimes recklessly. I drank too much; I met men at bars and parties and on dance floors; I didn't always practice safe sex. I would bring a man home with me simply because I liked the way he laughed or stroked my forearm or bit his lower lip as he listened to me talk. Today I remember my sexual partners, not their names necessarily, but the encounters themselves. I remember wanting them as much—perhaps more—as they wanted me.

For a time, the skin on my finger calmed and I resumed wearing my rings. But soon the irritation returned, even worse than before. I called a dermatologist and explained the situation. "Maybe you've developed an allergy to platinum," she said. "That seems the most likely cause. Come in for some tests." So I made an appointment, came in for the tests. Negative for platinum allergy. Negative for nickel alloy, gold, and a number of others I can't remember. She examined my finger and said, "Hmmm. Interesting." Then she wrote me a prescription. "Stop wearing the rings completely for two months," she said, "and apply this cream every night before bed. It should clear up. And then you can go back to being married." She grinned and handed me the paper.

Why do we get married? Historically, of course, love was not the point. The point was that one male head of household be-lieved that his financial or political interests would be furthered by legally joining forces with another male head of household. One daughter, one son. The daughters grinned and bore it. The sons did too, but they became heads of their own households and could determine the trajectory of their own lives and fam-ilies. Meanwhile, the wives delivered daughters and sons while also providing their husbands with the bonus pleasures of sex and home cooking, and the whole cycle repeated itself again and again *ad nauseum*.

Marriage still means the public and legal union of two in-dividuals, but in our enlightened modern world there's also the good stuff: loving each other, planning a life together, pooling resources to make that life happen. There's the shared project of raising children, keeping house, planning vacations. And of course there's the sex—sex that's not simply for procreation or male satisfaction but for mutual pleasure.

About a month into the period of applying the dermatolo-gist's cream, I began to develop an itch. Like the ring allergy, it came on slowly, so slowly, barely noticeable, certainly contain-able, and then blossomed into something that seemed very, very wrong. It was an internal vaginal itch that I could not scratch away. I tried, believe me. I tried over-the-counter yeast infection creams. And vaginal suppositories. Vinegar baths. Douches. Epsom salt. I googled "intense vaginal itch—solution?" and its variants. Hundreds of home remedies appeared on my screen. I couldn't possibly try them all, but I tried many. Boric acid. Yogurt. Profidius pills. Kombucha. This special vaginal soap. That organic vaginal cream. I changed laundry detergent, soap, and shampoo. My gynecologist tested me for every sexually transmitted disease, every hormonal imbalance.

"Well," she said. "It's a mystery. Maybe you should stop having sex for a spell. Give your vagina a break."

The idea hadn't occurred to me before. I'd been having sex with my husband for fifteen years, the itch for only a few months. But I agreed with my doctor's orders. Yes, I'd give my vagina a break. I'd stop with the probiotics and creams and stop with the hurried, lights-out, half-hearted intimacy that had become our sex life. It was only later that day, after I left the doctor's appointment and arrived home to an empty house—the kids with a sitter, my husband at work—that I realized how easy this would be. How much relief I felt. I couldn't remember the last time I'd honestly, genuinely wanted to have sex with my husband. Perhaps the night we conceived our third child? Could it be that long? Sometimes I found myself focusing on his lips or hands or voice—the specific facets of him that once I'd found most appealing—but now I felt nothing. No stirring of desire or attraction. If anything, I felt repulsed.

Legal scholar Robin West calls consensual but unwanted sex a personal, social, and political problem for women everywhere, from college campuses to long-term marriages.[1] The resulting condition—that is, what happens to a woman after repeated engagement in this kind of sex—she calls *consensual sexual dysphoria*. Dysphoria means a state of unease or generalized dissatisfaction with life. In West's analysis, unwanted, unpleasurable sex undermines a woman's dignity, her sense of self-worth, her subjective happiness, and her ability to assert her equality. West's work is relatively new. In her writing, she notes the limited empirical research available on the subject. She couches her conclusions in words like "it's likely," "it must be," or "it's hard to imagine." For example: "It is simply hard to imagine a healthy sense of one's own agency either developing or being sustained over the course of an adult life in which a woman as a matter of identity and habit bends her will regarding her own body for the sake of another's physical pleasure."

I've discussed the issue with female friends—all of them fierce, funny, smart, independent women—and yet nearly without exception we've all done it. Once a year, once a month, or every goddamn night. We grin and bear sex that we do not want and do not enjoy. We follow a tradition laid down (literally) centuries ago by women without our legal rights, education, or consciousness. Why? We do it to keep the peace. We do it because we love our husbands, even if we don't feel sexual desire for them. We do it because that's what marriage requires. That's what is expected of us.

"Why don't you want to have sex?" Our marriage counselor was speaking directly to me. This was roughly a year after that last visit to the gynecologist.

"I feel," I began—but I did not want to talk about the itching. The itch was long gone by then. Giving my vagina a break had indeed done the trick. Now the itch seemed inconsequential. A symptom of a much larger malaise. I had never returned to wearing my wedding rings. Even a few hours would inflame the skin, turn it red and painful. On my right hand, I wore other rings, rings I had chosen, without a problem.

"I feel as though I've lost my desire for him," I said to the counselor. "It was there, I had it, and then it was gone."

My husband stared straight ahead. A great surge of guilt swamped me. I'd had no affair, but it was as though I'd committed the worst kind of betrayal. A betrayal, deep and mysterious, that I could not make right with a confession or counseling, creams or drugs.

"Intimacy is important in any marriage," the counselor

continued. "Sometimes you just need to give it another try." She shrugged.

I remembered the feeling I'd get after sex: exhaustion, emptiness, a deep longing for something nameless and shapeless, something much more profound than passion or an orgasm. Intimacy? Connection? Power? Self-worth? I didn't know then what to call it and I still don't. West writes that the experience of consensual but unwanted sex "occasions an alienation of the choosing self from the integrity of the body [that] undermines one's sense of physical security in the social world, and hence one's equality in it."

"I think we should give it another try," my husband said.

I realized then that bit by bit, piece by piece, my desire for my husband had leaked from my pocket during those end days of our marriage, days that totaled months, then years. Days when I didn't know what was happening or why, but my body did. My body sent me urgent messages. The rash on my finger. The vaginal itch. The ten extra pounds I couldn't shake. The headaches. The lethargy and depression and, yes, the sense of dysphoria.

West is writing in the context of #MeToo and the rise of sexual assaults on campus. At this particular moment in history, we are blessedly and finally aware of the prevalence and impact of sexual crimes and misconduct against women. But the public discussion of both the problem and its solution focuses almost exclusively on the question of consent. Is it okay if I touch you here? And here? And here? Was she too drunk to say it? Was she too young to mean it? Did she nod or did she clearly say the word *yes*?

This, West argues, misses a very large elephant. Consent necessarily defines what constitutes a sexual crime, but if we're interested in well-being and happiness and equality and why women can't seem to find them at work or at home, then maybe we should start in our bedrooms and with our bodies. Maybe silence begins there. And resentment, self-sabotage, self-hatred, acting against our best interests, voting against them too.

What does it take to spread your legs, night after night, for a man to whom you are no longer attracted? To consent to a sex life from which you derive no pleasure, no satisfaction? It can only erode your sense of self, your mental and emotional health. It can only act as a kind of violation. And yet our counselor suggested that I continue to have that kind of sex. Even worse, I was the one who felt guilty that day in the counselor's office. I was the one who felt I had done something wrong.

I want to say here that a body doesn't lie. A body cannot twist and turn the truth around in the ways that a mind so often does. A body doesn't recognize expectations and habit, traditions and duty. Desire begins and ends in our bodies. Trauma begins and ends there too. They are linked, these two opposite feeling-states. One emerges from within, the other is delivered from without, but they push and pull against our most intimate selves. They turn us one way or another. Healthy or sick. In love or out of it. Can we control these forces? I don't think we can, not entirely. But we must listen to what they say.

I never told my husband why I stopped wearing my wedding rings or about the itch. I said only that I wanted a divorce. I had no desire or love for him anymore. I had lost it, somewhere, who knows where? The pretense of continuing to love him was ruining me. I needed to listen to what my body was telling me. I needed to change the external forces that pushed against me so that my internal self—my desire for sex, for love, for life—would return. And I will tell you this: they did.

1. Robin West, "Consensual Sexual Dysphoria: A Challenge for Campus Life," 66, *Journal of Legal Education.* 804–821 (2017).

Halls of Air

Laura Joyce-Hubbard

EVERY SINGLE DAY, I AM COUNTING: THE DAYS, OR hours, until Lloyd, my spouse, leaves our home. Or I am counting the days, or hours, until he returns. I check the weather, monitor the cloud ceilings and the visibility near Midway Airport. He has spent decades doing the same.

We have chosen to spend our partnered lives like this. For as long as I've known Lloyd, and as long as he's known me, one of us has just unpacked. Or one of us is packing to leave. Life as pilots has meant a life spent in transit. A steady stream of Arrivals. A constant walk toward Departures. The consistency in our relationship is in the partings—me curling into his tall, lean build in parking lots; smiling in another jetway threshold, like there's no lump in our throats; leaving a note on top of a flight bag the night before, to be discovered at 3:00 a.m.: *Fly Safe. Love you.*

When I first met Lloyd, I was a Second Lieutenant in the Air Force, a "butter bar." I deplaned from a DC-9, a military cargo plane, in Spokane, Washington, where Lloyd was assigned to fly out of Fairchild Air Force Base. I didn't know him yet, but I didn't like the sound of him: a bomber pilot, a bow hunter, a man who drove a Ford F-250.

I'd traveled to Spokane to do some research for my master's degree and to visit my best friend—also in the Air Force, also assigned to Fairchild. Although I was a pilot, I'd arrived as a passenger. I'd earned my AF pilot wings but was in grad school studying environmental policy because there was a "pilot surplus" at the time. In other words, the Air Force didn't need me yet.

It was snowing. I stepped off the plane in my black pumps, afraid I might slip on the stairs—each snowflake kissing the metal, creating a shiny but dicey surface. I'd been required to wear my dress blues to catch the flight from Colorado on the Air Force's dime. In a polyester blue dress skirt and light blue uniform blouse, my long brown hair pinned up in a French braid, I held the silver aluminum rail with my right hand and my Air Force–issue hat with my left. My cover, as we called uniform hats, kept sliding off my head.

My friend had come with her boyfriend, Lloyd, to pick me up from the base terminal. I wasn't moved by Lloyd's dark black hair, nor his hazel eyes. But I did notice an air of kindness about him, a softness I wasn't accustomed to among military Air Force pilots. It might've been the way he cooked for us. Or that we ate off a wooden table he'd made himself at the base woodworking shop, where he also made wooden canoes by hand. Or that he had a nice set of pots. I'd never met a man with a full lineup of cast iron cookware in assorted sizes.

I saw Lloyd naked. And he saw me naked, long before we began to date. This is not what you think. Or maybe it's exactly what you think.

I was also in a relationship at the time. My then-boyfriend had family in Spokane, and I'd arranged for him to meet my bestie, just as she had arranged for me to meet Lloyd. The snow still hadn't stopped—and wouldn't during my entire visit. Lloyd had a hot tub. After dinner, all four of us sat in the hot water under chunky, wet flakes of thick snow, our skin growing pink like boiling lobsters. We wore no swimsuits. When I look back on it now, I don't know why my painfully modest self sat naked with another couple. Maybe I didn't pack a bathing suit for a trip to Washington state in the winter. Or maybe it was the influence of my boyfriend, who proudly called himself a hippie—he had a thing about being naked in nature any chance he could get.

This sounds like it was headed in an entirely sexier direction. Instead, it headed toward me making my first snow angel. My Floridian bones had turned me into a giddy kid under a canopy of real winter. Shedding all inhibitions under the dome of flurrying sky, I couldn't believe the tall evergreens that surrounded Lloyd's log home were real—etched in snow, their branches wearing lace sleeves. I felt like I'd stepped into a picture book. I threw myself down, pressing my bare back into thick layers of snow, raised my arms above my head, my legs into an upside-down V, and carved wings. I was mesmerized and uninhibited. And freezing. Sprinting back into the hot tub, my friend and I squealed, skin prickling with the plunge from ice to steaming water—meeting the warmth like the welcome wave of heat from a bonfire.

It would be several months before the couples from that winter day broke up. Several years before my flight path crossed again with Lloyd's. But it was Lloyd who took me back to the base operations after that first trip to Spokane so I could catch my return flight. Little did either of us know that the way we met—our hellos and goodbyes sandwiched between my flying in and then out—would come to define the conditions in which we would fall in love, marry, and raise two sons. If our life could be reduced to a toy snow globe: shake it, and you'll see thousands of planes looping the watery sky.

When I started to fall for Lloyd, I wouldn't admit it, not even to myself. The Air Force was reassigning him to Texas. I didn't want a love story that began *When I met him, he was dating my best friend.* I blocked Lloyd from my mind's eye of possibility. What kind of person, I thought, writes to her best friend, deployed to Iraq, to ask for permission to date her ex?

Lloyd and I started to exchange handwritten letters. We shared a profession where most things happened quickly—from the speed we flew over Earth to the touch-and-go landings we practiced in our planes. In the air, things could turn into a crisis with one red light, one aural tone, or one flashing button.

Waiting for a letter to arrive, writing a reply, and licking an envelope required patience. A romance on slow burn felt somehow like a perfect antidote to the speed of movement in our respective cockpits and the corresponding speed of thinking required for the job.

Through our letters, I learned he came from a family of artists. His mother was, astoundingly, the first woman nominated for U.S. vice president on the Democratic ticket in 1984. He tied his own mayflies for fly fishing. But the thing that most caught my ear: Lloyd wrote poetry. And he *admitted* he wrote poetry. Had he been actively trying, he couldn't have been more different from the men with whom I flew on a daily basis.

I told him that his hunting made me feel uncomfortable. It wasn't the eating of animals, though I was a vegetarian; it was something else, something I couldn't name then but can now. I was already married to the military—a war-fighting institution whose mission condoned killing under certain conditions as a matter of course. I couldn't double-up on death—even in a different form.

Lloyd talked about his preference for hunting with a bow. I remembered the arrows he'd made that hung on his wall. He said that bow hunting was an excuse for him to be alone in the woods, and that he passed up many shots. For Lloyd, hunting was mainly about listening to owls and the flow of a river's current, watching a hawk's wings at sunset, or tracing the stars on the night's cape overhead. Watching the season change. He said he didn't care if he ever hunted again. And he didn't.

We plunged into time zone crossings and transcontinental meet-ups—a long-distance relationship defined by latitudes and longitudes. Continents and deployments. We spent our waking hours flying jet routes, transiting through halls of air. "Meet me in my dreams," I'd beg him over the crackling static of a cross-country landline.

Even after so many years of living in this liminal space, my want is so great I believe that we can compel our subconsciouses to meet when our physical bodies cannot. A space beyond what we can see. That our love can work like a turbine engine—propelling us to find each other in dreamspace, beyond the gravity of our own thoughts, if we just try hard enough. I fall asleep at night believing this. It's one of the many tricks I play on myself to endure the unending separations.

It's hard to admit that despite having one another, rock solid and committed—a fact I know is a gift, a privilege, a *something* that many people spend their lives searching for—I want more. I want *every day*. To not see his black leather flight boots lined up at our back door; his rollie bag parked near the dirty laundry bin after returning; his neatly folded white uniform shirts, rows of black socks, and white undershirts. I want to stash his Traveler Pro crew luggage in the attic. But most of all, I want to shed the feeling of inhabiting an hourglass turned upside down each time he walks through the door—impending departure, impending farewell. *When do you leave? I can't remember.*

Or I want to go with him. Every single day, I long to defy gravity. To defy earthly weights, to feel raw horsepower, vibrating thrust beneath my gloved hands. To propel myself against every law of physics that tries to keep me earthbound. I long to watch the sunrise from forty-one thousand feet. To peer down at Greenland, or across the expanse of the Pacific—into an infinity of indigo-blue. I long to slip through, to keep my company with the clouds. I want to admire, again, a cockpit windscreen developing like a roll of film from a dark Atlantic crossing into a tangerine-lavender sky. Then: a full-bodied blood orange.

For as long as I've loved him, for thirty years, I've left him. Or he's left me. While we were both in the Air Force, Lloyd and I flew different types of planes, and we were assigned to different bases—sometimes in different states, often different countries. I flew cargo planes that deployed worldwide, and he flew bombers, then jet trainers. We wrote more letters, bought more stamps. We spent our paychecks on long-distance bills and airline tickets to see each other at any chance.

The goodbyes took their toll on me. In an early stage of long-distance life, I started creating reasons to argue. I wasn't aware at the time, but I came to understand that I was picking fights before one of us left in order to try and make the parting easier. To soften the approaching swell of sadness with a possibility we might break up after all. That we would find relief in ending our endless long-distance, no longer burdened by seeking a future together. It felt like we were awaiting a watering hole in the desert of our service commitments. But one day, on my drive back to my home base from Lloyd's house, after a manufactured argument had wrecked particular havoc and left me bawling as I drove down the empty two-lane West Texas highway, I realized the leaving wasn't easier that way. It was just lonelier.

Our "dates" mostly consisted of talking on the phone and commuting. We tried to run the same number of miles in our separate cities, to feel we lived parallel lives. We'd pick a marathon and train for it together, but separately. We'd eventually meet up on race day in a city where neither of us lived.

Our relationship was like a marathon, an exercise of endurance, but we couldn't see the magnitude yet. We didn't know if, or when, we'd make it across the finish line—or how many years, like mile-markers on a racecourse, there would be ahead of us. But when we were together, we were infused with adrenaline. We kept going.

We'd talk about the mundane: what we ate for dinner. I thought if I scooped up every morsel of detail he lived without me, it would somehow span the loneliness. I convinced myself it did. Sometimes, we would watch TV shows simultaneously over the phone. Sometimes, we still press play on Netflix from separate cities, on separate laptops.

I held out on marriage because I wanted the sappy fairytale version of it. I wanted to marry, come home in my wedding dress, and be carried over the threshold into a home where we would live. Together. I wanted this because it represented everything I didn't do on a daily basis in the military. As an aircraft commander and then instructor pilot, I was one of the then 4 percent of female pilots in the Air Force. I was reminded at every turn that I was in the minority. I carried the knowledge of my minority status like it was something I had to defend and protect. I was in a proving ground: land the plane better, handle simulated emergencies more smoothly, find a way to get along with everyone. I carried myself across every threshold in flight like future women pilots were counting on me. Like past women pilots were watching me.

Everything in my work life, down to the essential—each urge to pee—reminded me of my gender. There was no place to urinate on the plane I flew other than a urinal designed for male anatomy. I carried empty Pringles cans, disposable coffee cups, and Tupperware to use in flight—all in the name of creating a makeshift toilet. I cried on the phone to Lloyd at night. I dreamed of the post-wedding homecoming, despite knowing in my heart that it was antiquated and silly, because in my daily life, I masked my gender to fit in, to keep the peace with the men I served with. I didn't highlight challenges like my physical struggles onboard and I steered clear of anything that could further define me as other.

My job also demanded my constant attention. I tried to carry the entirety of our squadron's safety culture, something others often wrote off, on my shoulders. I'd direct pilots to go around when they were headed toward an unsafe landing. I'd tell the Army jumpmasters when it was unsafe to send their grunts out the back of my airplane. I'd brief a squadron full of aircrew before formation flights. I was a trained crash investigator and the designated squadron safety officer. But in my private life, I wanted the wild abandon of unconditional love. I wanted to roll my long hair out of the bun or braid required when in uniform. I wanted to be carried over the threshold as a bride.

The Air Force told us they could do nothing for those in-relationship. Only if we were married could they arrange for us to be assigned together. So I married Lloyd after years of long-distance. We spent our honeymoon on horseback in Ireland. But there was no "Joint-Spouse," as promised when we returned to our separate bases. Our career paths were "incompatible," the assignment manager said, because Lloyd flew bombers and trainers and I flew cargo aircraft. The Air Force viewed us as entirely mismatched. We were reduced to alphanumeric codes: I was a "1CXX." He was a "1BXX." In Air Force math, we didn't add up. Instead of providing us a "Joint-Spouse," the Air Force moved the finish line to some unreachable point on the horizon. Our vision of marriage, instead, became a mirage. I'd never felt more affinity with anyone. Yet the Air Force had the codes and, with them, the last word: *incompatible.*

Lloyd and I couldn't fathom that we had to accept this ruling. He offered to fly a different plane, to cross-train and fly a C-130 like me. I offered to cross-train and fly trainers, like him. We said we'd go anywhere: Alaska, Japan, Little Rock, or Germany. The only answer we received was one word. *No.*

I arrived home to my house in Abilene as a newlywed, twisted my small silver key into the front door lock, and walked in alone.

I left active-duty Air Force because it was clear we would spend our entire flying careers never being assigned together. Driven by my want to be under one roof with Lloyd, I signed my separation papers. It would've been more accurate to call them divorce papers—I was done with the institution governing my personal choices.

My close friend's toast at our wedding was a beautiful tribute, her blessing for Lloyd and I to live as peregrine falcons— majestic birds that mate for life. I loved this toast. I replayed the memory in my mind whenever I was lonely.

But on a layover while surfing the TV channels in a stark hotel room, I learned more details about the peregrine falcons from the Nature Channel. Yes, they mate for life. But they're almost completely solitary. The peregrine falcons that migrate live alone for eight months of the year. Worse, they spend only about four months together with their mate when raising a family. *Dangit*, I thought. *I want a do-over. A different toast.* I needed a more ordinary bird—like the downy woodpecker. A toast about their sharing incubation duties would've worked.

When I left active duty and joined the Air Force Reserves, I also joined the airline world as one of the then 1.8 percent of women commercial pilots. I loved many of the differences from my military job. For one, all the planes had lavs. This was a major improvement. In uniform, I could wear a short version of the men's tie or the designated women's tie. The latter looked like an eight-year-old Girl Scout's uniform. I choose the male tie. Wearing my long hair down, instead of pinned above my collar as the Air Force required for fourteen years, was liberating. In my new line of work, I appreciated having choices about my appearance. Many of the men I flew with had daughters my age. I found more comradery with the new (older) generation I flew with, which surprised me—I guessed from the stories they relayed that it was because many of their daughters were trying to make it in male-dominated workspaces also.

For the first time in our lives, Lloyd and I lived under the same roof. I had to report to airline training straight from the last day at my Air Force base. Lloyd drove my car to our home in San Antonio while I flew to Dallas for training. We rendezvoused at airline headquarters for the Spouse Welcome event. My training lasted six weeks. Eventually, we spent a first night in our home together as a married couple, falling somewhere between my check-out probationary flight and a new assignment to fly Boeings out of a Washington, D.C., pilot base. I don't remember it.

I spent my career carving out a female place in the sky. It required independence, borne of fierce feminism and self-determination. And yet my longing for a more traditional marriage—or at least one that allowed me to spend time with the man I loved—didn't fade. Every takeoff was a rush. Pushing up the throttles into takeoff power, hearing the engines spool, and feeling the last bit of the plane's weight liftoff was a joy that never became rote. But through it all, I was always scheming our next rendezvous, our next night together, dreaming about the timing of our children's births.

At parties and dinners with friends, Lloyd and I heard the friendly chiding, how the key to our happy relationship was that we were never around long enough to enter a rut. That is true. It is also a gross falsity. What we have is compression. When a departure is always on the horizon, the calendar is a third party in every argument. When we fall out of harmony, we know exactly how long we have to resolve it, unless we want to part ways out of sorts. One thing we agree on without fail: the agony of departing for three days or two weeks—both possibilities in our line of work—while fighting is worse than the humility required to make amends.

Soon, my job transferred me from Washington, D.C., to Miami. Even though Lloyd and I were living under one roof, my commute and my change from domestic to international flying began taking me farther, longer. When I was sleep-deprived, arriving after long flights across the ocean, I wanted to fall asleep in the crook of Lloyd's arm, to dream to the rhythm of his breath. We shared the same street address, but we didn't share more time together.

After 9/11, our worlds flipped. My airline laid off pilots, talked about bankruptcy, and my family was thrust into relative uncertainty. Lloyd finished his career in the Air Force and was hired by an airline less impacted by 9/11. I took a personal leave from my job after the exhaustion of planning multiple crew member memorials, not knowing that I was actually leaving permanently. My partings halted, but Lloyd's continued. I stopped leaving but became the one who was always left. But our sons, I told myself, will have one parent at home. This will be the consistency. I will be the glue.

Lloyd sends me texts from his flights: snow-capped Rocky Mountains over Colorado, snow-clad ripples over Oregon's mountains, a waxing moon over a New Mexican cloud layer. I send him texts from home: Lake Michigan ice in January resembling a stack of cracked plates, a stadium shot from our older son's basketball game, a video clip of our younger son's solo in the choir concert. I'm solo parenting half their lives. I'm lucky and I know it. It's a privilege to have a healthy family. To have reliable income and health insurance.

But despite this knowledge, I want what I don't have: weekends as a family. I want to reserve two tickets for our son's spring choir concert. I want family birthday parties to always include Lloyd. I'm tired of being buoyant on Thanksgiving, at home in Highland Park, Illinois, with our sons, when he is on a layover in Seattle, Sacramento, Salt Lake City—and we are setting the table for three, not four.

In the air, pilots are bound by and forever overcoming drag. We are seekers of lift. But one flight maneuver defies the pursuit of lift: the slip. It can save you if you're too high on approach or if there's something tall in your landing path. A thrill to court physics like this—to work with gravity, instead of the usual: overcoming its grip. You can use it to drop out of the sky. *Press on one rudder pedal, put the opposite aileron down.*

In flying, there is no escape from danger. With great freedom comes great risk. In a slip, you fly sideways through the skies.

Made of Clay

Abigail Thomas

IN HIS ROOM AT HOSPICE WAS A CLAY STATUE SOME-
one had made, and she told her daughter she wanted to make
something like that too. This was before he died. Then he died,
and when she didn't know what to do with herself, her daughter
gave her a box of clay.

This is what she does, first thing, every morning now: sticks
her left hand into the plastic bag of terra cotta and starts grabbing. It isn't easy. She has to keep digging and digging with her
fingernails because even though it's damp, the clay can be stiff.
Her hand seems to know how much it wants. It varies. She looks
at the raggedy lump when she first brings it out, to see if there's
anything implied, anything resembling something else—maybe
there's the hint of a face, or a dog's head, or a dragon, or a fish.
(There's never actually been a fish, but she did do a woman's
face in silhouette that some people mistake for a fish. The face is
thinner than a flounder filet, maybe a sixteenth of an inch thick,
and she made a base to keep the face from tipping over.) Or
sometimes it's maybe the beginnings of someone's nose. That is
very exciting, because then she gets to look for the rest of who-
ever is there. She is enhancing the accident. She is in love with
clay. Head over heels in love.

Once it was the head of a dead baby elephant, its ragged
mouth open in a last cry, it was so sad, she saw its poor tattered
ears, she really hardly touched it, and now it's on the table. Its
tusks were gone. She thinks, *Fucking poacher.* If she points it out

to a visitor, they see it too. It's quite small. It fits in her palm with room left over. She wonders if she's crazy.

When she doesn't find something or someone right away, she gives it another squeeze, looks again. If still nothing, she rolls it around in both hands and starts shaping the raggedy lump into an oval on a breadboard in her lap. It gets messy. She doesn't know why it's always an oval, except she loves the word—*oval*—and the possibilities implicit in its shape. Sometimes there is the suggestion of a nose. She begins with that, pulling it out of the center, because once she has the nose, she has the cheekbones, and where the eyes will be, and eventually the mouth. She loves making noses, big ones, broken ones, pointy ones, and once most of it is done, she does the nostrils. Nostrils are important and delicate, and she uses her fingernails to pinch them into a mood. Flared, she has to be so careful. She also uses fingernails to make the eyelids, fingertips to make the eyes. She keeps a little dish of water to dip in when something needs smoothing out.

At first, they were always dead. Not because of her friend who died; she thinks that was a coincidence. She didn't know how to make eyes yet, that's all, so everyone's had to be shut. Some of them died badly, one with a crack in his forehead and a hole in the side of his head. Some of them died angry, or in pain, or sad. She also made a couple of dead women, but they were old and died peacefully in their sleep.

(She is eighty, she doesn't know how she wants to die.)

Now that she's figured out eyes, most of them are alive, and they are all ages and all moods. Some are children. The little boys always look puzzled, and she loves them. *Good boy*, she sometimes whispers. When a face is pretty much done, she uses the edges to curl over and make leaves if he's a god, or curls, or sometimes nothing at all. She tried to make horns on a couple of them, when she saw what they were, which was the devil, but the clay is always too thin above their foreheads.

Yesterday, out of nowhere, there was a dog's head. Then

another silhouette, thin as can be, and once she got to work it turned out the dog's head was surrounded by a great big umbrella, which was also part of the dog. Her daughter told her there is a Japanese word for this kind of thing, she can't remember what it is, but it means inventions that have no use whatsoever. The example her daughter gave off the top of her head was an umbrella that had a straw attached to it.

She can be in the middle of something else that interests her or something she has to do, when she just has to drop everything and go for the clay. Of course, she's had to buy more of it, some of it is white, some of it is gray, some of it is terra cotta. Pounds and pounds of clay. She is only really happy when her hands are covered in slurry and something is getting discovered or finished, or in the middle of being made, and it's almost always a face, and usually a man. Some of them she would go out with if they were bigger and they were real, some of them she would run from. It all depends. Not really go out with, but there are a few who might make her laugh. It amazes her that with her bare hands and a lump of clay, she can make the face of a man who looks like someone she could talk to.

So far seventy-two faces, four animals plus her umbrella dog, a dragon, a gargoyle, several groups of creatures kissing, with wings and sometimes beaks, all of them embracing, and an odd creature with an armful of eggs of different sizes. It's part turtle, part something else whose name she forgets. Her daughter wants that one.

Right now, she's out of the white and the gray but they are on order. She still has most of a fifteen-pound box of the terra cotta. But she really wants the gray. That's the color her daughter gave her in the beginning. That's how she began. She could get her money back because it's six days late, but she really just wants the clay.

After she has made something, she puts it on the radiator cover in the living room to dry, because it's winter and the heat is on. She loves this part. She used to lean over to see how they were doing, but now she has a little chair to sit on while she checks the progress of whatever she's got lined up. She visits them every couple of hours, and she picks each one up to get a sense of their half-doneness, or doneness, which is interesting. They weigh so much less. They are separating from her, turning into themselves. She is watching over them, really.

Sometimes she wonders what has gotten into her. She wishes her friend was alive, or he could come back in a dream and tell her what she's doing. He could explain her to herself and make her laugh. Because even late at night she feels the urge to make one last face. She calls it her nightcap. She can hardly wait to see who he will be.

Splitting the World Open

Lisa Taddeo

WHEN I WAS IN THE FOURTH GRADE I WAS IN LOVE with a boy named Jonathan. He had curly chestnut hair and was attractive in a way that would never be sexy. I don't know why I loved him. I see him now on social media and he looks smug and boring. But back then he was shaped like the hole in my heart. One winter he returned from a Telluride vacation with a ski goggle tan. I thought of the hills of bright white snow and the tall pines and Jonathan at the top of a run, looking out over the whole world.

For Valentine's Day we wrote each other cards. Everyone in the classroom. Inside of mine, nothing substantive. But on the envelope I spent too long on the letters of *Jonathan*. I went over them with multiple fat-tipped Crayola markers. The resulting pigment was the most striking art I will ever produce. A fine turquoise with overlapping traces of jade and sapphire. An ocean to which I'd never been. The accident of its beauty was met with my frightened, titanic intent. When I passed the envelope to Jonathan, he blinked. He said, "What color is this? This is so freaking cool."

"Jesus Christ," I stuttered. I said, "I don't know." He looked at the other envelopes in my hand. Stephanie G. and Grant R. and Jeff K., their names in staid, solid colors. Uncherished.

Twenty-odd years later, I wrote a book about female desire. It's not the sum of anything. In the beginning, it was meant to be. I spoke to hundreds of people of all genders and races and sexual orientations. I wanted, like Kinsey, to document. I never wanted to analyze. I didn't have a hypothesis. I didn't want to draw a conclusion. I'm not in any position to do so. I wanted to light candles in dark places. I wanted to be a conduit for the stories, which spoke very powerfully, not of the state of desire in the country but of their own.

The first several drafts contained a large group that eventually was whittled down to three who happened to be women. The reason those three remained was because they had given me so much of themselves, had described with intimate granularity the way hair felt in their fingers and the light of the moon the night they lost their virginity.

People have asked, *What do they have in common?* The same thing we all have in common—the will to live, the desire to love, the need to be seen. But another commonality linked them—which I didn't fully comprehend until later—and that was the way their communities had responded to their choices. The judgments were grotesque.

I found Lina, a housewife in Indiana, when I began a discussion group in the back room of a local doctor's office. Lina's husband had recently told her that he no longer wanted to kiss her on the mouth, that the very sensation offended him. Their couple's therapist nodded.

"Lina," she said, "the way you feel about wet wool is the way Ed feels about kissing you on the mouth."

That first meeting Lina, blond and quiet, the kind of woman who seemed like a very new mother even though she wasn't, told the group that she'd been raped by three boys in high school and that her husband didn't want to kiss her although that was the only thing in the world she wanted. There was a woman with Dolly Parton hair, cleavage the depth of a canyon. She delivered tissue after tissue with one hand and held Lina's hand with her other. Some of the women cried for her. But at the next meeting, Lina told us she'd reconnected with her high school boyfriend

Aidan, the only man who had ever made her feel sensual. Now the women physically retreated, sitting back in their seats. Privately, they told me she was a whore.

Maggie Wilken, a young woman in Fargo, North Dakota, brought charges against the high school teacher with whom she'd allegedly had an affair starting when she was a sixteen-year-old student in his class. He was named North Dakota's Teacher of the Year. Publicly, she was called a whore. Out on the streets as she protested his acquittal, his current students, little teenagers in little shorts, shouted, "You're a fat cunt and he would never have wanted to fuck you."

Finally, Sloane. A striking, enigmatic, powerful entrepreneur. I heard two rumors after moving to Newport—that her husband liked to watch her have sex with other men; that her husband wanted to have sex with her every day, and not only did she allow it, she *enjoyed* it. The latter was spat out with more disdain than the first.

"Wow," I said to the first woman who mentioned it.

"What?" she asked. We were eating greasy pizza under the roof of a general store. It was late summer and pouring outside.

"That seems like a good thing, doesn't it?"

She laughed at me. "It's bullshit. It's disgusting." Straight faced, she said that, as though jealousy weren't glistening like the grease on her face.

> What would happen if one woman told the truth about her life?
> The world would split open.
> —MURIEL RUKEYSER

I've been surprised by the women who call other women victims, who say with confidence that the women in my book are not representative of modern women but shadows of our past. Wraiths from which we must run.

These women are not victims. To call them victims is to

engage in the very same behavior as the small-minded people in their communities who judged them to begin with. They are the agents of their own passion. Sometimes they fall on the sword of that passion, but wherever there is deep passion, there is a profundity of pain, at least across the many hundreds of people with whom I spoke. The way in which Maggie's story, in particular, has been characterized by several women—with a lack of empathy I didn't think feasible—is stunning in its shortsightedness. The notion that describing the complex assertion of female passion at a young age is somehow a disservice to the gender is mind-boggling to me. Maggie and the other women in the book and the men and the queer men and the queer women across the country felt pain in their passion, not always at the hands of the ones holding the power, but often at the hands of their own desire, the desire they clambered toward because they made the decision to. Because they *wanted* to.

> Of all the female sins, hunger is the least forgivable; hunger for anything, for food, sex, power, education, even love.
>
> —LAURIE PENNY

Finally, as a gender we are speaking about what we don't want. But, perhaps more than ever, we are not speaking of what we do want. Because when and if we do, we're abused for it. I've wanted love in ways that can be, at times, embarrassing. I have, like Lina, upended entire days, weeks, in the service of being in the right place at the right time for a person I was after. I have, like Maggie, felt actualized by someone else's gaze. I have, like Sloane, been attacked for my involvement in something aberrant. For my happiness in the same.

In that fourth-grade classroom, in the swirl of doily-shaped paper hearts glued onto red construction paper, beholding my envelope and its storm-colored *Jonathan*, I shook in my seat. Not because Jonathan had noticed it, but because the other girls—I remember Stephanie G. in particular—investigated it. She took the envelope from Jonathan. She turned to me and said, "It looks like you went over the letters in, like, five different colors."

It was the first time I felt the bright hot shame of female meanness. The first time I felt hunted.

As women we are, indeed, at a biological disadvantage. We're meant to wait at home for the man, gestating, while he goes out to disseminate his seed over the hills of grass and the hills of snow. The women I have met don't prove that biological disadvantage so much as they prove that women are still punishing to other women. We still draw conclusions about lives that are not our own. We still project our own shame onto others. We fear the mirror. Men don't deserve our tears, but neither do other women, flailing at their own lack to reconcile themselves with their darker parts, with the parts that wanted things outside of their own bodies.

We don't want to hear that other women struggle with their weight, with their looks, with aging, with socioeconomic status. We want to pretend those struggles don't exist. We want to pretend we don't look for the lost or broken parts of ourselves in the shape of other people. I very often spoke to women raging against infidelity one moment and sending untoward emails to people who weren't their partners the next. I've heard that the women in the book are not happy. That their partnerships are depressing. Sloane's marriage is, in fact, one of the happiest I've ever met. There's confusion in it, as there is in any relationship. The confusion was interesting. Her self-awareness within that confusion was compelling. But some readers attack the aberration even as they sit in their swiveling chairs and bemoan the lack of representation of this group or that.

The key is not to ignore the history of the patriarchy, to pretend it never existed, to pretend that women in the middle of the country, in towns that have *still* never heard of #MeToo, don't need help, someone to light the way.

What it's all about is this. We don't want to hear about what another woman wants. If it's something married, if it's something brutish, if it's something we have wanted too. We don't want to hear a young woman feels actualized by the gaze of a man. Even if hearing that—and witnessing the fallout it wreaks—is the very thing that helps another young woman not make the same mistakes.

Oh my god, can anyone in the history of the world say they have not wanted to sleep with the *wrong* person? Or insufferably pined for the right one? Why do we think we have the power to make or judge that decision for others? Is it not, in fact, the same hubris wielded by the men who still control our reproductive rights?

I'll never forget the way I felt in that fourth-grade classroom. I've felt that way many times since. By men I have felt objectified, emotionally raped, physically raped. But by women I've felt shredded in a way that's difficult to describe. It's characterized by a coldness, by a callous quiet, the same way that the senior girls looked at Maggie after they heard rumors about her relationship with an older man. They were upset by her audacity, by the glint in her eye and the shine in her hair. One girl, in fact, told another that she was jealous of Maggie's hair. Of her *hair*. And that was why she called her a whore.

I've met countless women on this journey who I never saw judge another woman. These were often the ones who were the most candid and the best listeners. The ones who did judge never spoke of themselves because they were afraid; but they weren't afraid of dissecting the details of someone else's life. The young women in Maggie's community attacked her incoherently. They barely knew what they were attacking. They took a peculiar, childish pleasure in hating without really understanding why.

Some presumably intelligent women have tediously attacked the language of these women and not the content of their desire.

Lina's language for Aidan was unguarded and vibrant; she evocatively conveyed her hunger without fearing being called pathetic. *Pathetic* is a pathetic word to begin with. After being a body raped and then a body abandoned, Lina was finally inhabiting hers again.

But we don't want to validate some women's needs unless they're cloaked in language half of us have deemed socially responsible. Finding oneself via orgasmic meditation is fine, but driving three hours to meet the only person who has made us feel not raped or not ugly is not. If the thing a woman wants is a *bad* man or a *bad* woman, then maybe we can begin—if we really must assert an opinion—by excavating what that woman *actually* wants, what she is actually missing. It's likely not the other person. It's like some hole shot up in her, perhaps, as I saw time and again, by other women, by her own mother.

My book offers no conclusions. I began with no hypotheses. I think to make a conclusion, as a layperson, as a human being like all the ones I've spoken with, would be the most irresponsible, judgmental thing of all. Plenty of people draw conclusions about lives that are not their own. Plenty of people evaluate that which they have never accomplished. It's not for me to do that.

But the time I spent has brought up many questions for me. Among them: how might we expedite the path toward ascendancy? How might we be less forbidding to one another and to others who have suffered like us? Can we temper our jealousy over another woman's satisfaction in the bedroom, success in her career, finding the home she always wanted, or the ocean or the dog or the cure for cancer? Perhaps we don't realize what we do to one another. Perhaps we are so focused on the people or things for which we burn that we don't realize how we burn our sisters. Perhaps we don't see it. Perhaps there is a hypothesis to my research after all.

The Thief

Jane Wong

THE THIEF DREAMED OF OPENING A SET OF ENCY-clopedias. She dreamed of the gilded spines like the foil of chocolate coins, the fresh metallic ink, the pages falling open like the wings of some newly discovered moth. The thief went over to her neighbor's house to hang out and there it was: the *World Book Encyclopedia*, 1996 set, *A* through *F*. The encyclopedias were heavy enough to press four-leaf clovers or straighten out curling band posters or clobber a gluttonous cockroach. Even though her friend was missing the rest of the alphabet, even though this wasn't the highly coveted *Britannica* set, she wanted it.

As her friend talked on the phone to some middle school crush, a boy with so much hair he was practically a yak, the thief lay down on the rug near the bookcase, touching the oxblood spines. She dreamed about devouring these books, gorging herself with facts about fire ants and tectonic plates and Romanticism, the pages stuck between her teeth. She would need a toothpick for sure. Did it matter that these entries were often wrong? Or that the books lacked entries that reflected who she was, how she grew up, where her ancestors came from? Did it matter that the whole thing was a marketing scam, brought door-to-door via a salesman in a tweed suit or via a thick catalog that promised knowledge at your fingertips with a pay-in-installments plan?

The thief looked at her fingertips, glitter nail polish chipping like an old disco ball. The want was somersaulting inside her, an oil fire. The want was rollicking in her lungs, hay heavy. This is when it first happened. Yes, she thought about it, for a few brief seconds. Of tipping book *B* from its place like a trust fall, of the book landing into her hands, and then slipping it quietly into her backpack. Of pushing the other books to the left, closing the ghost-book gap. No one would miss the *B*s anyway—her friend could live without interrogating the beach, the barnacle, the beetle. Seconds of the thinking, of the longing, dragged on. The longing for what we can't have and what trouble this longing gifts us. The longing settled in her, the first firefly among decades of tall brush.

But the thief did nothing, and, when her friend gave her the receiver to talk to Yak Boy, the cord dangling like a long ramen noodle, the thief hung up on him, her friend screeching, "*OmgomgJaaanewhatthetruefuck!*"

When I was finally caught, I cried because I thought I should cry. The tears were like glue, sticky with empathy. When I was finally caught, I lied and said it was my first time stealing, that my friends put me up to it, that I had never thought about stealing before. When I was finally caught, it was in the jewelry section of a big department store in the Monmouth Mall in Eatontown, New Jersey. I was trying on a pair of earrings and moved my head back and forth like a fish to see the turquoise stones shine. I did not put the earrings back. I just left them on as if they were mine to begin with. When I was finally caught, the security guard walked me through every single department—women's shoes, men's dress shirts, bedding, appliances, hosiery—like I was on a grand parade of shame. I kept my eyes on my boots, which were wet with melting snow and sidewalk salt like blue pop rocks. When I was finally caught, I was led into a back room that was dimly lit and had blurry gray security camera televisions stacked atop each other. A chair swiveled behind a long steel desk and the manager was there with a goatee, looking at me with furrowed brows, and it was so much like a bad crime show, I laughed. "What's so funny?" the manager asked, placing both his hands down on the desk like he was pressing apples for cider. When I was finally caught, I sat there amid the spectral glow of the security televisions and thought about how the earrings I stole were on sale, 65 percent off. I almost laughed again, thinking about how I only stole things on sale. That even in my deep sinkhole of indignity, I was a thrifty thief, a clearance red-sticker shoplifter. An immigrant baby, always. The manager admonished me again as he took my photograph for the wall of shoplifters banned from the store. I closed my eyes as the flash went off. When I was finally caught, I couldn't stop laughing and crying at the same time. "This is not funny, young lady."

The desire to steal was like terrible metals fastening themselves to any glittering thing, swaying in wicked delight. The desire was almost romantic, almost swoon-worthy, akin to the crush I had on the homeschooled punk who also worked at the public library with me, stamping dates on newspapers in the periodicals section. During my year of stealing, I wanted so badly to be bad. I wanted to shake loose all the expectations placed upon me—quiet, sweet, "good." In my thirties, a disgusting man will say to me, after shoving his slug tongue in my mouth, "Are you a good girl or a bad girl?" How was I supposed to calculate the length of time it would take to let loose what others thought of me? He bit my ear and I pretended to like it. "We both know you're a bad girl," he said, eel-like. I've always been terrible at math.

At seventeen, I wanted to want, to be wanted, wanton in my wanting. I worked in the children's section at the Monmouth County Public Library, mostly reshelving dinosaur books, and I would sometimes stop by periodicals like I had something to retrieve. A stapler maybe, a misplaced issue of *Highlights*. Because he was homeschooled, the punk didn't know that I was a nerd in high school, or that I'd never been kissed or asked out, or that I spent my weekends reading novels instead of going to parties. Once, in his oversized ripped-up hoodie, he looked up from the counter with basset hound eyes and said, "I want to check you out." And when I stood there, slack-mouthed in my ugly-duckling stink, he quickly added, "Just trying out terrible library pick-up lines. Did it work?" I hope you're wincing too.

I didn't have to tell my mother. But what kind of immigrant baby would steal and then lie to her mother about it? I drew a line in my shame, a do-not-pass-go in the dirt. I didn't have a car and so I had to wait for my mother to pick me up from the mall. When she picked me up, she had to park far away because a large section of the parking lot was being paved with a fresh coat of asphalt, which shone like a beautiful onyx necklace I would be too afraid to steal.

When I told her, I said it simply; I said it without looking at her, for fear of seeing myself reflected in her face. "I stole something and got caught."

She said nothing. We walked back to the car, past the perimeter of the new asphalt, the dimpled potholes, the gasoline slush of January snow. My mother is not the quiet type. She's an extrovert, a total ham, someone who loves to talk and wraps you in the warmth of her talking. She will literally talk to anyone. Once, calling sick out of work, she thanked the automated assistant who told her to have a nice day. "You have a nice day too," my mother said and hung up. Aching with laughter, I told her she didn't have to talk to robots. My mother smiled and shrugged: "The robot is nice." Here, in the stinging cold of my failure as a daughter, my longing felt hot pink and nauseated with her silence. All I could hear was the sound of the car starting and snow crunching underneath the tires. I wanted any sound to come out of her—a tremble, a sigh, a growl. Nothing.

When we got home, she closed the front door behind us. In the hollowed privacy of shame, she spoke.

"I give you everything you need! Food, a house, clothes, everything for school! How could you do this to me?"

I felt my body go slack from everything she said, everything that was true. As the child of an immigrant single mother, how could I have slapped her in the face like this, ungrateful and greedy? When my mother arrived in this country, arranged to be married to my father—a stranger—she had only twenty dollars in her pocket. After my gambling father left and our restaurant failed, she fended for me and my brother. I thought about her working night shifts at the postal service, of poorly packaged mail getting jammed in the machine at 2:00 a.m. (read: please stop putting candy in business envelopes), of her reheating rice, string beans, and steamed fish on her lunch break at midnight, whirring in the alien light of the microwave. The same food I ate many hours prior, the black bean sauce delicious with the flaky white fish. How I funneled it into my mouth, scallion scented, mindlessly. At that moment, I touched my ears, which were no longer bejeweled, and started sobbing. I fell to the floor, a mud slop, sputtering apologies. I knew how hard my mother worked, knew what it meant to live paycheck by paycheck, knew why there were no baby pictures of me (we couldn't afford a camera). My mother's eyes were wild, disappointment flashing like telephone wires in a storm.

And finally, slowly, she said in both English and Toisanese, "You broke my heart." These words could have been stolen from any pop song, yet they stuck their spindle legs deep into my chest, finding footing for a kind of disgrace I couldn't bear. She turned away from me then, as if declaring we were no longer mirror images—our mouths, our noses, our eyes, our doubled birthmarks, no longer the same. Variations in goodness, in badness, in what happens in this country because of too much want.

That night, from my bedroom window upstairs, I watched my mother hack ice off the windshield of our car—the cold crystals flying off like strange, interior fireworks. The car huffed in its attempt to warm itself, clouds of exhaustion. I worried about my mother slipping away from me, skating off over a frozen pond. I leaned against a wall to brace myself, to feel something holding me up. I closed my eyes, imagining each brick falling away, tumbling into the bright blue distance, and there I was—still leaning against some invisible force resembling the face of forgiveness.

The thief left the books at home, piled wayward like a poorly built fire in her bedroom, and drove to the library punk's show at the Stone Pony in Asbury Park. She went alone and pushed through the forest of tall teenaged boys, to the front of the crowd. The library punk was a bassist, his hair spiked with gel; to be honest, the band was fucking terrible and the drummer kept losing the drumsticks. But he smiled at her like cracking the sugar of crème brûlée. His bandmates would tell him later to never smile like that because it was fucking cheesy and what was he doing liking a Chinese girl anyway, unless he liked Oriental sluts? The fear of being a fetish overwhelmed her so much, she felt like she was going to tip over and fall face first, and so she moved backward instead to overcorrect. Ever the nautilus, she moved so backward that she left the venue completely in that moment. The thief returned home to her books and, like heavy necklaces, she put them on, one by one.

The manager placed me in customer service at Marshalls on the first day of my job. It was the summer of my senior year of high school. "A smart girl like you can deal with stuff like returns and exchanges," she said, leaving me with a line of ten customers, snapping their gum and shifting their babies from one arm to another like judicial scales. I was still working at the library, only a few streets away, and my mother decided I needed a job with "people skills" too—worried I was just hiding in the book stacks like an awkward turtle. To be honest, she wanted the 15 percent customer discount. And to be honest, I was most definitely an awkward turtle, and I fumbled about my shell daily.

"I'd like to return this rug," my first customer said, her hair piled atop her head like a chandelier of curls. She kicked open a nine-by-twelve damask rug, and it unfurled like a wave on the floor, forcing the people behind her to step back. I peered over the counter and took a look at the rug. It was covered in footprints, cat hair, and cigarette burns in the corners. The hell was this?

"You speak English? I said I'm returning this rug," the customer said, now gripping her hands on the counter. There are moments like this, when a white person asks me if I speak English, where two things happen: (1) I feel immediately defensive and enunciate every. single. syllable, or (2) I feel bad about the impulse to prove myself to white people and move quickly toward rage against the racist hierarchy of English and say absolutely nothing and go into side-eye hibernation.

The second option is where I am these days. I chose the first option when I was younger, fumbling through the ventricles of internalized racism. "I sincerely apologize. Let me see what I can do for you," I said, as A+ AP Lit as possible.

During my time working at Marshalls, so much stealing happened. But this time, it wasn't me. Customers would try to return random shit, retagged with a price maker at home. "This is from the dollar store across the street," I told one of them, lifting a plaid cosmetic pouch. She kind of shrugged and didn't even try to disagree. Some people stole in the most blatant ways—shoving a pair of underwear into their purse while tying their shoes. Or sometimes it was more subtle, like moving a red-tag clearance sticker onto a full-priced item, which I honestly feel fine about. If you need the sale, make it happen. Once, one of my coworkers got caught stealing money and items from layaway. During a break, she told me she'd upgraded to a queen-sized bed. She shared half of an orange with me, peeling it in a perfect spiral. One of the items on layaway was a headboard. When she was pulled out of the store, she looked only at the ground, even when a few employees called out *we got you*, and *you didn't do it!* None of them knew I was in my year of stealing. That I had put on five pairs of Victoria's Secret underwear just the day before, hidden under sweatpants. That I carry scissors in my purse, at the ready. As my coworker passed by me, I thought about how sweet it was that she shared that orange with me, cleaning off the pith with such grace, care.

Ever since I told my mother I stole, I haven't shoplifted. When I watch a group of teenagers at a store motion to each other with their eyes, readying their moves, I can't bear to watch. I grow sticky with fear and want, and I have to leave the store immediately. These days, twenty years later, I keep thinking someone is going to catch me stealing something. Like putting shiitake mushrooms in a brown bag with cremini mushrooms at the grocery store. Like I'm-sorry-my-mistake. But then I worry: was it really a mistake? I've begun to suspect myself.

What the thief would like stolen from her: the tick her college boyfriend found curled up in her belly button; pairs of socks with holes in them that she can't bear to throw away; the moldy shower curtain from her first apartment; the memory of the man who told her "I could destroy you," biting her nipple so hard it drew blood; the memory of another man who held her neck with his hands, drunk and stewing in the suet of power and violence; the vast flood of her period during history class and the nonmemory of passing out in the hallway when she rushed to the bathroom; the swamp marsh of rotting bundles of cilantro in her fridge; all her throbbing mosquito bites past, present, and future; her pair of broken flats that flapped about like a duck; her college debt, each loan piled atop each other like kindling; each gleaming heartbreak in which men made it very clear to her that they did not want her—that no one would want a woman who wants so much and has too much to give.

Once, an ex-boyfriend drew me a card with a raccoon holding a heart on it. It had clearly been traced with a pencil and then filled out with a Sharpie marker and colored pencils. Written inside: "She stole my fucking heart." This was an ex of mine that told me he could imagine having babies with me. He also told me he was astonished that he could be with someone so beautiful and brilliant. He traced the corners of my mouth gently. He came so loudly during sex, I often blinked wide-eyed, startled by my own power. He wanted me from the very start, sitting front row at a poetry reading, fixed on me. He was so handsome and so bearded and I was a glutton.

Over and over, I rolled around in the greasy glut of being wanted. I longed for that look of theirs—that look where men can't seem to make sense of me, can't help but flutter near me. At a writer's conference, I met an older poet who clearly wanted me. He stared at me from across the room, whiskey in hand. He was a professor somewhere. He gave me his book, which I never read. I had no interest in him whatsoever, but I wanted to be wanted and so I spoke to him. He thought I was such a goody-two-shoes, asked me if I've ever done anything bad. These terrible men and their stereotypes, their Orientalist fantasies. I told him I used to steal. "Did you ever lay out all the things you stole on your bed? That's sexy," he said, trying to touch my hand. I stepped back and laughed in his face. "I stole on clearance." I left him there, gawking, and never spoke to him again.

After promising to move to a new city with me, after meeting my new colleagues, that ex of mine wrote me an email and said I was a fantasy. That our connection wasn't real. And he referred to me in third person, as if I wasn't real. He disappeared, his want disappeared, everything disappeared, as if a year didn't pass. There were so many men like this in my life that it became a sickening pattern, with varying degrees of cruelty. The obsessive, visceral want and then the sudden shutting down of that want. I was told so many things. That I intimidated them, that I wanted more than they could give, that I was worthless and ugly and stupid.

I grew terrified of want. I didn't want men to want me; I didn't want them. I slinked away from their looks, grew disgusted by their image of me and desire to toy with me. I called my mom often and she'd ask me: what do you want? At a restaurant, I'd catch myself staring into a bowl of beef noodle soup or tonkotsu ramen and ask these questions, my face steaming with answers I couldn't decipher. What makes me happy? What does it take to want myself? I slurp noodle after noodle, ravenous. The noodles bounce back against my teeth, deliciously resistant to the bite.

Each week, at 11:30 p.m. on Fridays, her mother would wash the thief's hair. The thief's hair was long. It grew way past her butt and was as thick and coarse as horsehair or a straw broom that never quite swept everything up. Throughout the school week, her hair would grow dirty and oily, full of grass and sweat and pencil shavings. She was eight years old and still loved it when her mother would sit on the other side of the bathtub, lathering her hair into coils of soapy songs. Her mother's hands were rough from chopping vegetables and frying eggrolls and scrubbing dishes at the restaurant, and this meant her hair was being scoured clean and kneaded with the strength you need to make a proper loaf of bread. Held under the faucet, water spooling over her hair and forehead, the thief would look up at her mother, who would look down at her, and there it was. The warm, clean depths of it in the lukewarm bathwater. The face of forgiveness has no sense of time. I sat there, listening to forgiveness do its work, the swirl of the bathwater curling down the drain. The sounds of which I eavesdrop upon from time to time, in learning to forgive myself especially. Even then, my mother seemed to say *we have each other.* Enough to loosen longing, strand by wanting strand, jawbone by jawbone.

Addiction

Susan Shapiro

"WHERE THE HELL ARE YOU?" I YELLED, BANGING ON his door at 3:00 a.m., freaking out he'd disappeared again. I couldn't believe he was mind-fucking me after he just told me to travel an hour to see him so late. What game was my guy playing?

No, it wasn't a past lover screwing me over. He was my pot dealer. I was waiting for him in subzero cold, wearing a flimsy blazer with one hundred dollars in my pocket, all alone in a strange Queens neighborhood that suddenly seemed dangerous. I'd rushed there to buy a little bag of strong light green Hawaiian weed, somehow surprised that someone I'd recently met who was often stoned and sold drugs for a living would be so unreliable. Finally, he let me into his vestibule, and we quickly exchanged my cash for his stash. Then, afraid to take the subway so late (years before Uber), I had to find another taxi to get home to my Greenwich Village studio to smoke my fix.

I was a nice single Jewish girl finishing my master's program who'd just landed a coveted (albeit low paying) editorial assistant job at a top magazine. Why was I risking my safety for this impulsive middle-of-the-night excursion? I saw no choice; I'd unexpectedly run out of my daily dose and couldn't find anybody closer who had any to share, loan, or sell me. After desperately sifting through the garbage cans in my apartment, I didn't find enough roaches for a leftover puff or bong blast. I used to buy dime bags in Washington Square Park blocks away—until somebody sold me oregano and I realized there was no Better Business Bureau to complain to. I wanted to get high so badly my brain flew out the window of the cab I couldn't afford.

Addiction is desire on steroids. You not only want something, but you'll do anything to get it, craving it so badly it feels like you'll die without it. In my case that involved repeatedly sweating, shaking, crying, and going through withdrawal whenever I couldn't find it. And yes, you can become physically dependent on marijuana. A recent study showed teenagers' addiction rates for cannabis were about the same as opioids.

Then again, I fit the textbook definition of an addict: someone with a compulsive physiological need for a habit-forming substance—many different ones actually. It originated when my sweet redheaded mother, who'd grown up poor and an orphan, constantly overfed her children, making us all insatiably hungry for food. In psychology class, I read about the Stanford marshmallow test that showed kids able to delay gratification would be more successful. I laughed because I'd literally eat a bag of marshmallows myself, as well as pick out all the Lucky Charms in the cereal the minute it appeared in our pantry. Was I doomed to failure?

By thirteen in suburban Michigan, I'd become a nicotine fiend like my difficult doctor father—who'd chain smoked Chesterfields—because it was a way for me to suppress my appetite. My first commitment-phobic boyfriend turned me onto Bob Dylan, dope (as we called it back then), and cocaine, which made me dance and not want food for days. Drugs led us to hell; he slept with two of my roommates while on magic mushrooms.

"To want is to have a weakness," Margaret Atwood said in *The Handmaid's Tale*. I had a variety of weaknesses over the years. Mixed in with the compulsive consumption of cigarettes and pot was twelve daily cans of Tab ("JAP Juice," my boyfriend called it) and forays into diet pills, vodka, champagne, rum (mixed with diet soda), Juicy Fruit gum, popcorn, and cupcake icing.

During years of therapy with a Jewish shrink who worked on a sliding scale, I talked about growing up feeling like an outsider who never felt I fit into my conservative Midwest family. She wondered if my mother's early losses, quelled by food, led to inherited trauma, or whether chain smoking with my father made me feel closer to him, bonded in our method of self-destruction. I hadn't ever considered my parents' role in my adult addictions before she suggested it, but my past continued to haunt my present choices.

At twenty-nine, I met a kind, older, curly-haired scriptwriter who was only addicted to me. I told the boss who'd fixed us up, "He's smart and sweet but not my type." She said, "Your type is neurotic, self-destructive, and not into you. Go out with him again." My shrink guessed I was ambivalent because he was unlike my father and thus not "cathected with past erotic energy." I didn't know what that meant, though I'd noted that a few of my bad boyfriends were born in August like my aloof dad, while my new beau's birthday was in May like my mother, whose love was more unconditional.

Then he took off for a job in California. Not being able to get what I wasn't even sure I wanted made me long for him. So I fought to get him back. We married when I was thirty-five. Right after we said "I do," he told me he hated the smell of smoke in our home and I had to quit smoking and partying. Can a mate insist you stop doing something you love? I threatened to leave him. The only problem was we'd just thrown big wedding parties for all our friends, colleagues, and relatives, then emptied our savings and borrowed more to buy an apartment. Plus, I adored him.

Luckily, he found me a brilliant new WASP male shrink who was an addiction specialist. This tough-talking paternal figure turned out to be a Leo like the original, except he was a head doctor—a different kind of internist—who'd quit tobacco. (My father eventually gave it up too.) "The problem with addicts is they depend on substances, not people," he said, insisting I had to shift my dependency to someone like him (and other "core pillars") to get clean.

This was weeks after 9/11, when we were both still in shock and mourning in downtown Manhattan. I'd just turned forty. While others were having trauma sex, I was having trauma sobriety. "I'm reading obituaries of people my age who were killed. I can't stop thinking that if I died tomorrow, I'd never have nailed what I really wanted in life," I selfishly confessed.

"What do you want most?" he'd asked.

"I want to publish my book."

I admitted feeling like a loser since the story of my self-destructive relationships that I'd spent seven years revising kept getting rejected. I'd helped so many students find agents and editors; I was like the wedding planner who couldn't get married. I ached for a book deal so badly I could taste it. Having found my desire to get healthier wasn't motivating enough, he said my memoir would only sell if I stopped smoking, toking, and drinking.

Ascertaining that having my book see print was my Shangri-la, he ingeniously brainwashed me to believe that the only reason I couldn't land a publishing contract was that "using" clouded up my brain too much to sustain a longer narrative. And merely by quitting would I be granted my career fantasy. (Never mind that many authors were known lushes, smokers, tokers, sniffers, and even heroin shooters.) He convinced me that getting rid of my small daily desires would allow me to achieve my biggest dream, refocusing my energy on a specific plan.

For the all-out assault against my bad habits, I avoided bars, parties, smokers, drinkers, and druggies—basically my entire social circle of writers and artists. I did weekly talk sessions with him, supplemented by emergency phone calls and emails he'd answer, often five times a day. I was itchy, twitchy, anxious, angry, lonely, and lost for months. I cried over nothing. He admitted I had the worst substance withdrawal he'd seen and that I was his most taxing patient. When I asked why, he replied,

"You have a chronic anxiety level connected to a hyperactive mind that's plugged into a very analytic level of consciousness. There's no rest or rhythm. It's all high pitch. There's a continual idiosyncratic intensity that's exhausting."

When I read the description to my mother, she said "That describes your father exactly," hinting that there might be a genetic connection to my intense addictive personality. My shrink guessed it was exacerbated by an over-feeding parent on one side and a chain-smoker on the other, giving the hourly dual message that difficult feelings could be immediately eaten, drank, or smoked away.

Some of my shrink's patients had luck with antidepressants, so he suggested a psychopharmacologist who prescribed Wellbutrin. It gave me horrible headaches. When I read the side effects were seizures I stopped taking it. Thinking I had ADD, he suggested Adderall, which is supposed to make those with attention deficit disorder calmer. It made me a speed freak.

"Get off now," my shrink told me. The only medication that helped was a high dose of the nicotine patch for six months, along with more of his weird behavioral modifications.

"Put everyone you know in two categories," he said. "If they're part of the problem, avoid them. If they're part of the solution, see them more." He wrote little sayings and directives on the back of business cards he'd hand me, like "Underlying every substance problem I've ever seen is a deep depression that feels unbearable."

I found therapy riveting, not depressing, and had always thought I had a very upbeat, vivacious personality. He said I put the word *manic* in *manically depressed* and the *high* in *high energy*, adding "Everything is too important to you."

"Make your husband hold you for one hour every night without speaking" was one mantra I shared with my mate, who obeyed. I guessed if we couldn't talk we couldn't argue (plus his arms were soothing). I became dependent on his touch to stay calm.

When I mentioned chewing on gum or veggies all day, my shrink worried. "Your personality is so habit forming, you could get hooked on carrot sticks," he told me, pushing me to halt chomping on gum and vegetables. "Diet and practice portion control. Don't overeat or you'll just do the substance shuffle."

"What can I have? Water? Tea?" I asked, exhausted from all the quitting.

"You could keep your mouth shut and not put anything in it for hours at a time," he told me, a choice that, up until then, had never actually occurred to me.

I took notes, scrawling his quotes into pages of my journal, asking him to repeat every word of his pithy adages, especially when they felt poetic like "You have to learn to suffer well" and "The only way to change is to change. Understanding follows."

Continually warning me that one could become addicted to anything, he mentioned other patients who'd gone down the rabbit holes of gambling, charity work, church events, shopping, adventure sports, cheating, and danger. "Beware all excitement because it takes you out of yourself, and you always have to go back to yourself," he said. For me, that meant regressing back to thirteen, before I found the instant gratification Band-Aids of two packs a day of More Menthol Lights to fill in the fear and emptiness.

"Lead the least secretive life you can" was his mandate, a cross between AA's "You're only as sick as your secrets" and a paraphrase of Robert Frost's "The only way out is through." I was so substance deprived that a girlfriend emailed me, "Hey let's get together and have some water." Yet my goal-oriented obsession cleared my mind of clutter. I wrote for hours every day, becoming a workaholic.

Surprisingly, a critical persnickety Leo made a better head doctor for me than a partner, and the treatment was wildly successful. After nine months, a poetic time frame, I sold my memoir about the five past self-destructive relationships I'd quit: *Five Men Who Broke My Heart*. Then I sold a sequel about five self-destructive substances I quit called *Lighting Up: How I Stopped Smoking, Drinking and Everything Else I Loved in Life Except Sex*, chronicling our addiction therapy. By the end of the first year, I had three book deals I analyzed endlessly with my therapist, making him read a new chapter every session. I pined for his feedback on every page. If he canceled a session, I went batshit. When he was late I'd fume and pace in his waiting room. I'd become addicted to him.

A neuroscientist whose book I read argued that we don't help addicts by ministering directly to their brains since people learn to be addicts and thus they can learn not to be. Yet based on my own experience I doubted that an addict could become a nonaddict. Instead, you just switched addictions by refocusing your powerful energy elsewhere. (That's why AA members often guzzled coffee and donuts and puffed cigarettes outside their meetings.) Meanwhile my shrink insisted that using substances did not make you pleasure seeking, they made you pain avoiding. If that was true, then dodging painful feelings had become such a fanatical quest that it ruled my senses for twenty-seven years.

When my addiction specialist moved to another state, I went through withdrawal from him too. He'd been charging two hundred dollars a session. Therapists on my updated insurance cost only twenty-five dollars a session. Desperate for his replacement, I saw eight shrinks in eight days. Instead of speed dating, I was *Speed Shrinking*—which became my first comic novel.

Publishing books substituted for other dependencies. Hearing an editor say yes was so exhilarating, I felt like I'd found God or at least a power higher than nicotine, alcohol, marijuana, gum, or soda—substances I haven't touched in twenty years and no longer felt any desire for. Sometimes I missed wanting something so badly it made me crazy.

Last summer I celebrated my twenty-fifth wedding anniversary to my screenwriter soulmate. By this time I was the author/coauthor of seventeen books. Interestingly, a new study revisited those adults who'd taken the 1972 marshmallow experiment and disavowed the original results, showing no difference between kids who waited versus the ones who gobbled up the white fluffy candy. Additionally, it was easier for children of privilege to wait since they knew more treats were coming.

I saw flaws in the premise that delaying gratification was a key to success. I'd called my journalism classes "the instant gratification takes too long" method, where the goal of the class was to write and publish a short piece by the end of the course. As a long-time *New York Times* editor told my class, the writers he'd seen who became most famous were the ones who were most obsessed. Someone imbued with passion went farther than a brilliant, patient person with no drive. Desire was the presentiment of our abilities and the forerunner of our accomplishments, according to the philosopher Goethe. We wanted to want. My worry was that all the yearning would wane.

Yet in my fifties, I kept waking up every day as hyper as the Energizer Bunny, drinking green tea and rushing to my computer to check what my agent, editors, or critics had to say.

"Book deals and press is your new cocaine," my shrink warned by email.

The substitute seems safer and more benign. Except during the months when I can't make a new clip happen or years when a book deal isn't forthcoming. Then I feel like I'm still banging on doors at all hours, frazzled and frustrated when they won't open to give me my fix. In these cases, I go back to teletherapy for emergency tune-ups, a less fraught addiction that involves limits, boundaries, and dependence on another human being. Yet I'm still paying him to help reshape the waves of my endless hunger to get what I want: the thrill of nailing the next prize.

Where It Starts, Where It Ends

Terese Svoboda

DESIRE BEGINS BEHIND THE STERNUM AND RADIATES
through the body but especially to the wrists, where depression
sits later. And lower of course. You are glowing already—desire
is an emergency—when you open the door and see the lump in
his front, this Chilean god of heat. I'll be right there, you tell
someone on the phone an hour later and then sink back to the
bed, where he pulls you to him again and again, so impatiently.
When he leaves, you are standing behind the door raw, the air
sort of loosened around you, your hands little useless claws.
You are not consumed by desire, no it hasn't eaten you down
to nothing—yet. Instead you are filled with a physical intensity
that surely no one else has ever felt before.

It must be the same for him: he says so. He's so in love,
he says. *Incredible*, he says in a tone that sounds as if he's been
cruelly captured. All complimentary, indeed, but besides being
five years younger, he can't really speak your language. Really,
he says very little, being sensitive about his English, he lets his
handsome, rugged face with its dark eyes talk. Work-study has
sent him to labor beside you, and you have barely progressed out
of the study part of life. Besides, the office is very small, and
it's back when there were file cabinets breast high and women's
thighs swished with sausage encasements of nylon reminding
everyone every time you move that you have a body, topped with
lips that say whatever, who can remember? That leads to ripped
nylons at lunch when the boss is out, and the sure knowledge

you'll be caught. But no, you aren't. Then you don't leave together, you stall, all agony, watching him exit, checking your
purse for the appropriate synthetic pale prophylactic just in case
completion is possible, knowing what part of this is your business. A street corner later, appearing casual, you meet and repeat
that kiss, the one you'd left hidden behind the cabinet.

What this leads to, in a matter of weeks, is black and blue,
is him shoving you against a wall so hard you can't think what's
next: he hits you. He's told you his father hid in a closet while
Pinochet's soldiers searched the house with guns and how he
felt such shame when his mother couldn't get rid of the smell of
urine. Your country paid those soldiers! You don't listen or you
do and the story floats off amid him at you again with desire
so great you are drowning in it. That he touches you there so
tenderly afterward says everything. You avoid the mirror in the
morning, you go to work in sunglasses.

You have a small child from your ex and split custody. Two
weeks after the Chilean hits you, he totes the child around on
his shoulders and it's the three of you, off to his mother's, the
mother who scrubbed out that closet, who now owns half a block
of Manhattan. She inspects the boy as if he's a math problem
that will never yield an answer. You can't imagine her moments
of desire, except when she kisses her son goodbye, your own son
set down from his shoulders and free.

Her grilling leaves the Chilean happy, most of it so fast you
can't follow her. Afterward, he insists your son call him Daddy.
That is when you discern the difference between love and desire.
The son is love. He looks like you already, it is as if he came to
be strictly through the narcissism of desire, a perfect imprint
changed into love. If you can't protect yourself, you must protect
him. You start to pick him up from his father's at odd hours,
you tell your ex you have to skip some weekends, you imperil
split custody by staying away, you endure a cuff, a slap from your
lover, but you keep them apart.

You miss your son terribly.

One Monday your lover slams the file shut on your hand. No one hears your squeak. You say you feel sick at lunch, you'll just work through. He pushes you with his torso, the soccer-thick torso where it should be pliant but instead blocks. He wants to know if you're pregnant, something you might inflict upon him, as if it's a disease he might suffer from. He demands you test yourself. You say you're not that sick, there's no problem, what about a cheese sandwich? You eat but can't swallow.

Still, you buy a dress with just enough cleavage.

Your boss has a name from some Texan town, Austin or Houston, and she's lanky and brash, older, certain of her attractions. She has enjoyed watching the ricochet of all this desire, its strains, such torment in such a small office. She invites you to dinner to discuss it.

You tell her nothing, no girl talk. In the dark of the restaurant, you don't need sunglasses. She says, opening her purse for her card, she has a lead on a better position for you. You hem and you haw, you say you'll consider it.

You pick up your son at the sitter's.

His father has him the night your lover won't let you flee, the night you threaten to phone for help, the night you phone the cops while he's pissing. Terror runs to your wrists, waiting, and you turn so talkative, so seductive—until they finally come to the door. His English has improved over the months you've been at this, and when the cops swagger into the apartment, after a short volley of questions, the bond men make with their first exchange is palpable. Besides, they're Latino. They might as well have shaken hands. The cops smirk, say there's nothing they can do, it's domestic, take her out for dinner or tell him it's over.

His fingers on the file cabinet, his fingers on you in the hall. What is it?

When you don't find a new job, the boss hires her own sister, squeezes her into the office on a folding chair, just for the six weeks between terms. She is more his age, she is blond with hair she can sit on, and oblivious to you. Your boss takes him off the files. He will sort, the boss says, at the desk beside her sister's. He sorts and he sorts. He misses a day of work. Her sister is sick on that very same day. Your boss offers you a week of pay while you look for work.

You gaze at the clouds where they're collecting just outside the one office window, you hesitate. She fires you.

Naivete and stupidity are the chief assets of the young, causing mountains to be climbed and wars to be waged. You knew what to do but why couldn't you leave? The only thing that was clear at the time was the moment he cracked your head against a wall: violence was not you. Only now do you understand the boss' machinations. You thought it was punishment she was inflicting, but it was rescue: she knew her sister could handle him. Under the lash of such desire, you could not see how your son would inevitably be put in danger, whether he was around or not, to be used by the lover in any battle with the ex because violence was all he knew. He would not be his father in that closet, scorned by his mother for the rest of his life as a coward.

It isn't but three weeks after three weeks of not seeing him, not even in the pickup soccer games at the park on two very nice Saturdays, of not calling him once so you can hear his deep voice and then hanging up, of not loitering around the office after five to at last glimpse him wandering, so petulant and sulky, after that blond sister, that you meet someone else and the same little flame lights your cortex, prefrontal or snake brain, or lower, and, coaxed and stoked, it flares white-hot, however primed. You don't put it down for the next forty years, you're still holding it, embers in your hands, blowing on it.

Control Freak

Domenica Ruta

"DO YOU KNOW WHY THEY SAY THERE IS SO MUCH breast cancer in the United States?" the nurse asks me. A small medical device like an ugly sadistic broach pierces the skin just above my heart. It hooks me to several bags of chemo, including one known colloquially as the "red devil," that have been dripping into my veins for hours. I am a captive audience if ever there was one. And I have breast cancer, so yes, I want to know.

"Because of all the abortions," the nurse says.

"That's not true," I snap, fury on a taut leash. Once upon a time she would have scared me witless, but I know in my body what is true. I always have, though it took time to get here.

Access to safe, affordable legal abortion freed me from the burden of raising a child at a time when I was too young, too alcoholic, and too broke to do it. It allowed me to continue living an adventurous life of interesting temporary jobs while I was figuring out what it meant to be a working artist. It made space for me to leave a relationship with the man I was dating at the time, years afterward, without the lifelong tether of joint custody to complicate things for either of us.

The socioeconomic impact of abortion cannot be overstated, but for me, it engendered a transformation that I think of as sacred. In another universe, another life, abortion would be a secular sacrament, bloody, holy, a threshold that people could walk through on the way to becoming the person they were born to be.

For the first two and a half decades of my life, my body did not belong to me. I grew up with a narcissist mother who gouged away any and all boundaries between herself and me to such an extent that I still find myself, decades later, a mostly self-actualized adult, picking tendrils of her flotsam out of my hair. During this childhood under her reign, I was sexually abused by a trusted adult, a firebomb to the central nervous system, to any sense of bodily safety. "If I feel this I will die," I thought in the wordless lizard stem of my brain. And I lived. I wrote my spelling words three times each, I cleaned my parents' ashtrays and folded the laundry, I watched thousands of hours of television, I grew up. To do that—*live*—I had to elect a hazy mental erasure, though this, like so much else, didn't feel like a choice. My mind, like my body, was something I had no control over; it did what it wanted, remembered what it wanted, blacked out what it wanted.

For years and years it was like this. Things *happened to me*. I *got* my period, a passive reception, inevitable and shameful. I threw away my underwear at those first streaks of blood, as though this could make it go away and never come back. When I realized I was powerless to stop it, I tried to hide it from my mother. I failed, and she humiliated me by telling everyone she could. Hair *just grew* all over my pale skin, not in the downy light brown and neatly contained areas like other girls but black, coarse, persistent, growing back less than a day after I shaved. I *had* sex as a teenager (luckily enough by choice, sadly in a world where such autonomy is considered "lucky"), but *having* is not the same as *doing*, because first, there was a rotating cast of good and awful boyfriends to whom I was always ceding control, then there was that moment when I took off my clothes, when someone touched me, and little earthworms of repressed memory wriggled into the bed, mucking up the sheets, exposing to my partners, to myself, what trash I really was. I never touched myself. The thought didn't even occur to me. How could I? All this stuff hanging off my head, my body, that wasn't really mine to touch. That wasn't really me.

Until my abortion my body existed in three states—hated, terrorized, or numb. What little agency I believed I had I used in pursuit of numbness. Here was a thing I could *do*, an action I could *take*: alcohol, Benzos, opiates. Anything from the family of downers was my chosen family. They didn't make me feel good. That was never the point. Drugs and alcohol gave me something more important than pleasure—relief. Once relieved of all the fear and pain, the nagging questions, the shame, I could do anything. I was free.

Then, at twenty-four years old, having avoided gynecologists for years and trusting foolishly in the precision of my menstrual cycle, I got pregnant. This was the final betrayal. I was enraged. My stupid disgusting body, never following orders. As soon as I saw the positive pregnancy test I went and bought a pack of cigarettes. I had quit smoking two years earlier, and those first drags made my head feel both bludgeoned and detached from my body. I sat smoking on my windowsill, looking at the dumpsters in the alley below, on that horrible edge of needing to vomit but holding it back. "I hate you," I said out loud to my stomach. Not to the blastocyst inside but to everything surrounding it.

Again, I was lucky, and again, it is utter stupidity that we still live in a world where a totally normal, safe, affordable abortion should be considered lucky. But I was particularly lucky, because Boston's central branch of Planned Parenthood was a short walk from my apartment. I passed through the metal detectors, still lightheaded from my first cigarette in years, and got an appointment on the spot. The staff there was professional and kind. After taking another pregnancy test I was assigned a counselor, a woman a little older than me but lifetimes away in term of coolness. She had short bleached blond hair with deliberately dark roots, pierced and tattooed at a time, the early 2000s, when not *everyone* was pierced and tattooed yet. She was beautiful and sexy and looked like she actually ate food when she was hungry, like she did whatever she wanted on her own terms because it felt good.

When I told her I was certain I wanted this abortion, she did the most amazing thing: she believed me. I was so used to doubting and numbing and repressing my own feelings, let alone desires, that her calm acceptance of me at my word was revolutionary. A new way of existing became possible, even if I didn't know what that meant yet.

She presented all my options for terminating a pregnancy with perfect equanimity and in a cool and empathetic way asked me how I was feeling. "Honestly," I said, "I feel bad about not feeling bad about this." Lots of women she worked with felt the same way, she assured me, invoking that magical combination of words where all healing begins: *you are not alone.*

The method I chose was a combination of misoprostol and mifepristone pills, known then as the French abortion. The counselor told me it was 97 percent effective, noninvasive, relatively painless, and that I could do it myself at home. She encouraged me to stock up on ice cream and other treats and rent some movies beforehand, which proved to be the wisest of prescriptions, then sent me home with a follow-up appointment scheduled for a week later. Because of my income at the time, the whole thing cost me around fifty bucks.

I did exactly what she said. I told my boyfriend what was happening and that I wanted to be alone, so he made himself scarce while I watched documentaries and comedies, ate Thai food, and napped. I bled enough to know that the pills had worked but not so much that I was scared something was wrong. I didn't feel like running a marathon but I experienced no pain. All in all it was blissfully ordinary, just a pleasant Saturday alone with myself, alone with my body.

For years I chased what I thought was relief through drugs and alcohol. If there was anything I desired it was that escape. I now know that what I had wanted all along was control, and getting high offered a believable substitute. The equation was deceptively simple. Drink this, wait twenty minutes, feel better. Snort this and seconds later feel something new, something I bought and paid for, something I chose. It worked well until it didn't. At a certain point in my progressive alcoholism, I could no longer manipulate the formula for the desired effect. My body had betrayed me again and then all I wanted was to die.

I've spent the past thirteen years in recovery from addiction. As passive as abstention seems on the surface, sobriety is a conscious daily rejection of both the passivity and the delusion of control I found in drinking. It requires work, lots of it, and a fearless consciousness of myself and my desires inside that work. I have to choose to be sober every day, which is another way of saying I choose to be here, in this life, in this body: the one where I am pregnant with my first child, opting for single motherhood over a more traditional life with a partner who is not right for me; the one where I am pregnant with my second child, conceived on purpose with a partner I loved enough to marry; the one where I am telling the surgeon that I don't want a lumpectomy, I want to remove both my breasts, because they are mine and I get to decide what happens to me; the one where I am fighting for my life in a little cubicle of the cancer center, hooked up to all those bags of chemo, immobile but no longer powerless, telling the nurse with the sureness of everything in my body that no, abortion does not cause cancer.

Love can be just as excruciating as fear in the body of a trauma survivor and reality in all its vagaries is fucking bleak even in the best of times. Despite all my growth, all my tools, what I desire now more than anything is that feeling of control I first discovered in my abortion. I want the power I felt then, the knowledge that my body would do exactly what I wanted it to do. I would happily sign away all my money, forgo every word I will ever write, give up all sex and bliss for the rest of my life to know that I had the same control over my children's bodies in the way I had of that first pregnancy. I want the power to ensure that they will never get sicker than I have the ability to cure with the generic syrups I have in my bathroom cabinet, that their bodies will never be broken by a careless driver, or a falling air conditioner on a New York City sidewalk, or the craven gunshot of a racist cop. Give me a 100 percent guarantee that no human being will ever touch their bodies the way my childhood abuser touched mine, that they will only have sex when they want to, and that it will never feel shameful and frightening to them in the same greasy, sinister way it can sometimes still feel for me. I want them both to explore our planet, or what's left of it by the time they are adults, and feel nothing but a combination of curiosity and compassion for the life that surrounds them, instead of the dogged anxiety that follows me to this day, whispering mostly, sometimes screeching, "You will never be safe, not in that body of yours."

I want that, forever—the power of choice not as microcosm or metaphor in a Planned Parenthood office but a discrete and tangible act, a bloody rite, a routine procedure I can undergo that will allow me to keep my family whole and happy, sane and productive, adventurous and safe, for the eight or so decades I feel is our due. I want control, both inside and surrounding us, a magical placenta where we have not only the right but the power to choose what happens to us.

The work of smashing my delusions never ends. Life makes sure of that.

The week my second child was born, the death toll for the Coronavirus was at its peak in New York City, where we live. I walked into the hospital with a plan for how this baby would be born—as naturally as possible, at his own pace and mine—but the hospital staff had other ideas. A nurse whose face I never saw because of our masks told me that yes, my birth plan was wonderful, realistic even, but not today, not with a pandemic and morgue truck parked outside. They were going to force me to have this baby as quickly as possible, which meant administering Pitocin, which meant getting an epidural, all the things I was hoping to avoid.

If abortion taught me for the first time that I had control over my own body, childbirth taught me how to let go of that control, and cancer was a lesson that neither of those things, control or surrender, are mutually exclusive. So I did what the nurses said. I agreed to their plan. My baby was born, an act that was both totally mine, of my body alone, and in collaboration with forces outside me. Something I did, something that happened to me, happened to us.

On Not Getting What I Wanted

Elisa Albert

WHAT I WANTED WAS A BABY. IT WAS NOT A LOGICAL or defensible want. I already *had* a baby; a wonderful son I hesitate even to mention for fear of exciting the evil eye. But I wanted another one. Another baby. All the mom-people I knew kept having other babies, more and more babies. Everyone knows you have to have *at least* two, otherwise it's not a *real* family, and why even bother with the whole endeavor in the first place?

We were lust-crazed morons when we'd had our first baby, our wonderful son, but we'd learned so much, risen to the occasion, grown up, evolved, and now we wanted another baby, a celebration baby, to come from our hard-won stability and contentment.

By "we" wanted, I mean *I* wanted. *He* wanted another baby, too, and claimed he was very much looking forward to the existence of the other baby. But the thing is, he never wept inconsolably when it didn't happen. The inconsolable weeping was all mine. It's really surprising how many tears a person can weep.

I didn't tell a lot of people about my wanting because (a) I did *not* want to be defined by it, and (b) it hurt so, so bad. Of those I did tell, a few were kind and circumspect, but most were somewhere on the insensitive to fucking-asshole spectrum. So it goes. Do you know that there are people in the world who, given any opportunity, are ravenously eager to pity others in attempting to make themselves feel superior? They're called sadists, and they're everywhere!

It crushed me when people said crappy things, and boy did people say crappy things. *Well I'm just so glad* mine *have each other. Don't you think it's cruel to just have one? Only children are weirdos! I know how you feel because I only had three boys and what I* really *wanted was a girl.* It was pretty astonishing how much cruel, stupid shit people said to me. A reflexologist said I didn't want it bad enough. A nutritionist said I wanted it too much. A foul douche cousin said, "I would never trust an only child." One time, I overheard a kid from down the street in conversation with my son: "What's it like being an only child? Seems like it would be super lonely." I had to clutch the kitchen countertop, close my eyes, and take a very deep breath to stop myself from popping in to say *Hey kid, what's it like having an alcoholic for a mom? Seems like it would be super toxic!*

Here are the kinds of people who have only one child: people disallowed more under fascist governance, coldhearted selfish career-obsessed bitches, people who loathed the experience of having the one, people with biological incapacity, and mothers of such advanced age that having even one was a dystopian miracle.

You *have* to have *at least* two. Why did I constantly look at other families with multiple children—even when said families were wildly dysfunctional and/or broken and/or blatantly miserable—and think: Well, at least they're a *real* family. Needless to say, I had to mute everyone I know who uses social media exclusively as a means of showcasing offspring. (No big loss there, though, and honestly, people: cut that obnoxious shortsighted exploitative shit *out*.)

Let us pause to remind ourselves, in spite of our sitcom brainwashing and general cultural programming and absurd devotion to some bygone bullshit Rockwellian lie, that *there is no such thing as a formula for a happy family.* Some of every stripe in every configuration manage to fuck it up, and some of every stripe in every configuration manage to rock it. Maybe family happiness exists on a spectrum, like gender. Suck it, Tolstoy.

Anyway, anyway: I wanted a(nother) baby. And when the (other) baby declined to appear, I felt cursed and punished and blighted and tragic and enraged and impotent. I screamed into the void. I told God to eat shit and die. And I found out some interesting things about myself. Such as: I am in conversation with God!

Also: I did not want that other baby bad enough to sign my ass up for industrial fertility treatment. I can almost, but not quite, imagine wanting it that bad. I one hundred percent did not want it that bad. This certainty was like a towering stone wall in my heart. I often rested my forehead against that wall. Its coolness and solidity provided comfort and reassurance. That wall had always existed, long, long before I did. It was a primordial wall. It was covered in moss. It was an ancient, quiet, verdant, merciful, restful place. I spent a whole lot of time there.

Like I said, I already *had* a baby. A beyond-wonderful baby. And still, I wanted *another*. How greedy is that? To "want" life itself. The more I thought about it—and hahahahaha, *man*, did I think about it—the more indefensible it seemed.

My job, then, was to learn to surrender want. I threw myself at this monumental task. I wanted to be worthy of it. What a badass undertaking. When you surrender want, you join the ranks of great priestesses and seers. When you surrender want, you became a guru and a beacon. (But, like, ego-less.) I wanted to be *totally fucking at peace with exactly what is*. I wanted not to despise God whenever some odious jerk-off announced the birth of their second/third/fourth/fifth child. I wanted not to care when sadists parroted nonsense to me about "only" children. I wanted not to feel mortally wounded whenever some intimate stranger went on some dumb caption bender about how it's Harlowe's fifth birthday today and goodness gracious we don't *deserve* her but *God sent* her to us and we're just so grateful that she *chose* to *complete* our family, or whatever thoughtless nonsense noise.

I wanted not to want. I wanted it so, so bad.

I thought maybe the *mikvah* (Jewish ritual bath, look it up,

I'm not your ethnic shortcut) might help me in my progress toward relinquishment of want. Or . . . maybe . . . the mikvah
would be the magical key to open the door to the desired pregnancy! *Ugh*, so annoying, that reflexive, automatic want! Fuck
off! I wanted to stamp it out, extinguish it. It caused me nothing but pain. Enough! No more! I was a prisoner of want, and
I wanted to be free. Do you see my quandary? Wanting was
everywhere.

I have a friend who bore thirteen children. I can't even
fathom loving thirteen people that much. How full can a heart
get? Most everyone I know recoils in horror at the thought of
thirteen children, but I stand in awe. Not just because she *bore*
thirteen children (although, uh, superhero much?) but because
she *raised* them all, with strength and decency and humility
and love and self-sacrifice, which is something like governing a
small country and something like running a school and something like being a top-notch nurse/administrator/teacher/CEO/
cook/housekeeper. This woman has her shit *together*.

My friend with the thirteen children agreed to tutor me
regarding mikvah. She gave me books: *Taharat HaMishpacha*,
The Waters of Eden. I already knew the gist; I'd immersed once
before, in advance of a reckless starter marriage at twenty-three,
but the real-real turned out to be a fair bit more complex and
interesting than I'd previously understood. I read up and went
over to her house on Tuesday evenings to study some more. We
sat side by side at her table and read aloud together. She was a
good teacher, a gentle woman. There was nothing in it for her.

The laws of family purity get a bum rap for seeming to
imply that menstruation is dirty, and that women need to be
cleansed/purified because we ourselves are metaphysically dirty/
bad. Cue the automatic assumption that religion is inherently
misogynistic and observant women must be an oppressed bunch
of self-hating victim/slaves. I believe this to be a pile-up of ety-
mological misunderstandings, but what can I tell you: look at
the texts and the texts about the texts and make up your own

mind, or don't. No skin off my nose, as the old saying goes. (I
mean, a personal no thank you to the part about sending one's
used panties to a Rabbi for inspection if unsure about the precise
color/nature of vaginal discharge, but to each their own.)

My studies left me dazzled and delighted. To my mind,
mikvah is as radically feminist a ritual as they come, and by
"radically feminist" I mean: enormously insightful with regard
to personal freedom, the rhythm and care and lifespan of a soul
inside a body with an unmediated menstrual cycle, hard truths
about fertility, life, death, and power dynamics within long-
term monogamous intimacy.

Sex with the same person for years and years and years gets
boring, no matter how much you may adore and respect and
like that person. Without mystery and newness and romantic
intrigue and the psychedelic dance of courtship, how can you
possibly stay jazzed? *Taharat HaMishpacha* has some answers:
You quite literally do not touch your spouse for two weeks out of
every menstrual cycle. You separate, and then you reunite. Said
reunions are glorious. You cherish your weeks "on" and you savor your weeks "off." You take clearly demarcated, finite breaks
from being sexually desired and/or desirous. A human being
cannot have or be had on every whim.

The mikvah is often described as the marking of transition.
A movement from one place—one identity, one role, one state
of being—to another. Marital sex, which for me had become
routine, an exercise in futility, a hotbed of grief and anxiety and
failure, could be thusly honored and reframed. *Yes*, mikvah said:
sex *can* be boring and rote and pointless, and yes, it *would* be
easy and fun to find someone new to do it with, but instead *you*
are going to become new, which in turn will make your spouse
feel new, which will ideally allow you to anticipate and enjoy
relations for a long time to come.

Bleeding, which had become the embodiment of heartbreak
and injustice, could likewise be thusly honored and reframed.
Yes, mikvah said: bleeding *can* be a recurring funereal curse.

Now come and enact this ritual that belongs to you and belonged to your ancestors (oh ho, you thought we were going to get out of here without acknowledging the *ancestors*?), and allow it to wash away heartbreak and injustice, so that you may emerge fresh and intact and whole and fine, just as you are. You are *not* cursed or broken or blighted; you are alive in your very own body, which is, itself, an Eden, holy and sacred and worthy and fine, just as it is.

So, for the first time in almost two decades, I visited the mikvah. A little unmarked building in the far corner of the parking lot at my local JCC. How many times had I seen it without registering it, without even wondering what it was. A lovely *shomeret* was there to observe and assist. I said the *brachot* and completely immersed, three times, in the collected rainwater.

I won't bore you with tales of mystical rebirth; it's feckin' private. Suffice it to say, everything about it felt good and right. Every bell was rung.

The wanting didn't magically go away, but it did fade some. Wanting's a tricky bitch; it waxes and wanes. Wanting is like an odor; it can find its way through the tiniest cracks. Wanting is like a weed; it self-sows. I am a person of some privilege who came of age in late-stage capitalism, so I am not well conditioned to, like, chillax with not getting what I want. (Dial up cinematic Veruca Salt from the original *Charlie and the Chocolate Factory*: "I want a party with roomfuls of laughter, ten thousand *tons* of ice cream . . . and if I don't get the things I am after, I'm . . . going . . . to . . . *scream!*")

I kept thinking I'd return to the mikvah, dip on the regular, make a proper habit/practice of it. But you know how it is . . . there's soccer practice or the dog hasn't been walked or you're going on a trip or there's an event you have to attend or—whoops—pandemic time. Or you're just too beat from trying to meet a deadline or advance yourself in some way or keep abreast with everyone and their mother on whatever platform holds you in thrall.

Still, my awareness continues to shift. I keep distance from my spouse during *niddah*, the days during and immediately after menstruation, and I notice that I tend to instinctively dress differently during that time too. Less likely to put the precise contours of my body on public display. Less likely to advertise what nice tits and ass I have. During that time I do not exist for the pleasure or approval or appraisal of anyone else. It's my time to be an independent creative entity, a fundamentally human animal more than a socially constructed and perceived "female" object. (I'm happy to show off my lovely tits and ass the rest of the time, though, rest assured! I'm not like an *anarchist* or anything.)

I'll probably always have a very tender spot where resides the lack of what I wanted, and that's okay. I might even go so far as to say it's *good*. Does the world really need more checked boxes, more acquisition, more staged Christmas cards, more general smugness? Have we not seen the devastation wrought by certain classes of people in certain sorts of societies *getting everything they want*?

Not getting what we want can leave us softer, bruised, gentler, quieter, and maybe a little more watchful and humble than perhaps we'd otherwise manage to be. Maybe not getting what we want can make us more grateful for what we *do* have. Isn't that just so nice and tidy? Well, no: it's also hard, messy, awful, and frustrating. It really is quite insanely hard. I still admittedly have a lot of trouble with certain Instagram narrators.

I sigh the lack of many a thing I sought, quoth a Shakespeare sonnet I scrawled on the inside cover of my diary as a lovelorn teen. Back then I was pouting over unrequited love, as yet unschooled in deeper realms of thwarted desire.

I. Wanted. Another. Baby. For a long time it was impossible to even speak the words out loud: I was too desperately vulnerable: you could snap my spine in half like a twig. Even now, I can type it, but I probably still couldn't say the words out loud. How unfair it seemed, how *wrong* it felt that I didn't get that other baby. Only *losers* don't get what they want. And I really did not want to be a loser. But I also did not want to be lost in a vortex of thwarted desire forever, so. You find ways to move the fuck on, and you thank god you aren't one of those programmed shmucks who think there's some prefab equation for a full or happy life.

By the way! The essential nature of want is that it is infinite and can't ever be fulfilled. Visit an AA meeting sometime and see for yourself.

I know people with two children who yearn for three. I know people with three children who yearn for four. I even know someone with four children who yearns for five. I wonder if my friend, my kind teacher, the mother of thirteen, ever indulges in wistful imaginings of what number fourteen might have looked like, or smelled like, or how it might have felt to press her lips against that nonexistent baby's sweet, sweet brow.

From Woe to Wonder

Aracelis Girmay

GWENDOLYN BROOKS, IN A 1977 INTERVIEW, DESCRIBES an ongoing argument with her husband about the fate of a running Black child:

> Once we were walking down a road and we saw a little Ghanaian boy. He was running and happy in the happy sunshine. My husband made a comment springing from an argument we had had the night before that lasted until four in the morning. He said, 'Now look, see that little boy. That is a perfect picture of happy youth. So if you were writing a poem about him, why couldn't you just let it go at that? Write a poem about running boy—happy, happy-running boy?' [. . .]
>
> So I said if you wrote exhaustively about running boy and you noticed that the boy was black, you would have to go further than a celebration of blissful youth. You just might consider that when a black boy runs, maybe not in Ghana, but perhaps on the Chicago South Side, you'd have to remember a certain friend of my daughter's in high school—beautiful boy, so smart, one of the honor students, and just an all-around fine fellow. He was running down an alley with a friend of his, just running and a policeman said "Halt!" And

before he could slow up his steps, he just shot him. Now that happens all the time in Chicago. There was all that promise in a little crumpled heap. Dead forever.

For every sorrow I write, also I press my forehead to the ground. Also I wash the feet of our beloveds, if only in my mind, in the waters of the petals of the flowers.

I cross my arms and bow to you.

I cross my arms in armor wishing you protection.

On August 23, 2014, I joined thousands to march for the life of Eric Garner and against the police who murdered him one month before. The blastocyst that would become my son was multiplying inside my darkest me unbeknownst to me.

Time moved through us. It is now 2020. Ramsey Orta, who filmed Garner's death and bravely shared that record, is imprisoned on trumped-up charges and beaten by guards. Eric Garner's eldest child, the activist Erica Garner, has passed at the age of twenty-seven from an enlarged heart after giving birth just three months before.

It is summer, then all the leaves are falling. My kids are two and four, then they are nearly three and nearly five. My son's birthday, now I know, falls between the birthdays of young Ahmaud Arbery and the poet Kamau Brathwaite. I hear Gwendolyn Brooks: "You just might consider that when a black boy runs . . ." My partner and I teeter in that argument between Brooks and her husband, our own sight touched by both things: the happy in the happy sunshine and the policeman saying halt. We dance in the circle following both these men—Ahmaud Arbery, ever-becoming, and Kamau Brathwaite, the elder, who wrote in *Elegguas*:

How all this wd have been one kind of world.
   perhaps—no—certainly—
kindlier—you wd have been bourne happy into yr
   entitlement of silver hairs
and there wd have been no threat

My partner and I do not yet speak to our children about racism and such threats here looming. We speak of justice, diversity, fairness. The kids love the story of *Malcolm Little: The Boy Who Grew Up to Become Malcolm X*. They read a little at first, then a little more. We give them the large brushstrokes of the burning house, but we talk for long about Malcolm's brilliant family, their commitments and work, the ladybugs in the garden. In *Mae Among the Stars*, when the teacher dismisses Mae's dream to become an astronaut, our son is shocked. "Why would a teacher say that to a child?" He asks this very question, out of what seems to us the blue, over several weeks, then months. We do not mention that the teacher is white. We do not mention that the people who burn Malcolm Little's house are white.

My partner and I talk to other Black parents, including our own. We get advice, ask questions, work, and think about how to nourish and fortify our children. It does not occur to us to talk to our kids about whiteness just yet, but increasingly I think we must. For example, I am startled, in February, by my son's white schoolmate who runs into the hall to announce to his parent that Martin Luther King Jr. was killed because of the color of his skin. These months later I am again startled by the very young white children who speak openly and, it seems, without fear about George Floyd's murder.

We are on a Zoom call with my child's class. One of his white classmates has gone to a march with her family, in the middle of a pandemic, to march for Black Lives. The power of this is not lost on me. I am moved by their family's investment and risk, a risk I do not take. I study the child's face. The baby still in her voice, her cheeks, the way she holds her mouth. She says, "George Floyd was killed because . . ." And I click the sound off. My youngest says, "I can't hear, Mommy." Just a second, I tell them both, just a second.

The rest of that sentence might go a hundred different ways, might say something about the brutality, profit, and racialized terror on which the police state is founded, but this is not the sentence I expect. The sentence I expect is a variation on a theme: George Floyd was killed because of the color of his skin. People are mistreated because of the color of their skin. George Floyd was killed because his skin was brown.

Our skin is brown.

We stand in the light of the sentence but the perpetrator is under cover, cloaked. But by what, and in whose service?

It occurs to me in an instant that we have insufficiently prepared our child for the threat inside this fog.

I imagine a seesaw. My children are on one side and this white child, my son's same age, same height and weight, is on the other side. She is one child, my children are two. And yet they are the ones hovering in the air, ungrounded. He was killed because his skin was brown. So goes the sentence that holds my children, dangling and subject, and that grants the white child her ground, her safety, her natural habitat, and close-to-the-earthness. The consequences of white supremacy are named only in terms of my child's suffering or potential suffering, named only in terms of the suffering of our beloveds, but not in terms of the causes, the perpetrators, the inheritors, not in terms of the consequences on the minds of the white children who have already been failed, have already been taught wrongly to stand outside of the equation with their families.

Our son already knows the basic principles of physics on which a seesaw is designed. He knows that one and one is two. He knows: from the chicken, the egg; from the apple tree, the apple; and so on. So why should we teach him such a distorted logic that goes out of its way not to name the other subject in the sentence? If we do, the sentence itself becomes a kind of captivity. If we do, he will have no chance of knowing what it is he's trying to get free from, and white children, too, will think the problem is out there, someone else's, even his, and not the water they drink, the cleanish air they breathe.

Gwendolyn Brooks writes, in this excerpt from the persona poem "The Near-Johannesburg Boy," written during apartheid:

> My way is from woe to wonder.
> A Black boy near Johannesburg, hot
> in the Hot Time.
>
> Those people
> do not like Black among the colors.
> They do not like our
> calling our country ours.
> They say our country is not ours.
>
> Those people.
> Visiting the world as I visit the world.
> Those people.
> Their bleach is puckered and cruel.

She begins to pull whiteness into the frame. And there is something here for us I think.

When a white person with a white child points to my child, even lovingly, as an example of a Black life who matters, I would also like that person to teach their white child about white life and history, and about how they are going to have to work really hard to make sure that they are not taking up more air, more space, more sidewalk because they have been taught wrongly that the world is more theirs. I would like to give my five-year-old words so that when he is told "George Floyd was killed because his skin was brown," he is able to say something like, "Well, actually, there is an idea called whiteness. Some people think that they are better and deserve more of everything because they are white and their ancestors are from Europe. Their ancestors hurt people and hurt the land to get the power that they gave to their children and that their children keep keeping, and keep using to hurt, even today. Isn't that terrible?"

I want him to be able to say something like, "Those people. Visiting the world as I visit the world."

This spring, we are, in our apartment, two kids and two parents, always together. By the time the last minutes of Ahmaud Arbery's life are all over the internet, and we have begun to mourn the news of police officers killing Breonna Taylor inside her bedroom, and the news of the police murdering George Floyd, and the people, including children small as my children, have begun marching in the streets, my son and his sister are in their parent's skin again, consuming only what we want them to consume. For a few months nobody, not even the puppets on *Sesame Street*, say in front of our children, "He was killed or she was killed or they were treated unfairly because of how they look or act or who they are." There is a little more time to work on our children's armor before they go again out into the further world, which, yes, we also love and want them to be in. We want them in the world with our family. We want them running in the sunlight with their laughing friends.

Ahmaud Arbery. Breonna Taylor. George Floyd. I move fast through the house, then slow, trying to listen for my mothers. The kids and I spend an afternoon boiling peony petals in water, then they take turns mashing them in the pilón. We wash the paper in the pigment and the color goes from a nearly invisible violet to a purple so strong it is like medicine. It gets darker and darker through the night, even in our sleep. They know this now. And they know how to pull the smoke over their heads in blessing. But more protection, more. And not just protection, also truth, also dreaming. Violet inside the petal. Purple inside the violet. Truth inside the purple. Dreaming inside the truth. Freedom inside the dreaming.

Time repeats through us. Time moves. My son was born, then he was two, and then my daughter was born. This spring they are almost three and five. In April I begin to say, as I do each year, "Right about now we were getting ready for you to be born. My stomach was enormous. My heart was pumping so much blood. The buds were bursting from the trees. The grass was high and green." I do not mention Eric Garner. I do not mention Mike Brown or Tamir Rice. "Five years ago now we were getting ready." I do not mention Walter Scott. "Papa put the stroller together, we went on walks, we were followed by a squirrel. We waited for you to be born." He likes to hear this story and asks questions about the squirrel, the dark, the ice cream, the blood. He asks for all kinds of details from his gestation.

This year we go to the marsh. It is cold and so windy that almost no one else is out there, so we take off our masks and turn our backs to the wind. What was here before us? Who was here? What is here still though we maybe cannot see it? We are teaching the children to ask. This is Lenni Lenape land. There was a wilderness once. When the Dutch arrived in the seventeenth century, they began their colonial project by waging war with the land and its people. The tide is high, and we do not see the crabs or clams or snails, but we know that they are there.

Days later, it is warm again. The kids move up and down the marsh quietly seeing what they can see. The scurrying of the crabs. Their father says, "Gentle, gentle, you don't want to frighten them."

When I was eleven, I watched a crab scurry upright and frantic across the cobblestones in a small plaza in Colima where my aunt lived. I remember still its panic, how I felt seized by it somehow. With it I shared a skin. I swear, I thought something like, "You are my ancestor. I am you. Until I learned to also become the one who hunted, no longer feeling for your loss of life. At first I said, no, no, and was so sad, crying and snotting into my hands. My parent told me, Shh, eat, because we were hungry, and so then eventually I did. I began to eat your meat not just out of hunger but out of greed, without thanks, without prayer, without guilt, as something to do."

My way is from woe to wonder.
A Black boy near Johannesburg, hot
in the Hot Time.

Those people
do not like Black among the colors.
They do not like our
calling our country ours.
They say our country is not ours.
Those people.
Visiting the world as I visit the world.
Those people.
Their bleach is puckered and cruel.

I try to follow the boy from woe to wonder, but these years move often from wonder to woe. It is the thing that animates my quiet. It blazes like lightning through all my branches. Wonder to woe. LaQuan McDonald, age seventeen. Kwame Jones, age seventeen. Trayvon Martin, age seventeen. Ramarley Graham, age seventeen. Tamir Rice, age twelve. Aiyana Mo'Nay Stanley Jones, age seven. Given names by their families. Names to be called from another room. Names to be taught to write and read. Names to, maybe, be shouted in a circle while their beloveds clap and clap for them to dance.

Woe to wonder. Needing to survive and to survive—my country—for my children: Get up. Put the water in the pot and boil the egg. Wash the faces. Empty the trash. "Where are your shoes?" I say. "Let's count your fingers. Mommy loves you," I say, and across our lines I hear the other mothers coming through.

My mother, for example, used to tell us, "Death and life is in the power of the tongue."

Death and life, our mother said, about any number of things and in any number of ways. Part of what I understood was that language could help us to live and could help us to die. That rebuking Satan and anointing our heads and house with oil actually *meant* something. Whether Satan lasted was not the point, though, yes, we wanted Satan gone. The point was she was teaching us to fight.

This spring our son begins to read. He works on words, their smallest sounds, sometimes guessing, sometimes repeating what he hears us say about English: You know *laugh* is a funny word. It looks like it would sound one way but it really sounds another way. *Without* has two words inside it. He is tickled by what surprises. How the silence of some *e*s is not so silent because they change the sound of the vowel before. *Hose* is one letter away from *nose*. I begin to imagine that to learn to read English is to begin to know something also about this country. Something hidden, something shown. Something sinister, something joyful. Some things are not what they seem. Other things are what they seem. In the letters I find the shapes my brother's body makes uprocking inside the circle. I trace the shapes my sister's body makes as she plants trees. And a million configurations of this letter in front of that one, marching in the streets this spring, this day. My son teaches his sister. *W* looks like water. This letter looks like that one. Maybe they are a family, maybe not.

With the pigment my son makes a birthday card to mail to his beloved friend. He writes *treehouse* very neatly in nine brown letters on the bottom of the paper, I don't know why. Maybe because it is the most wonderful idea he can think of to offer. He asks me, "Have you ever seen a treehouse!?" I am tickled beside his joy that such a thing exists. I take note with my own paper and pencil. A house inside a tree. Oops, it looks like I wrote *free*.

I am late in my thirties when I hear for the first time, from my friend Ross, that one of the strategies of *petit marronage* for enslaved people was to go into the tops and trunks of trees, finding and keeping a refuge there.

Whenever it is that my partner and I begin to teach our children about the brutality, by design, of this moment and this country, the continuum of catastrophe we are alive and loving and breathing in, I know now that a vital part of what we teach them must have to do with the beauty and power of the imaginative strategies of Black people everywhere. Maroons planting cassava and sweet potato, easily hidden, growing secret in the ground. My best friend's godsister, Brandy, who, when we were small, knew how to disappear into thin air by opening a book. *Tegadelti* freedom fighters on the front lines in Eritrea, making pigment out of flower petals, to paint. Palestinians who, when Israeli forces criminalized the carrying of the Palestinian flag in 1967, raised the watermelons up as their flags. Red, black, white, green. The mind that attempts, and attempts again, to find a way out of no way.

It occurs to me that what I right now want for my children is to equip them with fight and armor and space for dreaming in the long, constant work of our trying to get free. I am trying to think like a poet, like a maroon—to tell our children that there were people who, even while under the most unimaginable duress, had the mind to find and *keep* refuge in the trees. That they are all around us still. Some of them are named Gwendolyn. Some of them are named Kamau.

I am trying to learn with and for the sake of my children. To help them move, even in their woe, toward wonder. To resist the seal of a sentence so complete, and to find, in the syntax, openings through—so onto a ground of their own dreamings, again and again, they alight.

Leaving the Palace

Ann Tashi Slater

TWO AND A HALF CENTURIES AGO, PRINCE SIDDHARTHA Gautama slipped out of his father's palace in the north Indian capital of Kapilavastu. Twenty-nine years old and dissatisfied with his pleasure-seeking existence, he wanted to find the deeper meaning of life. He traveled the roads of India, living as an ascetic and studying with renowned spiritual teachers. After six years, he experienced an awakening and became the Buddha while meditating under a bodhi tree. His insights included the recognition that all life is suffering, and suffering is caused by desire.

When I learned about Gautama's journey and his realization that desire creates misery, I felt confused. Hadn't desire driven him from the palace, leading him not to sorrow but to enlightenment?

In any case, I didn't need the Buddha to tell me desire caused suffering. There was so much I desired—I'd lived in a state of desire for as long as I could remember—and this just seemed to have made me unhappy. When I was a girl, I met with a Greek chorus of disapproval, at home and out in the world. I wanted to know a lot of things and was always asking why. "If you don't stop asking so many questions," my mother said, "no one will like you." I wanted to be kinder, and I worried whenever I thought I had hurt someone's feelings. "Don't be grandiose," my father said, cautioning me against overblown belief in my power. I wanted my own clothes instead of my sister's hand-me-downs;

I wanted second helpings. *You're a greedy girl.* I wanted my parents to reconcile after their divorce. *You think it's all about you.* I wanted to be taller, to have blue eyes and blond hair—instead of my Tibetan-American brown eyes and brown hair—to blend in better in white American suburbia. *You're never satisfied.* I wanted to be heard and wanted my opinion to matter, so I didn't hesitate to speak up and out. *Who do you think you are?*

In school, I wanted to excel and went all out to win the running race, the spelling bee, the poster contest. I spent long hours crafting shoebox dioramas to illustrate my book reports, laboring over the paradisaical miniature worlds: cotton-ball clouds, paper moons and tin foil stars, Lilliputian clay chairs and beds, embroidered fabric people. Classmates called me "Little Miss Perfect" and "Miss Goody Goody" (no boys were known as "Little Mr. Perfect" or "Mr. Goody Goody"). I wasn't one of the girls considered "foxy" or invited to play Kick the Can or go steady by a cute guy who gave me his St. Christopher necklace. In high school, boys started noticing me in a more enjoyable way and I began to feel sexual desire. "Don't flaunt yourself!" my mother said if she caught me exchanging heated glances with a boy.

I felt sullied by my desires and struggled to hide them, loathing the differences between how society characterized boys' and girls' desire-driven behavior. Boys were determined leaders, studly go-getters; girls were stubborn and bossy, slutty and selfish.

On a spring evening in London almost forty years later, in 2020, I saw "Nora: A Doll's House," Scottish playwright Stef Smith's stunning adaptation of Ibsen's nineteenth-century play. Three women, wives and mothers—in 1918 (women's suffrage in the U.K.), 1968 (legal abortion and the pill), and 2018 (#MeToo)—are choking on their alienation and rage, their desire for selfhood. Devoting herself to pleasing her husband, to meeting his and society's expectation that she fulfill her roles as wife and mother for the larger good of the institution of marriage, each woman comes to see she's been living like a doll in a doll's house; she has cast aside her self. As they undergo this awakening, they tell their husbands again and again, "My heart beats for me." At one point the women chant this in unison, over and over, over and over, their fury and passion mounting and reverberating in the dark theater. You can hear their hearts beating as their chant swells like the voices of so many women over time: *my heart beats for me, my heart beats for me*. Not for my husband, my children, my mother, my father. My heart beats to keep *me* alive.

Walking back to the hotel that night, I thought about the desire that's always roared in my heart. I'd discovered there are different kinds of desire when I began learning about Buddhism after college. I came to see that what the Buddha meant is *craving* causes suffering. Craving is represented by the *preta* hungry ghosts that populate one of the Buddhist realms of existence, wretched beings with stomachs as big as the Grand Canyon and throats as thin as a piece of hair (*never enough drinks or eats for them*, my Tibetan grandmother liked to say). *Preta* desire— *tanhā*, or thirst—is a compulsive striving for objects, qualities, and traits we think we need in order to feel happy (like being taller or whiter). We're hamsters racing around and around in our wheels, trapped in an endless cycle of hungry ghost longing that spirits us away from our authentic selves.

The drive toward selfhood, on the other hand, is a healthy, mindful desire that leads us within. This isn't a search for a fixed, coherent self but instead an embracing of who we are (rather than who others want us to be). If, as a girl, I'd understood the difference between *preta* craving and the desire for selfhood I would have felt better (I was fighting a battle for survival that had to be fought) but, in the end, more miserable (the battle seemed unwinnable). Like many—most?—girls, I was taught that the quest for individual authenticity is selfish. I was taught to please, to seek approval no matter what the cost. I learned to pretend I didn't want another helping of dessert, didn't know the answer to the teacher's question, didn't notice boys, didn't have an opinion. Ignoring my inner voice—or, better yet, killing it off—would make others happy, which would make *me* happy!

If we stifle our desire for selfhood, the urge may, in time, disappear. Then we, too, may vanish, spiraling into the schism between who we are and the self we present to the world. Or we may be consumed by the tension between the force of our desire for selfhood and the force of our exertion to hide it. Growing up, I was constantly exhausted. As a girl and a young woman, I felt I was performing a role on stage, waiting and praying for the curtain to come down. For years, I dreamed that I was trapped in a basement where the pipes were leaking and bursting, that I was trying to squeeze through a trapdoor into an attic; I dreamed I was lifting off and flying free over towns and forests.

In "A Doll's House," Nora's husband attacks when he realizes she is determined to leave: "How unreasonable and how ungrateful you are, Nora! . . . To desert your home, your husband and your children! And you don't consider what people will say!"

To his horror, Nora replies, "I cannot consider that at all. I only know that it is necessary for me . . . I believe that before all else I am a reasonable human being, just as you are—or, at all events, that I must try and become one."

Ibsen said that when writing "A Doll's House," he hadn't "consciously worked for the women's rights movement" but rather, for "the description of humanity." His view speaks to the larger issue at hand: the longing for authentic selfhood as a yearning for full humanity. Nora doesn't say, "I am a reasonable woman," but "I am a reasonable human being." Her desire to leave the doll's house is like Gautama's wish to go beyond the palace walls, to break free from the life he's living and seek the potential of human existence. For me, "leaving the palace" was a going-forth—from the U.S. to Japan, my adopted country—where I left the houses of family and society I'd grown up in. Seductive as staying in the palace can be, because of the strength of habit or the fear that others will be angry with us, I realized somewhere along the way that staying wouldn't reduce suffering, only deepen it.

My journey to Japan turned out to be a wandering pilgrimage that was similar, I like to think, to the Buddha's journey. In college, I'd majored in comparative literature (French and Latin American) and planned to make my home in Paris as a writer. When I graduated, I first went to Darjeeling, my mother's hometown, to stay with my grandmother for a while and learn more about my Tibetan side. The following year I left for France, stopping off in Japan to teach English for a few months so I'd have money to launch my new life. I've now lived in Tokyo for over three decades.

As a girl, I dreamed of a world where I could feel free— Japan turned out to be that world. I got a job as soon as I arrived and, for about three hundred dollars a month, rented a converted one-room teahouse in the northwest part of the city with no hot water, no bath, a straw tatami floor, shoji-screened windows, and a sliding wooden door that opened onto a tiny garden. Alone in my monkish little house, the wide blue Pacific between me and the Greek chorus, I could finally rest. The feeling that I'd found sanctuary was intensified by the orderliness and safety of the surrounding environment. My neighborhood had a mom-and-pop grocery store, flower shop, bakery, rice merchant, and public bathhouse; in the morning, salarymen headed to work, housewives hung out the laundry, children set off to school in crisp uniforms. At night, I could ride the last train home by myself and no one even glanced at me. Coming from America, where bad things happened to women on their own, and from India, where, as in the U.S., women were preyed upon, I was in paradise. I did whatever I wanted whenever I pleased, exploring shrines and gardens, gyoza joints and fish markets; lingering in jazz bars and cafes. For the first time, I experienced what it was like to be at home in myself and the world. I felt as I thought Flaubert must have felt in Egypt, the country where, he said, he could dream and feel well.

———

Entwined with the desire for selfhood is the Buddhist principle of renunciation. At first, this seemed paradoxical: isn't desire about attaining and renunciation about relinquishing? But if, like Gautama, we are to succeed in realizing our full humanity, we have to let go of what lies between us and our authentic selves.

In the final moments of "A Doll's House," Nora tells her husband she can no longer be his "little skylark." The performance ends with the sound of a door slamming as she leaves. For me, the curtain started to come down when I arrived in Japan. Around the time I began living in Tokyo, a friend told me that a plant I'd given her years earlier, which hadn't died but hadn't thrived, had at last bloomed. In a similar way, I felt, my life was now unfurling. I'd expected to live alone forever—no man could love me—but in Tokyo, I met someone and we got married; I became a wife and mother, a writer and professor.

Who do you think you are? When I was a young girl, the meaning of the refrain I heard so often morphed into a different kind of question, one I spent many hours pondering. I knew I was someone but didn't know how to find her. I sensed her presence sometimes, like on winter days when I skated at the town pond with my friend Kathleen. We were faster than all the other skaters, driven by the unchecked joy of sprinting across the ice, the electrifying power of being in and of the world, nothing holding us back. There were kids who fell through into the dark water, broke arms and legs, but we never did. All these years later, I can still feel the cold air and the sun on my face, smell the damp earth and woodsmoke, hear our shouts and laughter, see the bare trees silhouetted against the clouds sailing past.

Approximations

Nicole Hardy

"I'M HAVING AN INTENSE PLATONIC ROMANCE WITH the sound of my upstairs neighbor's footsteps," I confessed to a friend over Zoom, forty-four days into solo quarantine. There's no knowing when science will deem it safe for someone like me—single, childfree, and living alone—to touch anyone outside of my household of one, even casually, accidentally, in passing. There's also no knowing when the pressing, desperate need for human contact will outweigh the risk of infection, potentially death. I lasted sixty-seven days.

"Nothing's weird in a pandemic," my friend said, trying to reassure me. I shrugged, looking out the window to Elliott Bay, the blue-gray emptiness where cargo ships should be lumbering toward Harbor Island; to the silent sky where airplanes once traced nonstop routes to business now ground to a halt, weddings now canceled, vacations now called superspreading events. On some level I believed her. I also knew this would be my last Zoom call. Pixels couldn't bridge the distance, and I'd lost the energy to pretend.

Everything I know about James, my neighbor, is what drifts through our shared walls and open windows: the smell of bacon wafting from his kitchen Sunday mornings, the waterfall of his shower cascading through the pipes, his bare feet padding to the kitchen at 2:00 a.m. when we're both up too late, scrolling: infection rates, death tolls, field hospitals, infographics showing the dozens of people who'd still be alive if just one person had stayed home.

The drift of him has become my lifeline. Even the flush of his toilet is soothing, somehow; so's the muffled roar of his vacuum tracing patterns overhead. It's hard to explain the swell of affection I feel in response to his chores, how much it helps to know that he's standing ten feet above me, doing dishes or eating toast while I'm wrapped tight in a blanket, bingeing on *Breaking Bad*—something, anything to distract me from feeling what's real. But even in the midst of a pandemic, even on a plot of land once designed for life in quarantine, there's no world in which it's normal to say *Your vacuuming helps me feel like I also exist.*

I told my friend all of this. What I didn't say is that this oppressive isolation has dug hooks into my oldest, deepest fear and begun to drag it like a shipwreck back to the surface. Here, again, are the habits of abstinence I'd mastered as a woman, girl, child born and raised in the Mormon Church. Here, again, is what it's like to feel half-alive.

Men speak for God in the LDS Church. They prophesy. This was the only world I knew growing up, so I trusted. I believed, when they said that sex as an unmarried person is the worst sin I could commit outside of murder. My choice was celibacy until marriage or death, whichever came first. I stayed single because I could never connect the thrum of desire inside me to the purpose of motherhood, their definition of (house)wife. I stayed celibate because the flipside was a long list of threats: eternal punishment, self-loathing, my family wrecked by my weakness. I stayed crouched in that fear-based, disconnected state, created a safety net of emotional withdrawal and physical distance—until I nearly suffocated beneath it. Turns out there's more than one route to spiritual death.

When I finally left my church, I swore I'd never live that way again. I didn't think to account for a virus that would also—because I'm single and live alone—rebrand the *even if God chose to forgive you, how could you forgive yourself* I'd heard from the pulpit every Sunday since birth. Now, every social media site wants to know how I'll feel if I infect my immuno-compromised mother. If I leave the house and end up killing someone's grandma. We've all seen the memes.

That Zoom call was in April; it's now June in Seattle, one of the nation's pandemic hotspots, and we're still locked down tighter than most places in the nation. As the weeks trudge on, I feel myself flattening, fading into a paper doll version of myself, the color leaching from my clothes and hair and face. Gray as I feel, I keep reminding myself I'm lucky. I have friends who send postcards, drop cookies on my doorstep, pop up on my screens wanting to know if I'm okay.

Not really.

I appreciate the calls. And I often avoid them. It's humiliating to admit I'm worried about myself. Also I don't want to add to anyone else's problems, which are almost always the opposite of mine: too many people crowded in too small a space plus the relentless demands of parenting, kids' schoolwork, workwork, and housework hanging like anvils over their heads. Everything we loved most about our lives has turned on us; I'm not unique in that regard. Besides, I can't say "skin on my skin, fist in my hair, breath on my neck, sweat in my mouth, tongue and cock and fingers inside me, the full weight of a man pinning me against a wall," when they ask what I need. Instead, I depend on James, though he's unaware of our relationship.

I mark my days by the movements of his parallel life, his footsteps tracing the same routes as mine through our identical one-bedroom condos built on the former site of the Laurel Beach Tuberculosis Sanatorium. The hospital was an intentional quarantine area established in the early 1900s when TB was the leading cause of death in Seattle. There was no vaccine, then. No effective treatment beyond hope and isolation. Prior to COVID-19, these facts were distant pieces of trivia.

Now, when I read news stories that predict our current distancing measures could last for years, I wonder how those patients survived it—the quarantine on top of the disease. Then again, they had each other.

Some lived for years on this steep, waterfront hillside separated from their spouses, children, family, and friends. In grainy, black-and-white photographs you can see their flat, gray faces gazing out toward Puget Sound or combing the rocky beach at low tide, looking for shells or sea glass—the same things I do now, wondering how many patients died here, or miraculously recovered; how many became best friends, had shattering affairs, or fell in love. How could they not, given the close quarters and constant presence of death?

Some days, I think I could do this forever, too, if I could just eat a meal in the same room—at the same table—with someone I love. Sip out of the wrong wine glass, tear hunks from the same loaf of bread, share the knife that spreads the butter, and pass the shaker of salt. Those days, when all I want from life is another heartbeat in my house and the collapse of laughter into someone else's shoulder, the absence is a wrench in my chest, tightening fast and deep. It can crush me, out of nowhere.

Day sixty-seven was one of those days, like every other at first. Breakfast for dinner after too long in the tub. Upstairs, James stood shifting his weight in front of the stove, also making dinner for one. But for the first time, the trick of his nearness didn't work. Time to flip the omelet, but I couldn't move. Out of nowhere, black waves of panic doubled me over, buckled my knees. I needed something to steady me, but there was nothing to catch. Just the too-hot handle of the pan still gripped in my hand. Just the familiar braid of fear, sex, and death weaving back together again, pulling tight. Heavy enough to drag me under.

I watched my eggs turn rubbery, then brown. I watched my palm burn until reflex jerked my hand away, pan clattering. The pulse of pain under cold water brought me back to the kitchen.

To cedar trees through the window, and Etta James through the speakers. My lungs eased open.

The cool stream from the faucet brought me back to myself and the knowledge that prolonged isolation is so contrary to human biology that men have used it for centuries as a weapon, a method of torture, and a tool of coercion. My religious life is long past. Its threats (disguised as love, disguised as revelation) turned out not to be real. This was not that.

Also, James was not what I needed, not anymore. It wouldn't help to put on gloves, a mask, and a garbage bag and hug someone, *anyone*, as one friend suggested. I needed to press my living body against another living body. I needed someone else inside me. Fuck all these sad approximations.

I walked to the front window and pictured the way it would happen. We'd meet on the waterfront at the end of the steep driveway that was once a grassy hill on hospital grounds. I'd choose a man, and make a promise: if there were chemistry there'd also be pandemic monogamy, obsessive handwashing, conscientious mask-wearing. A household of two. As much pleasure and kindness as each of us could give, for as long as we both agreed.

Just before sunset, I'd walk down warm asphalt and breathe him in. We'd cling to each other as if we'd just been given a cure. We'd sway a little, not speaking. Finding our rhythm. I already knew I'd remember it forever—the blinding orange sun over the Olympic mountains, the smell of wet seaweed, and the shiver of coming alive again in the arms of a perfect stranger.

TEACH ME HOW TO WANT TO LIVE

by Teresa Wong

In the kitchen we have a plant wall that does not get enough light.

So all the plants have started leaning to the left, towards the window.

Normally, succulents are compact and symmetrical — the most orderly and low-maintenance houseplants you can get.

But mine are grotesque, misshapen and sort of embarrassing...

so naked in their obvious desire for sunlight.

Just getting through the day takes almost everything I've got.

So I look to my ugly plants and try to learn from them.

Somehow you find a way.

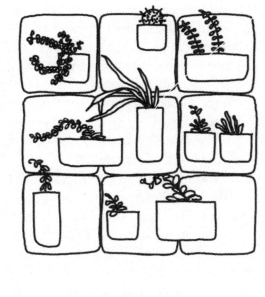

And somewhere there is light.

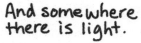

Notes Toward a History of Desire

Merritt Tierce

I AM A FORTY-TWO-YEAR-OLD WOMAN AND I HAVE been sexually active since I was sixteen. Over twenty-six years I have had intercourse, and other sexual experiences, with many men, and a few women. I have been married twice. Last year it occurred to me, for the first time, that I could try to consistently enjoy a sexual encounter from beginning to end.

This statement may cause you to imagine a woman who has never enjoyed sex, who isn't in touch with her body. I think something like the opposite is true; when I have enjoyed sex, I have enjoyed it so much, and have experienced my own erotic energy and sexual physicality so fully, that a great deal of my life force and my time on earth has now been devoted to trying to find someone I can rely on for continued and deepening access to this realm of experience.

I am single and I feel straight. I'm interested in men, sexually, and I don't want to give up on them emotionally either, though I've been encouraged to, by people who think I would have more relational success if I dated women, and by myself, owing to my own disappointments with men. Those disappointments have mostly landed in the field of unrequited desires. I have wanted to connect and to emote and to bond and to continue, and I have wanted a partner in exploring sexuality, and the men I have known have not wanted those vulnerabilities or expectations or structures they tend to see as strictures.

But back to my realization that I could try to enjoy a sexual encounter all the way through. The problem has been that almost every time I have sex with a man, I feel things I don't like feeling, and I choose not to tell the man. Here I am using *feel* mostly in its simplest straightforward physical sense—either a sensation hurts, or isn't pleasurable. It could be that most of the experience is fine, or even good, but there will almost always be something or other that isn't. When I am single, often I sense that the men I have sex with think that either I am not gorgeous enough to deserve their effort or, for those for whom I am sufficiently appealing to look at, that showing me they want me to feel good will be misinterpreted as a desire for greater intimacy and life-weaving. Life-weaving they will then have to retreat from at some point, which they imagine will prove tiresome or chaotic. Or I sense that the man doesn't care about me enough to care if I don't like moments or entire passages of the sex I have with him. My instinct (and my experience) is that the man will feel threatened or turned off by my saying that something doesn't feel good, that if I said *That hurts* or *Wait* he would adjust or comply but would punish me somehow. Either by being slightly colder to me for the rest of it or by not wanting to see me again. So I can have sex that is not as good as I know it could be, and sometimes hurts, or I can have sex that is even worse than that, which is the slightly colder but more navigated sex (because coldness directed explicitly at me is worse than whatever I experience when I don't speak up), or I can have sex less often.

I don't ask for what I want because what I want is to be asked what I want, and/or to know that if I talk about what I'm feeling or what I want my words will be received with curiosity and attentiveness. Perhaps this sounds maddeningly passive, and you're thinking *Has this person not discovered kink, or polyamory, or any of the sex-positive hyper-languaged communities/trends/ frameworks that proliferate in all directions to serve all needs these days?* I'll come back to that.

I have elaborate fantasies about what I want and what I like. I know exactly what I want, by which I refer to a quality and type of experience rather than a position or a scenario, though of course I have some specific desires and preferences there as well. But when I say I know exactly what I want, I want to be clear that I am interested in the kind of experience that would be expansive, that would allow me to discover new desires; to be clear that I am not at all imagining some completely prefigured, choreographed sex play. I know what I like, but everything cascades from the man's interest in my desires. I don't want to simply instruct another human about which buttons to push in what order to generate an orgasm from my body. That's not the point and has no appeal for me. I love my orgasm but I'm not after that release. What I seek is connection, not performance. I want a cosmic experience I can't have alone.

And now it may seem that, rather than someone who doesn't know what she wants, has not discovered herself sexually, perhaps I am someone who wants too much, and certainly I have been told that.

Here is something I want: I want to go back to one of my first sexual experiences, with my first boyfriend. I had just turned sixteen, had just left home, had just started college. Until that month I had lived my entire life sheltered among evangelical Christians who did not speak about sex except to exhort young women to maintain their own purity in order to protect young men from their own uncontrollable baseness. I had not been taught anything about sex in school, except that sexually transmitted diseases were to be feared. In sixth grade we were shown graphic images of sores and told not to have sex. In sixth grade I was eleven years old and had no understanding or knowledge of sex. I had never seen a sex scene on television or read one in a book, except for the obliquities of the Bible: he lay with her, he knew her.

Apparently she didn't know anything, and I didn't either, when I arrived at college. My body had not awakened. My mother had given me a book about the human body, which contained a few pages about human sexuality. She gave me the book open to those pages and told me to read them, before I went to college. But we never talked about what I read. She may have asked me if I had any questions, but if I did I'm sure I would have been afraid to ask them. The mechanics of it didn't really make sense to me; it seemed abstract, difficult to imagine. We didn't talk about how I could protect myself from pregnancy, infection, or heartbreak, and we didn't talk about what I wanted for myself as a sexual person. We didn't talk about consent, and we didn't talk about desire. So I was raped, and I got pregnant, and I got diseases, and it seems I still don't know how to negotiate my own desires. Surely some people who have been adequately educated about sexuality and reproduction are also raped and experience unplanned pregnancy, etc., and people who aren't educated aren't always raped. But my ignorance probably didn't help.

My first boyfriend came from a family of liberal intellectual atheists. They were white Americans, but the parents spoke French and made sure all three of the children spent enough time in France to become fluent. His mother had grown up in various places in the Middle East, because she was the daughter of an oilman. His father had been an attorney before kidney failure kept him homebound. His father studied German for two hours every morning while he did his dialysis. My boyfriend's mother worked as a computer programmer at IBM beginning in the 1980s, before there were many jobs as computer programmers and long before there were many women doing them. My boyfriend's brother was also an attorney, who'd attended the London School of Economics. The sister rebelled by changing her beautiful name and having relationships with women and eventually marrying a Muslim man and naming one of her American mixed-race sons Osama, after 9/11.

My parents were both public school teachers. My mother's parents were a nurse and a helicopter mechanic, and my father's parents were a mean Southern Baptist preacher/carpet salesman and a housewife. Almost everyone in my extended family on both sides worked blue-collar or lower-middle-class jobs. Everyone was conservative and religious, of some Protestant stripe. We were Southern Baptist, but there were also Methodists and Assembly of God relatives. No agnostics, atheists, Catholics, or anyone who believed in some other religion. We were all monolingual white people and few of us had traveled very far from home.

That description of my extended family is no longer true; with two more generations have come other races, other languages, some diversity of sexual orientation, quite a bit of travel and higher education, and a few of us have left religion. But that description is to give a sense of why my boyfriend found me provincial, twenty-six years ago; I was provincial. I hadn't encountered much culture, urbanity, or cosmopolitanism yet, though my father gave us the great gift of orchestral music, because he was a band director, and my mother, a librarian, gave us the great gift of a love of books. When I was still at home I often woke up to a strange symphony: the clattering clinking domestic sounds of my father's unloading the dishwasher, made supremely dramatic by the epic thundering battle hymns of Gustav Holst's *The Planets*. But otherwise, I grew up in small towns in west Texas and central Texas, and there was no internet. My boyfriend grew up in cities and went to a French high school in Aix-en-Provence.

The first time I took a drive with my boyfriend and his father, my boyfriend asked his father to tune the radio to the NPR station, and I asked what NPR was. I'm not sure what could have appealed to my boyfriend about me, beyond my being an easy foil for his sense of worldly superiority. When we met, he had a girlfriend. I was sixteen, he was seventeen, and his girlfriend was eighteen. He and I went to the same university in north Texas, and his girlfriend went to a different university in Houston. They had been dating for a year but had not had sex. He had no intention of breaking up with her but pursued me from the first day I moved into our dorm. His attention was exciting to me, and I wanted to be loved. I did not have a strong sense of self and was completely vulnerable to exploitation. But I wanted a relationship, and to spend time with him, and mutual expressions of affection, so I became attached to him; I did not want anything with my body yet. It was dormant, the pilot light had not been lit. When I took a shower I would avoid looking at my naked body, either in the mirror or while I bathed.

My boyfriend, who at the time was someone else's boyfriend, wanted to make out with me, so I let him. I felt stiff and didn't understand how to do it and he made condescending observations about my inexperience. Because everyone who lived in our dorm was underage—we had all begun college two years early—we weren't allowed to be in opposite-sex rooms with the door shut. So my boyfriend would lead me to parks off campus or dark corners under stairwells on campus almost every night of my first weeks at college. Each night he took his sexual experience of my body into a next new territory of discomfort for me, gradually but aggressively culminating in his rape of me, about a month after we met. Most nights we'd stay out until our 11:00 p.m. curfew, often running back to the dorm to make it right before they locked the doors, including the night he raped me.

But the experience I want to go back to, to get at where this all began, after it began in my religious upbringing, and before the rape: we're in a park. It's dark. We're lying atop a concrete picnic table, looking at the stars. We're making out, which I've begun to be slightly more comfortable with. I'm wearing thin nylon Umbro soccer shorts the color of diluted orange juice, with the diamond logo embroidered in purple. He slides his hand inside the leg of my shorts and his fingers inside my underwear, and he rubs my vulva. He hasn't done this before. My body tenses. It doesn't feel good to me at all. It feels like a violation; I have a moral reaction. I don't want him to touch me there. So I feel ashamed and afraid, and repulsed. (That it felt gross is a feeling I can't really reconstruct, because it doesn't feel gross to me now, if the circumstances are right, but I remember very clearly that it seemed gross, then—in the sense that everything between my legs had to do with excretion and nothing to do with erogeneity.) What he's doing to me feels wrong but it also doesn't feel good, physically. It hurts, it feels abrasive. My pelvis tries to move away from him, but I instantaneously dissociate and force myself to let him keep touching me. It doesn't occur to me that I could tell him I don't like it. It doesn't occur to him to ask me if I like it, or if it does occur to him, maybe he's afraid I'll say no and he'll have to choose between stopping or continuing. Perhaps he could tell I didn't like it and he didn't want to acknowledge that, because then, again, he'd have to choose between overt violation or not getting what he wanted.

It's hard for me to either believe or ignore how many damaging precedents this one relationship set. There's Unavailable Man, for whom I pine, for whom I think *If only he'd choose me, why doesn't he want me, why am I not good enough for him?* And there's Suppression of Own Desires. Before I ever had specific sexual and relational desires I felt prohibited from asking about, I had, first, the desire to *not* be touched in certain ways. And there's this Automaticity of Dissociation that allowed the man to have his way with my body.

If I could go back to this experience, the change I'd make would be so minor, and yet so cataclysmic: I'd speak. I'd say *Wait, this feels wrong to me, I don't like it. Please stop touching me like that.*

If he had continued to touch me, had responded with words that belittled me or dismissed my discomfort (as he would do later when I did try to resist), I would have stood up and walked back to the dorm alone and refused to spend any more time with him. If later he had admitted fault and requested another chance, had promised to behave more respectfully, to be more patient; or if, on the concrete table, when I said *Stop* he'd said *Oh, I'm sorry! You don't like it?*—in either scenario I would have told him he already had a girlfriend and I didn't want to date someone who had a girlfriend, or someone who would break up with a girlfriend to be with some other girl. If he had stopped by my room in the dorm during open-door visiting hours to plead his case, I would have been able to see down at the end of the hall the part where my future second husband is ending our marriage to be with his girlfriend, and before that ending his first marriage to be with me, and before that, closer, just a few doors down, my future first husband's suffering when I slept with other people while we were married. I would have said to my first boyfriend *This was never a good idea and I don't want love in any of these ways.*

If I had had the self-awareness and confidence to hold these boundaries, I might have also understood, in that moment on the concrete table, that I needed to educate myself about sexuality, that I needed information and I needed to find someone safe to talk to about these things; but maybe I would have needed the information and the education first, to have the confidence and self-awareness.

If I had been taught to value myself and my desires, with a more serviceable approach than abstinence, and had been able to form and speak my true thoughts to my first boyfriend in the moment when they were most relevant, I believe so many things would have been different, and I would have set myself on a path toward sexual fulfillment and liberation, if (though I do have doubts) sexual fulfillment and liberation are possible for a heterosexual woman. If I could have said *Stop* to him when I was sixteen, maybe I would not be writing an all-caps note to myself at forty-two that says *I DO NOT WANT TO EVER AGAIN HAVE A SEXUAL EXPERIENCE I DO NOT ENJOY,* and maybe an essay about desire would not have to be an essay about rape.

———

Here I am thirty-nine. What happened in the years between sixteen and thirty-nine? I broke up with my first boyfriend. I got pregnant by someone else, I married him, I had a baby, I got pregnant, I had a baby, I got pregnant, I had an abortion, I got pregnant, I had a miscarriage, I got divorced, I met up with my first boyfriend again and he raped me again (I think), I had dissociated sex with a lot of people, I had a volatile five-year involvement with a cruel and hostile professor of literature, and the sex with him was the best I'd ever had. I got pregnant, I had another abortion, I got my tubes tied so I could have sex without getting pregnant. My married, upstanding mensch of a mentor crossed lines he shouldn't have, using me to inject some transgressive thrill into his life, many times over many years, and I didn't say no. I got married again, my second husband didn't want to talk about our relationship or sex but was afraid I would leave him, or cheat on him, so he preempted infidelity by pushing for us to start having sex with other people, by inviting me into a theater of betrayal and then feeling hurt, and crazed with jealousy, to see me attracted to other men. He fell in love with someone else, we got divorced, I moved to California, I started dating. When I am thirty-nine, I have been on dates with thirty-six people in a year and a half of online dating, but I haven't lined up with anyone yet. I don't want casual sex; I want to be in a fairly traditional long-term relationship. There have been a few people who've wanted more with me, and I haven't wanted them, and a few people I've wanted who haven't wanted me. So it goes. I've had sex with nine of the thirty-six, but only one of those nine do I feel good about having had sex with, in retrospect. Because he seemed present and tuned in and I respected him and there was potential for a relationship and I didn't dissociate. But he was one of the ones who didn't want to continue with me.

So now I am thirty-nine, I am in Cuba, rock climbing with a French economist, who has been on online dates with seventy-four people and has had sex with eighteen of them, even though he's not yet legally divorced. He doesn't think of me as a potential mate, which I know and feel diminished by, but he is captivated by this new experience he's having with me: enjoying the company of someone he's not very attracted to. He finds me interesting and easy to be around. In the shower I ask him what he cares about most in life. He says *Success* and he asks me what my answer is. I say *Love* and I wonder whose answer is more depraved, more loathsomely gender normative. We rush back to the U.S. so he can see his kids before he has to go advise the prime minister of France on some banking measures. He wants me to sit on his face while I'm on my period and have a tampon in, which I think is kind of nasty, and besides which I don't like that position, but I do it anyway and grind out a weird orgasm, staring at my dissociated self sitting in a swivel chair across the room, twirling back and forth, bored of all my weaknesses, watching me get older, watching me insist on remaining untreasured, unchosen, watching me come in what we both know is a rather restrained performance. There's too much light in this room, you can see all the ways my body is not enough for him.

Later that year I am still thirty-nine. I am about to have sex for the first time with the man who will become the love of my life, though I have never been tempted to deploy that schmaltz. He will become my dybbuk, my white whale, my unscalable mountain of projections, the latest avoidant to my insecure, my boyfriend. He will write a letter to the government of Israel calling me the love of his life. But when we have sex for the first time it's only our third date and we barely know each other. I do know my desire to have sex with him is full and true, I have no uncertainty about it whatsoever, and this is evident in how I respond to him. His desire for me also seems complete and real. He has cooked a wonderful nourishing dinner for me and then we kiss on his couch until he asks if I want to go to the bedroom. We move to the bed and take off our clothes. I will never get over how amazing it is to be naked with someone you like. He puts his fingers on my vulva the way my first boyfriend did, and my pelvis moves away from him because it feels too rough, the way it always does when someone tries to touch me like that. He tries again and again my hips shift away from him. It's not a big or dramatic motion. It's subtle, maybe almost imperceptible if you aren't paying attention. He is paying such close attention. The third time, he stops and says *What can I do to make you more comfortable?*

This moment is imbued with so much significance for me, because of my history, that it's possible the entirety of my obsession with him, at the time of this writing now in its third year with no abatement in sight, arises from it. But that's ridiculous! Shouldn't it be so unremarkable, to be attuned during a sexual encounter, to notice someone's discomfort, to speak about it, to try to make each other comfortable?

It's not that I recognized the significance of that moment, of his words, at the time. It was much later, deep into the woods of my entanglement with him, after countless hours spent ruminating on why the attachment felt so intense and unbreakable, after realizing there had to be some unplumbed subconscious force at work because how could it possibly be about him? It was too powerful to be anything but a displacement of something else, even if my interest in him and hope for a life with him was also real, was never completely delusional. What had been displaced? What had struck me so hard, with him, why did it resound the way it did? What was it? When he said no to a relationship with me the first time, when he said *I'm going back to Israel and this cannot continue*, I felt a tectonic traction in my chest. I felt actual movement, as if all the prismatic sides of my heart fell away from all the others for a beat. My dissociated self said *What the fuck was that?*

Maybe it's only that he gave me back that other moment, on the concrete picnic table. When I resisted, however slightly, he didn't ignore it. He wasn't so focused on what he wanted that what I wanted didn't matter.

I didn't want to take off my shirt for my first boyfriend, but he took it off. I didn't like it when he touched my breasts, I felt ashamed and exposed. I told him I didn't want to have sex before I got married, and he made fun of me. I didn't want to perform oral sex on him but he wanted me to, he expected me to, he didn't ask me if I wanted to. I did it and I hated it and I felt debased. He tried to penetrate me one night and I said *No* and he stopped.

A few nights later we went to the place we called The Spot. It was a narrow brick enclosure behind the Speech and Drama Building. I'm not sure what its purpose was; it was enclosed on three sides, there was no roof, and the brick walls were about twelve feet high. There was just enough room in one corner of the enclosure to not be visible to people walking past the passageway that led into The Spot, but it was also dark, because it was night. We had carried a wooden platform, probably part of some theatrical set, from the back dock of the Speech and Drama Building into The Spot. It fit perfectly in the corner. It had a triangular top just big enough for me to sit on, and two steps. I was sitting on the platform, with my feet on the bottom step. My boyfriend was standing in front of me, making out with me. I was wearing a white cable-knit short-sleeved sweater and jean shorts and underwear. I was wearing white socks with lace at the top and brown leather penny loafers with pennies, head side up, in them. He pulled my shorts and underwear down around my ankles and tried to push his penis into me. I'd like to say he tried to push his penis into my vagina but that's not the way I think about it. I said *No* and he pushed inside me anyway. It hurt a lot and I was temporarily mostly concerned with the physical pain. There was a pop of intensity, a sharpness flashed inside my brain. I was being stabbed with a penis. It hurt. I was only with the pain and the shock of it until he said *Don't worry, I won't ejaculate inside you.* I didn't know what the word *ejaculate* meant.

We ran back to our dorm. He was so happy. He had done

it, lost his virginity, had sex for the first time. It felt so good to him. I was in shock. The world was shattered, different. I was focused on how incomprehensible it was that he could be feeling so happy and up, when I was feeling what I was feeling. As we ran I thought about how I would have to marry him. My vagina hurt. When we got back to the dorm we both got a drink from the water fountain and then he patted my butt and said he was going to play foosball. I went upstairs to my room.

I didn't think to call this rape, or wonder if I was raped, or say *I was raped*, until I was thirty-six, twenty years later. By then I had been with my second husband for five years. I don't know what prompted the new categorization of those events with my first boyfriend, but I was always reviewing them. I thought about what happened with him every day, even though I hadn't been in touch with him for more than a decade. My mind needed me to think about it every day, my mind needed me to not forget about it. But it still bothers me to say I was raped, to call what happened rape. I knew that if I was raped it was the least violent version of rape, and rape is such a violent word. I knew he might say he thought I loved him, he thought I wanted to be with him, he didn't realize I meant it when I said I didn't want to have sex until I got married. I knew he might want to say it couldn't be rape if it was a misunderstanding. He might say *If I raped you why did we stay together for two and a half years after I raped you?* My deepest fear about it is that he would say *You didn't say no*, even though I know I did. So I couldn't let myself think of it as rape when I thought about it every day. Maybe the reason I told my second husband the story when I was thirty-six was because I finally felt secure enough with someone to settle, to calm down, to sit still and survey my life and try to figure out what had happened in it. I told him the story, without using the word, and he said *Well I guess you were raped then*. I couldn't parse the way he said it. His flat delivery could have indicated a matter-of-fact assessment. He was a lawyer. But some part of it sounded disinterested, or even a twinge annoyed. Because he thought I was fishing for a diagnosis of rape? But he gave it to me. So it was a man who gave me permission to think of it that way.

After I got married for the second time I thought *Now, now I will be able to explore what I know is possible within and through my sexuality, because I am in a love relationship that will last the rest of my life. My husband will want to know what I want in bed, and I have the emotional context I have sought, and we have all the time in the world.* But he didn't really want to know what I wanted. He said he wanted it to be simple, and lighthearted, and it didn't mean as much to him as it meant to me. I kept trying to talk about what I wanted, assuming my husband would be interested. He wasn't interested. He felt criticized, even though I was careful to never say anything about his technique and I tried to explain that it wasn't about technique. When I say *He felt criticized* I am afraid it will be assumed that I was mean or thoughtless, because we are all conditioned to believe a man's perception of reality. We are all conditioned to work to make that perception make sense. But I wasn't thoughtless. I spoke about our sex with nuance and delicacy, in a manner designed explicitly to avoid hurting his feelings. Most of all I spoke about it with enthusiasm. I put the emphasis on what I wanted, not on any lack. I wanted to make the sex as good as it could possibly be, and I had all kinds of ideas, and I had been waiting my whole life for the partner who would finally let me explore them and help me reach for what I imagined. But my husband just wanted me to want whatever he already did.

I want to believe that being raped, in the mild way that I was raped, can't possibly have obliterated my sense of self and my sense of my right to my own desires the way it did. I hate it when rape is unthinkingly referred to as "the worst day of a woman's life" or similar, because that reifies this notion that a woman's value *is* her sexual intactness, her purity, her unrapedness. Rape couldn't be the worst thing that could happen to you if your virginity and your sexual wholesomeness weren't the most important things about you.

But I can't come up with another way to explain why I have felt so silenced in my sexual encounters with men, because this way is so blindingly obvious. I know I've already said I didn't have a strong sense of self before I was raped, I've said I couldn't speak up before I was ever raped. So what am I saying? I suppose it has to be that the rape made the silencing worse, turned distributed sexist conditioning and ubiquitous, diffuse, subliminal socialization into one acute event, a bullet of silencing. I said *No* and he shoved his dick into me anyway. What I wanted didn't matter. So of course, when I am lying down with a new man, or a man I've slept with many times, or a husband, my dissociated self is hoping I'll say what I want so she can come back and be with me. But she doesn't have to do the saying, she doesn't have to feel the pain I felt when I said *No* and she had to go away and I had to feel her leaving. It's still all scrambled in my psyche; I can always hear what I want to say to the man in my head, but if I say the words aloud he might ignore them or do what he wants to do with my body anyway, and then I'll have to feel like I'm not a person, I'm only flesh to serve his purposes, my words are unhearable or not worth listening to, or he'll have a defensive response I won't know how to defuse. So I usually don't risk it, and when I do it usually doesn't go the way I hoped it would. But shouldn't my sexual partner *want* to know what I'm thinking? Shouldn't he *want* to know what I want? Not out of obligation or responsibility. Out of desire. I want to know what he wants. Why doesn't he want to know what I want?

And shouldn't it be fine for me to reject someone who ignores my words and what I want? Why do I keep ending up in this place where it feels like the choices are to be alone or to be with someone who won't listen to me?

I don't want anyone to care about my consent. I've already been raped. I want someone to care about my pleasure. But it seems like it would be much harder to breach someone's consent if you cared deeply, sincerely, about their pleasure.

I said above *I'll have to feel like I'm not a person*. That implies that the man's treatment of me, his orientation toward me, carries the authority of truth for both of us. I know that's not right. A man could treat me like I'm not worthy of respect and I could continue to know that I am; for that matter I could be worthy of respect even if I myself don't know if I am, or regardless of how I behave. But this is the thing that was disfigured: somehow I feel like holding to my own perceptions, with respect to sex, is the same as rape. That sounds preposterous, but I think that's what's going on. Because I don't have a good experience of collaborating or negotiating with a man, around emotionality, relationality, or sex, this my-way-or-your-way system persists. He wanted to have sex with me, so it didn't matter that I didn't want to have sex with him evokes: I want to believe I deserve respect, so it doesn't matter that he doesn't respect me goes to: But I don't want to do to anyone what was done to me, I don't want the unilateral. Turns into: I'd rather stay on the same side, with him in his bad world, hoping he'll change his mind someday, than be alone in mine, thinking I deserve respect.

So maybe monogamy is the problem. Maybe if I expanded my search to look beyond the confines of the conventional romantic dyad, if I relaxed my hopes for that old thing, if I weren't trying to have it all with one man—maybe a universe of sexual fulfillment would open up to me. I do admire the practice of ethical nonmonogamy. And I respect the communities of kink and polyamory because they have invented a vocabulary for talking about sex and negotiating individual and mutual desire that is unacceptably lacking among the unenlightened vanilla hetero-sexuals, even if the language itself turns me off: the fluid bond-ing and the hinge and the NRE and the ORE and the wibbling and the polycule—it's useful but I cringe. Regardless, in theory, when a man says he's into kink or he practices ENM, I can as-sume his baseline attitude is something like *It's okay for everyone to want what they want, and for everyone to say what they want so everyone can get what they want.* Though there's nothing keep-ing monogamous people from espousing this parity, I've found I can't expect it. So shouldn't the poly world be a place I want to explore? Shouldn't it be a place where I'm more likely to have my magical unicorn of a sexual experience I say I've never had?

I've tried. I'll try for months to find a partner who wants me, and wants the kind of relationship I want, and eventually I'll get lonely, and need a hug, and think *Fine, why not just pick someone hot and intelligent to sleep with now and then?* And then I'll stop swiping left just because I see *ENM* in a guy's bio. I tried to be with a married man who was excited about me be-cause he didn't have to talk about his kids' soccer uniforms with me. I tried not to care that he had an impressive, interesting career and an impressive wife and adorable children and they'd just bought an eighteenth-century stone farmhouse they were renovating. There were orchards, but I coached myself not to feel jealous about any of that, and I coached myself to feel com-persion—happiness for him that he seemed to have a rich and rewarding life that I could be a small part of. He'd come over and have attentive sex with me, and once in a while he'd even spend the night and I'd feel held and wanted for a few hours. Nothing went wrong, except I kept waking up and thinking *This isn't what I want.*

I still keep hoping I'll get over my hang-ups, that when a man says he's ENM and he has a primary partner he's been with forever I'll stop hearing *You'll never be the most important person to me,* but it hasn't happened yet. When I've gotten in-volved with men who identify as polyamorous, all of whom have had long-term primary partners, it has felt like I'm giving up on myself. Like I've decided I don't deserve to be the most important person to someone, I deserve to be the side door, the other woman, the fling, the thing he reaches for because he already has everything but he can't stop wanting more. Maybe my frame is all wrong and that's not how I should think about it, maybe my attitude is so close-minded and I'm missing the point.

Or maybe I'm just not cut out for polyamory. I don't want the sex I want with someone who doesn't love me in a certain kind of primary-partner no-other-partners way. That's my kink. My sexual desires won't turn on unless I feel like my heart is in it too, and my heart does not feel safe when my boyfriend has a girlfriend. I've tried to force myself to just go in and get the sex so many times, and it does nothing for me. Or it harms me. But why do I need to love someone in this possessive partnered way? Don't I realize possession is a construct, a projection of insecurity? I don't think of it as possession. I think of it as commitment.

In one of my giving-up gaps I found myself sending a man, practically a stranger, a long list of all my specific sexual preferences. We'd only been on one date but everything was very upfront and forthright, and, as usual, it felt weird to me to let the transactional live on the surface of the interaction, but I told myself those were just my fuddy-duddy roots showing and I should proceed like a wild woman, like someone with a sense of adventure, like the woman the men online are all seeking: *if you're chill, laid-back, don't take life too seriously, good vibes only, hit me up lol!*

That wasn't the way this particular man spoke. This one said lots of things about *our sacred tantra practice* and was very clear that he had a primary partner who *allowed him to play* but he wanted to make sure I was comfortable with the reality that practicing tantra meant excluding emotional attachment. I said I understood. He read carefully everything I'd said about what I liked sexually and asked me some clarifying questions. He asked me if I thought I'd be into a feather duster. I said I didn't think so. When he came over, he brought a feather duster.

I'm forty. It's the second date with another professor of literature. I should know the second date is too soon to have the kind of sex I want to have, but I am trying to erase the Israeli man from my body, from my desires. The literature professor and I are on my bed, making out. I'm still wearing my jeans. He unbuttons them and tries to put his hand down my pants but I resist because I know it will hurt. I see in his eyes that he has gone somewhere else. This is an absence I recognize. A generous interpretation would be that the man is slipping into a state of blissful hypnosis, a kind of flow state. To me it feels impersonal, like he is getting drunk and I am the drink, I am being used. In theory there's a way this could feel good to me, or I could be using him too, for my own escape, but usually it just feels like he is gone. I want to have sex with a man who can be present, whose eyes don't go away, who knows me. I keep resisting his hand, squirming away, putting my hand between his wrist and my pubic bone. He keeps trying. It seems he thinks we are doing something together. I am supposed to yield, to make that be the truth of what's happening. I am not supposed to speak. I would be fine with not speaking words if he would pay attention to what my body is saying. But clearly he thinks he is paying attention, and this one part of my body is saying *No*, and he thinks it means *I'm teasing you to increase the excitement when I finally give in to you.* So I will have to use words to explain that's not what's happening. Softly, trying not to disturb the mood, I say *I'm trying to show you I don't want that yet.* He stops. His eyes come back. He says, with petulance, *How do you think that makes me feel?*

I am careful not to react. After a few moments of lying quietly together in the broken connection I calmly refasten my bra and put my shirt back on and we act mostly normal and polite until he leaves. He behaves as if everything is fine and nothing awkward or problematic happened, and he says something about seeing me again. I say something benign that will not tempt him to argue with me or ask me to explain anything, something that I know has the best chance of resulting in his stepping outside my house so I can lock the door, something like *Sure, just text me. Take care.*

The troublesome part is that as far as I know, in his reality it's possible that nothing awkward or problematic happened.

I want to step away from the height of all this, it's too much. I want to laugh at it, and be modern and cynical and chill. We're all just animals, there's no place for all these feelings, good vibes only. And what's with my retro, conservative angle on marriage and monogamy? If sexual fidelity is the sine qua non, that's about controlling women's bodies as much as all the rest of it, and I've been sold a bill of goods. I don't know how to blame my first boyfriend for raping me. It was what he had to do in that moment, for some reason that couldn't possibly be entirely his fault, in the same way it couldn't possibly be personal, some formed malice directed at me; in a way it didn't have anything to do with me, which is the exact problem, though I've tried not to become overfocused on the banal horror of that. It sounds like I'm trying to excuse what he did, but I want the space to try to understand it without being accused of excusing it. He was only a seventeen-year-old kid. I'm mostly sure he doesn't think of it as rape. Someone taught him French and didn't teach him not to rape, like someone taught me Bible stories and didn't teach me to know myself and speak up, or anything about sexual desire, but those someones are no ones. Why would his parents have thought to teach him not to rape? He was their darling, their baby, cherished by his parents and his older siblings. Why would my parents have taught me about sexual desire? That wouldn't have made sense within their world or their values. At what point in a child's life do you instruct them in attunement to themselves and to the autonomy of others?

All along. But I think I must have failed there, too, as a parent. Did I ever teach my children about how to negotiate desire? No. I was too consumed with my own quest for love while they were growing up to think about it. I slipped them books, just like my own mother did. I didn't raise them in any religion, but I sent them to the local Unitarian congregation's Our Whole Lives sex ed program for a few weeks, when they were in middle school. So I had more conversations with them than my parents did with me, but that was a low bar, and I wouldn't say we covered the topic anywhere close to thoroughly. I do talk to them about dating and relationships a lot, but it wasn't until I had this thought I had last year, about trying to consistently enjoy a sexual experience from beginning to end, that I realized I hadn't educated my children about desire.

I'm forty-one. Now I live in Israel with the love of my life. We have somehow penetrated a hardcore-closed, absolutely no-entry border that has separated many unions more established or familial than ours, to be together during a pandemic. After both of us weeping through miserable I'll-never-see-you-again partings in three different cities, after a year and a half of being apart from him, after yearning for him the way I have not yearned for anything ever in my life, I live with him. It's a miracle. *Now*, I think, *Now I am with the person I love and finally we will be able to talk about our relationship, and about sex, because we are finally in a real relationship so of course we will both understand that we both deserve a satisfying sex life. What I want will be important to him.* I have never felt so completely alive and available and present and interested with anyone else, sexually or emotionally or romantically or intellectually, not even close. But he won't talk to me. Not about our relationship, and not about sex. He feels threatened if I want to talk about sex, he doesn't feel safe, he doesn't feel in control. I make gentle attempts that don't go anywhere. The two times I try harder to talk about sex, he disconnects from me, he barks at me, he withdraws, it is so painful. But his sexuality had been violently repressed for the first twenty-five years of his life and he had been made to think that was ordinary and righteous. He is coming from a place of severe cultural contortion and damage. And yet the sensuality in him is so intact and beautiful and powerful that I will do anything, have done anything, for a chance at connecting my own powerful sensuality with his.

It's a miracle that we sleep together every night, spooning, my foot on top of his. It's a miracle that we can have sex whenever we want. Married sex, or partnered sex, is so much better than sex as a single person. It's part of your life together, and you know each other, and you don't have to stay in this tendentious mode all the time, constantly open to the possibility of the guy in line at the grocery store, or the guy at the gym, or the guy fixing your bike, or the guy selling potatoes at the farmers' market, or the guy you're interviewing, or the guy who's interviewing you, etc. It's a miracle that I know who the person is, now. I wake up with him and there he is, his beautiful face. He usually smothers me with kisses when he opens his eyes and sees me, there next to him.

But I make myself wait, I don't initiate sex because I want to be certain he wants me. And I don't initiate because I know men think that because I've had sex with a lot of people I'm insatiable, and my insatiability makes my desire suspect and impersonal. I know they think the promiscuity in my past means it's just an appetite and I am vulgar, monstrous, unpredictable, out of control. So I don't initiate because I don't want to give my boyfriend any evidence that I love sex too much. Almost every day I am hoping he will want to be sexual with me, it never ebbs. It is so exciting for me to know that he wants me, and I love our sex so much. Because I love him, not because I love sex, and also because I do love sex when I can have it with someone

I love. But my desire for him to let the intimacy and love into our sexual connection never ebbs either. It was there between us, sometimes, in other countries, but not in this one. In this fucked-up trauma-state I am too unknown, he doesn't trust me, I'm too close, I could blow up his heart so he keeps it to himself. I love our sex but I wish he wanted to talk to me about sex, I wish he enjoyed talking to me about our sex, I wish he wanted to listen to me talk about sex, I wish we could have an open conversation about it. I try to snuff these desires because I'm getting to be with him and that's the important thing. But don't men want to be with a woman who wants to have sex? Aren't they sad and resentful when they're with a woman who won't have sex with them? I am so receptive whenever he wants to have sex with me, I don't make him struggle for it, because I also want it, I want the way he makes me feel and I want to show him the love I feel for him, with my body, and I want to see the ecstasy he feels when he touches me. But I still want to talk about it too. I try different ways of broaching the subject; I try showing him some OMGYes videos. We rub our fingers around on Zoe's clit, on the screen of my phone. She says *Mmm, like that.* My boyfriend doesn't know what to make of her, or that website, or my desire to talk about sex. Like my second husband did, he thinks it means I'm unhappy with something, rather than understanding it's because I'm so glad I have someone to have sex with and I want to talk about it because it's one of my favorite activities. But I know he's interested in sex—in the desert in Ezuz he reads to me from *Awaken*, a book about Jewish women's sexual experiences. It's in Hebrew so he translates as he reads. It's fascinating to me, I wish we could read from it every night. When we are naked in bed together all I want is for him to talk to me while we're having sex, to let me connect to the icaro of his voice, so I know that he is present with me and I am in reality. I think this is because, in addition to the fact that my brain is my most responsive sex organ, I imagine it would be hard for a man to rape me if we were talking ourselves through the experience. As long as he is talking and we are engaged in a call and response he has to be aware that he's interacting with another autonomous individual, right? He has to hold in his mind the me-ness of me, he has to stay in the connection, right? But the love of my life is always silent while we have sex. I know it's partly because he is so focused on how good he feels, and he doesn't know how to be in that state and talk to me. But it also feels like a way he can get what he needs and stay in control, a way he resists a more intimate emotional experience because he's afraid of losing himself. I wish he could welcome my radiantly sexual, erotic self without fear, so that I could share her with someone. I open up to him as much as I possibly can inside our limitations; when we have sex I drop into a state of such willing vulnerability, and I know he feels the power of my wholehearted *yes*. Sometimes I say things like *You feel so good to me*, to give him an opening to respond, and he does, but I get the feeling he wishes I wouldn't talk during sex. I can't help thinking that the women in porn don't usually talk during sex. But I know he loves the other sounds I make with my voice when we have sex. Why isn't that enough for me? I want to tell him *It would make me so happy if you would tell me what you're feeling*, but I have to leave him and his country before I can ever say the words.

I don't know what all this adds up to, except that now I am forty-two and I exercise for two or three hours every day, trying not to become invisible to men, trying not to lose my shot at having the sexual experience I want to have before I die. Now I have been on dates with ninety people in five years, and it has begun to feel like an extended piece of performance art. How many times can you meet a stranger on a street corner and say how many siblings you have and where you're from? I feel like I can't control much about how or when I'll be able to be in a relationship again, so I default to controlling the shaping of various muscle groups. But why is it so important, this experience I'm still seeking? I don't know. It's just what I want. It's something I want with no effort or consideration, and most things I want in life are not like that. Usually I'm trying to make myself want things I don't, or stop wanting things I do, or stay focused more on purpose than desire, doing things that are good for me or important no matter how I feel about them. But my desire for the sexual experience I know it would be possible for me to have in a loving, committed relationship is a pure and passionate want. The desire is so strong and organic I don't question it and I don't care if it's wearing a hideous cloak of psychological scars after all these years. To be held, to be naked, to be known, to connect, to be desired, to want, to satisfy, to cry out in ecstasy, to be intimate with someone you love who loves you, to know they want to know what you want.

There was one afternoon when my first boyfriend persuaded his roommate to leave their dorm room for a couple of hours, and he snuck me in and locked the door. We had sex on the bottom bunk while we listened to a Platters album on a cassette tape. I was sixteen. I didn't know how to have an orgasm yet but I was so happy to be connected to him, to be wanted, even though he had raped me and our sex was never satisfying for me. In fact our sex usually put me into a melancholy, mournful state, because I would just be approaching something like arousal, with no idea what to do about it, and then he would climax and the interaction would be over, leaving me there, stranded on a windy cliff of energy whipping and sparking and thrumming throughout my body. He didn't know what to do either, he didn't understand why I cried with frustration, he didn't like it that we had to deal with this emotional backlash at the end, every time.

But that afternoon after he came he fell asleep next to me; it was so new to me, what happens to a man after his orgasm. I liked being the only witness to how he'd spent himself, and I felt tenderness toward his post-coital vulnerability. I lay there staring out the window at a giant sycamore tree, my boyfriend's head on my chest, my hand in his coarse curly red hair as I watched the caramel light of Sonny Turner's voice play off the broad green leaves. *Smoke gets in your eyes.*

Caught in the mid-coital swirl of my own physiology, I was the opposite of sleepy, but I tamped all that down to appreciate the moment with him. I felt haunted and sobered by how important it was to be connected to him like this, by how deep the desire was, by how vital it felt. Like something I needed to survive. I was only sixteen and yet I understood my powerlessness in the face of my own desire to connect, to have a true experience of mutuality and pleasure, expressed through sex. It was a moment of farsightedness, when you sense yourself inside your own history, one of those moments of no apparent significance that you know nonetheless you'll remember forever. He was with me, I had given him what he wanted. I waited for him to wake up, hoping he'd want to give me what I wanted too.

Coming to Be

Sonia Maria David

I REMEMBER SWEATING. MY EYES MUST HAVE LOOKED like fledgling sparrows had danced on them with painted feet; they were closed so tightly. The heel of my left hand met my mons pubis, splitting hairless lips with the pressure that my body was begging for all day—mind you, it was probably about 1:00 p.m., but I could hardly wait to be with me. After all, it was Saturday, and this weekend luxury was my gift for going to every class and getting good grades in middle school. I deserved this reward.

So when I heard my father's voice yelling, "What are you doing in bed? Get up!" you wouldn't be surprised at my sense of inconvenience and ignominy. Jumping out of bed with my jeans undone, I yanked down my T-shirt and stood dumb, hoping my haste was explanation enough; then he asked what I was doing in bed at that hour.

Now, without getting too deep into my relationship with my father, please understand that he is not a monster or a pervert—I had no privacy as a matter of fact rather than malicious intent. God and I both knew he did not *want* to know what I was up to. However, he was one to bear down on me arbitrarily and aggressively—so this kind of question was standard in our interactions. It would be the first and last time we stood to be mutually punished for his intrusion into my doorless bedroom.

My chestnut doe-eyed stare begged him silently *Please don't make me answer that, Dad.* I sincerely doubted that my father would be ready to hear me say *Coming, Dad, I was having an orgasm!* I was around twelve years old in the early 2000s. It would be nearly twenty years before I would understand what a privilege this humiliating and exciting period of self-indulgence and discovery had been.

For about twenty-five precious years, my relationship with pleasure remained the same. Yet, occasionally and increasingly, my clitoris betrayed me. Sometimes, it would become inflamed—seemingly out of nowhere. It grew a tiny bump around the age of twenty-two. The bump grew to a short grain of rice at twenty-three. Each bout of inflammation would end in a nondisastrous resolution. Until it did not.

I remember sweating. My eyes must have looked like ravens had been clawing at my eyes; they were so red. I tried to seal them closed to quell the nausea I was experiencing. My overblown clitoris had then ruled my every waking moment for about a week at that point. Nearly annually, my clitoris grew randomly and resolved as unpredictably on its own, but not this time. I could not wait to be by myself. The bulge was so taut that I could see where the pus had built up beneath my ever-thinning yet resilient skin.

Sitting on the toilet on a Saturday around 1:00 p.m., I turned off the hot water that I brought to a temperature that might burn desensitized hands, placing it on my pulsing clitoral hood. I removed the cloth to see the defiant skin refused to release. At this moment, the pain of this bulge was second to none. Nearly without thinking, I took off my blunt earring, breathed deeply, and with my opposite hand covered in the hot cloth, I punctured my clitoral hood, praying that my pain would be replaced with relief.

I heard my body make a sound akin to that of bursting a grape. Aspirating the bulge sent a sharp scent of sickness directly to my nose despite its distance from my injury. I caught most of the pus in wadded toilet paper in my hand, yet I distinctly recall spraying Clorox on the floor and bathroom door at least three feet in front of where I sat.

If I cried, it was from joy; my body was mine again. I stepped into the shower, wrapping my fingers around the neck of the showerhead, bringing my body down to the tub, and ran a slightly pressured stream of water first over my mound—ensuring the temperature was neither too hot nor cold. With my left hand, I peeled back my labia, now bloodied by the gore from moments before. I rinsed them first. I let the water wander over the coarsely punctured skin of my hood, remarkably painless. Too painless for the ordeal. Streams ran down my body as they simultaneously stained my cheeks.

Am I okay? I thought to myself as I inhaled smoothly, wishing I had a smoking habit for mollifying racing thoughts. I ran the jet gently over my clitoris and instinctively moaned my next breath. *I am okay*, I thought to myself. I thanked Jesus and came in his name in that shallow bath mingled with my blood.

According to the World Health Organization, two hundred million women alive as of 2020 have experienced some form of female genital mutilation (FGM) in their lives. These women reside in thirty countries across Africa, Asia, and the Middle East. FGM ranges from severing the nerve that sensitizes the clitoris to a procedure encompassing the entire vulva—labia minora and majora, vaginal opening—and at times even the urethra when left to the unskilled surgical skills of the family member.

Somewhere, on the same day that I was discovered bringing myself to climax as a kid, and every day since, another girl in her living room was sitting with her relatives. At the same time, the steadiest among them split her labia to find her clitoris, with the unyielding patriarchal pressure their principles required for her clitoris to shudder, bleed, and die, alongside any hope of experiencing the fullness of even a single orgasm.

I do not know any of these girls. I have not done any advocacy work in this area. This essay is my first confession. I need to note that, until sharing my story in this public way, I was not an activist with personal knowledge of girls and women who are survivors of FGM. I also do not know anyone else with my specific problem.

My relationship with desire itself drives the passion on these pages. Yet, when I think of orgasms, I think of them as my basest form of self-expression. I reflect and radiate myself to myself in my ecstasy—two mirrors with my desire in between. The rhythms that yank at my hips like marionette strings are my birthright.

My situation is unique because I am safe from my culture, but not from fate. I am intimately aware of what my orgasms are to me in ways that the girls who are disfigured will never understand or miss in the way that I would. I know that ravaging is taking place, not from uninformed empathy but a visceral personal lived experience. I understand this tragedy as neither a victim nor a victor. For no reason that medical science could discern, I've lived in a constant state of threat.

I needed to affirm and reaffirm my sexual existence like how most twentysomethings need whatever ordinary people want. Nothing overshadowed my commitment to completion with every ounce of my being. Of around forty partners and one hundred liaisons or so later, I remember maybe twenty partners either by name or by the quality of my pleasure spasm.

Every time she (my body) squirmed, she would recall each gleeful flush that filled her chest and rushed to her belly. She remembers every sensual kiss and soft thigh. The smile on the face of the most beautiful woman I had seen who inexplicably wanted to sleep with *me*. She contemplates every erection she caused over a webcam. Every vibration against hidden seams as she rode the subway to work. She remembers my first boyfriend's

fidgety fumbling fingers chasing me on his father's bed. She remembers every foreign object that found its way inside her at
bath time in my tweens. Through touch, she remembers what
my mind cannot. She remembers every point of contact as if it
might have been the last time she might well up with a flood of
peaceful shuddering as she was both worshipped and adored.

She lived in unabashed transparency. Pleasure was her purpose, and she lived that purpose in vibrant color. Her hunger
would not be sated, and I fed her appetite without shame, never
knowing when the next inflammation episode would interrupt
her banquet at knifepoint. I refused to let her be slowed. After
all, she did nothing wrong. Yet, she was constantly at risk of
indescribable pain, the likes of which are inflicted on innocent
girls who have never so much as had a morsel of what she consumed as a matter of flippant wanting.

I learned precisely how fortunate I was to explore and enjoy
my clitoris in 2020. I sat in the living room of a man I barely
knew. My eyes scanned the empty sidewalk made quieter by
the pandemic. I could feel the heat from my nose and cheeks
call tears to soothe my sorrow. I explained to him that I might
never again come—the way I had done most days since I discovered my enthusiasm for sensual pleasure—at the ripe old age of
twenty-eight. He did not comfort me, and I did not want him
to hold me. I only needed a witness. I wanted someone to know
that the defining features of my sexual pleasure center might be
brought to a cold, abrupt end.

My clitoris was the second largest it had ever been. The
pocket of infection had grown beyond its past boundaries. I had
visited doctors throughout the decade and was dismissed or met
with vague curiosity. These men observed my clitoris, told me
they had no idea what was going on with me, encouraged me to
use a compress and "let it resolve itself" at home.

There is no telling when the infection will worsen and no
guarantee that it will rupture. I had no way to safely manage the
symptoms at home over the days and sometimes weeks when it

would take over my life. At its worst, sitting, standing, and walking all incapacitated me, so I avoided going outside, even though this would be the best chance for a doctor to assess the extent of my abnormality. It felt fruitless because the pain I experienced was never worth the embarrassment of having to explain *why* I came to the office in a waiting room full of patients.

"Sonia," my mother said frankly over the phone, not leaving an inch for the rebuttal she could sense coming from across state lines. "I know you hate to go to the doctor, but will you please go to the hospital this time?" I cannot imagine being my mother and having me as a daughter; she mastered the art of coaxing me into championing my well-being when I had long since lost hope. "I know you don't believe they can help you, but they have to see this at its worst to understand what you're going through." My mother was correct on both fronts.

I was afraid that the infection would rupture before they saw me—this had happened twice before. American emergency rooms are not known for breezy wait times. But I got into an Uber and held my breath over every bump to the University Health Service building. Once I was called in to see a doctor, he let me know that he knew nothing about what was happening to me. Though, he did offer to *try* and lance the infection. I looked that man directly in the eye and told him that he would not be performing surgery on my clitoris in this urgent care office— respectfully. I threw whatever loose-fitting, noncrotch-rubbing pants I had on and made my way to another Uber at my mother's insistence, this time to head to Mount Auburn Hospital in Cambridge.

I checked in, explaining that I was in pain because of my clitoris. The nurse motioned for me to sit and wait. Placing my tailbone at the very edge of the chair, I leaned back, barely balanced, for maybe an hour. A nurse called my name, and I did my wide stance walk to the examination room. I entered the space and gingerly undressed, donned the gown that said *I'm here for help*, and waited.

Two empathetic nurses came in to check on me and observe my condition. Immediately, they ordered pain medicine for me. I asked if we could wait until I found out what parts of the treatment would be nonnegotiable; they agreed, but with the kind of hustle you hope no medical professional uses on your behalf paged their general surgeon, who had a specialty in skin abscesses. He very thoughtfully approached me—a line of medical professionals silently stood outside the door—and he said to me, like a mother who needs to keep a child from moving and injuring themselves, "I cannot help you with this, but we are going to call someone who hopefully can." He also did not know what it was. He had never *seen* this before. I cannot emphasize this enough: there is no medal for the patient for being a medical first.

A new specialist and one of the compassionate nurses from earlier returned with papers and a needle. The doctor took a seat by my side, and the nurse cleared her throat. She fished for my attention; gravity was her bait. She said something like, "There is no shame in taking medicine to help you with this pain. I have morphine here. It will help you." I must have seemed listless with a languid din shading my usually bright demeanor because I could sense my anguish reflected in her gaze. I nodded, accepting her logic. She injected me as the doctor explained what had been happening to me sporadically that decade.

The doctor explained, "You have what is called a spontaneous peri-clitoral abscess. It is typically located on the labia and areas where hair grows. And while those are uncommon, your case is particularly challenging. Medically speaking, we tend to see this in women who have been subjected to genital injuries like those caused by female circumcision or female genital mutilation. In your case, it is not clear what has caused your infection. The placement makes any interventions risky. I am not equipped to perform this procedure tonight, but I want you to know your options. It is called marsupialization. Effectively, we make a small incision and use stitching to help the wound heal open. This prevents any fluids from building and will help you in the long run—we hope."

He continued, "There is no telling whether this procedure will have the outcome we are seeking because there is a very small population of women who have experienced this, and we don't understand when, why, or if it will resolve itself. I can make an incision on the area and flush the wound today. After that, I would insert a small balloon into the incision and inflate it to help keep the wound open for the next few days and hopefully prevent you from needing the other procedure. However, if I cannot complete the second part of the procedure, then there is a good chance that you will have to wait until this happens again for us to attempt a second time." At that moment, I was twelve years old again and entirely focused on my clitoris. But this time, I was in a room full of strangers who instantly embraced me with the best care their training could provide.

A fog hung over my head as I tried desperately to force my brain to process each word this doctor shared with me. The morphine must have been working well. I held the papers he must have handed to me at the beginning of our conversation; my mind does not remember—according to my medical records, it was 2:00 a.m.

Bewildered, I asked if I could think about the procedural options. My surgeon had a perfectly healthy and uncomplicated baby to deliver, so he said I could take my time. He was the surgeon you'd want your daughter to be with alone in the wee hours as she learned she was a case study. He had the bedside manner matched perhaps only by the angel who told Mary not to be afraid.

I looked over his handouts as he walked away. The fluorescent lights flickered between blinks, leaving me in a kind of trance. I lost track of time, but it must have gotten quite late because my mother sounded like she was about to pass out when I called her. Although she could not sleep from worry, she miraculously lit up with me on the phone as we waited. Having my mother's voice in my ear was just grounding enough to know that I was, in fact, in my body.

"Well, Mom," I chuckled—feigning a sigh—"turns out, I'm way more than just one in a million! How does it feel to have a truly exceptional daughter?" I highly recommend getting yourself a mother who can look into the abyss with you and laugh when you know she wants to get on a plane and hold your hand through the scariest moments of your life—it's incredible.

After hanging up, I rested, watching myself in my mind from a chair in the corner of the room. The trauma of ten years was validated, yet this could not be my body. That sexist, dismissive doctor who likened me to his wife (in a way that made me wonder how long he was from being served divorce papers) could suck it. Something novel had been happening to my body, and if he had taken me seriously, maybe my case would have been recognized sooner. Momentarily I wished I could have been stronger. I wondered if I should have spoken for myself more fiercely and showed my clit to any MD with a GYN in their specialty.

A couple of hours later, a new baby joined the land of the living nestled with their mother, and I cheered for my surgeon as he came in with the goddess nurse who cared for me earlier. I don't remember the hallway having any curious professionals; I was singularly focused on what was to come.

The nurse sat beside me as if she knew exactly how terrified I was and had me focus on her and her alone. She took my hand in hers and said, "You cannot hurt me," I suddenly imagined her five-foot-four frame standing taller than Athena and equally armored. She said, "Focus your pain on me. I am here." I practiced holding my pelvis down as she coached me. One slip of my hips and I would never again feel a clitoral orgasm.

I lay flat on my back with my right hand beside my ear, palm up. She held my hand, lacing her fingers with mine. I do not remember how the doctor confirmed beginning the procedure;

I only recall a searing pain as the doctor inserted the needle from the tip of my clitoris and drove it up toward my navel. Every muscle below my waist pressed down into the bed as I attempted to shotput the nurse across the room. She pressed with her entire body weight, giving me every pound she had, producing much more force than I could have imagined for her size. I was grateful.

I must have cried out because I remember my chest feeling exhausted, and the needle had only gone *in*. The medication was slowly plunged into my body as the surgeon meticulously delivered the anesthesia. I was on fire. I made a sound I'd never heard before. The nurse's skin and mine formed a spiritual synapse. Her nerve endings seemingly pulsed through my fingers entwined with my hyperstimulated system. I did not know agony until that moment.

Moving quickly, the physician reached for his scalpel. My mind snapped at the way my skin felt as he sliced into me. "*Stop!*" I cried, "Please stop. I need a break. Please. I can't take anymore right now, please I need a minute. Please. Just one minute." His hands were up. He assured me that he had stopped. Like a wounded animal, I buried myself into the bed, unable to control my tears from falling. "I am so sorry," I said. "My mind . . . I couldn't take the sensations. It was all too much for me. I am so sorry."

Sobbing from weariness, I caught my breath as my nurse praised me. "Are you kidding me?! You didn't curse either one of us out. You didn't kick the doctor in the face. I'm still in one piece. You did amazing." My surgeon concurred, gently patting my knee, breathing for the first time himself, it seemed to me. Even in that awful moment, I was worried about taking up too much space and not considering *their* feelings.

I nodded, resolved to keep going through the hell we were in together. The surgeon continued to manipulate the hole he created, and I held my breath. When he finished his incision, I exhaled and craned my neck to look. He explained to me how unique the discharge was. The gray-colored fluid indicated that my body was trying to metabolize the infection, healing itself.

Now the ballooning phase could begin. This part was a nuisance. The balloon would not stay in the wound once inflated. We tried twice, and I gave up, confident that we had done all we could with our time together. Defeat or a taste of despair seemed to wash over my surgeon's face; it was clear he wanted me to have the best chance at never going through all this again. I thanked him for his efforts and humanity. He took care of me as no one else could have. My nurse that night held my hand in a way that would have given my mother peace since she could not physically be there with me. I love them, and my mother loves them too.

That night in the emergency room, the team I had was comprised of the best people available. What I experienced was by my request and consent. I wanted every girl to have the same odds for being cut as I did—one in several hundred million. Intentional female genital mutilation has always been preventable. I wanted every girl to have the opportunity to orgasm for years undisturbed—a chance to learn her desires in the safety of her home. I hoped that when the medication would wear off the next day, I might too.

Numb between my legs as the sun began to rise the following day, I made my way home. Clad solely in a medical diaper of sorts, I slept undisturbed for hours. When I woke up, I was grateful that I was not in any significant pain; though I was bleeding and there was some—understandable—tenderness at the incision site. I tried to ignore the fear of recurrence, opting to let the nightmare slip away.

I padded to the shower, stepped out of my recovery garb, still getting acquainted with the look of my clitoris. Filling the tub one-third, I made my way into the water like a leaf floating down a current to a field of yellowed grass, unsure of what I'd feel—death, life, or anything. The water lapped the squish of fat between my legs that spread naturally as my knees rose and my hips splayed. I was a backstroking frog. I brought the shower-head to my chest, spraying a stream that matched my tempera-ture. From below my clitoris, I peeled apart the skin now thinly coated with blood, letting the bath's tide wash over the valleys of my vulval shores. The touch of the jet, though muddled with a mild sting, had kept its original sweetness.

Song of Songs

Melissa Febos

> My dove in the clefts of the rock, in the hiding
> places on the mountainside, show me your face,
> let me hear your voice; for your voice is sweet,
> and your face is lovely.
> —SONG OF SOLOMON 2:14

I CALL THEM "THE FEVERS," THE WAVES THAT SURGE
up my back and arms, break into electric foam at the jetty of my
neck when her fingers move at a certain depth inside of me. A
momentary influenza of pleasure.

The word *frisson*, from the twelfth-century French meaning
"fever, illness, shiver, thrill," was used in a 2011 study on the
psychophysiological effects of music to describe what subjects
experienced in reaction to certain musical provocation. In this
study on "Strong Experiences with Music (SEM)," participants
reported phenomena referred to as "chills," "thrills," and "skin
orgasms," in addition to "frisson," which implies both physical
and emotional sensations.

In all studies (that I encountered) the element of surprise,
or the upset of expectations, seemed integral to this kind of
pointed physiological pleasure in music. Music that strays from
the brain's anticipated next notes, but without disrupting musicality to become simple noise, is that which produces emotional
surges, goosebumps, and electric sensations on the skin—*frisson*.
Common culprits? Rachmaninoff's "Piano Concerto No. 2" and
Adele's "Someone Like You."

I am not a scientist. Nor am I a musician. I am a writer at
an artist residency in the Midwest. I simply want to know if the

sounds I make during an orgasm mimic those that elicit frisson, of which I have a rich and varied experience. I am also newly in love with Donika, my body sparking with desire for her. For the first time in some time, I feel that thrum in my limbs, the twist in my center when I think of her that makes my eyelids flutter. It is a kind of ceaseless frisson, and it feels different. *Doesn't it always?* a part of me retorts. And maybe it is some hunger to know that finds me so eagerly accepting this assignment from an editor to investigate the musical qualities of the female orgasm. Though as a lifelong music obsessive, I have often observed the similarity between my own frisson, chills, and thrills at favorite songs and those elicited by lovers. In many ways, my connection to music has been much more sustaining, my passion for it marked by a more complete abandon than that with any lover. Perhaps, in the heat of a new love affair, I hope to chase out the parallels. If I can quantify them, might I borrow some of that more lasting appreciation?

I have had partners who would object to this assignment. I can't imagine it is easy to be the lover of a writer whose lovers tend to make their way into the writing. Or of the kind of writer who writes about such subjects as the musical qualities of her own orgasms. I don't yet know how my new love will respond to this experience. And perhaps that question is what gives this assignment the sense of risk I feel in my gut as I accept it. Or is it a fear of what I might find should I discover a way to measure love's affect?

However, when I say "music obsessive" I mean music listener. I have no background that would allow me, by any musician's measure, to determine the similarities, or whether there is a correlation between the music that causes physical pleasure and the music caused by physical pleasure. But I intend to try.

Unfortunately, my studio/dorm is adjacent to a shared kitchen and though I am a person who will record herself masturbating, the idea of a fellow resident overhearing me while reheating their mug of tea makes me blanch. I may be a pervert but I am not an exhibitionist. I run through my options (the soundproof conference room, no, too many windows; the rental car, possible, though it's raining and I didn't pack rain boots) and figure if I sit on the studio-adjacent bathroom floor with the door closed, drape the largest blanket over me completely, and turn on the fan, I feel reasonably soundproofed.

I press record on the Music Memos app that I've recently downloaded to my phone and hold the microphone in front of my mouth (with my left hand). It is a slower than usual start, due to the cold tile floor and my performance anxiety, but I try my best to vocalize naturally, if more freely than I otherwise would out of concern for my New York City neighbors. The cold air when I finally throw off the heavy blanket is a thrill all its own.

Music Memos, intended for musicians, translates the sounds into approximate pitches and determines the meter and tempo of any recording. It is a stretch to apply the tool to human vocalizations that are not intentional singing and occur less as notes than as sliding pitches, but this is a creative exercise, not a scientific one. My first recording reveals an emphasis on F4 for the first seven measures, and if I subject it to A440 (the general tuning standard for musical pitch), my pitch appears somewhat flat overall. No surprise, the pace picks up as I near orgasm, with increasing emphasis on F4, D-flat 4, and G4. I climax at F4. As for rhythm, the entire forty-six-second "song" plays in a 5/4 meter, with a tempo of ninety bpm. The 5/4 tempo is unusual, its most familiar adoption found in the *Mission Impossible* theme song. The ninety-bpm catalog, however, is vast, and includes such hits as 50 Cent's "In Da Club," Billy Joel's "River of Dreams," and Buju Banton's "Champion" (my favorite of the three). As I listen to the songs, I can't help feeling that some combination of Buju's dancehall classic and the *Mission Impossible* theme does seem apt. Whether that's accurate or wishful, the idea pleases me.

Listening to myself masturbate, I should say, is excruciating.

Fortunately, the app will play the recording and show me the pitches "played" even while the volume on my phone is so low that the sound emitted might be a cat trapped under a distant neighbor's porch.

"It's odd," says a friend on the phone later. "That you can write so explicitly about sex, your sex, but can't listen to it."

"I mean, it's not *sex*."

"Do you think you could listen to a recording of yourself having sex, then?"

"Oh no, definitely not."

The volume at which I must play Rachmaninoff to hear it under my fort is easily detectable by my musical app, so I forgo the recording and try to assess empirically if my orgasms are influenced by the music or accompanied by any "skin orgasms." While I don't have "better" orgasms, or any definitive epidermal corollary, I do feel that my Rachmaninoff climax is a dramatic one—perhaps a redemptive moment at the denouement of a film whose primary conflict is the postponement of orgasm. The Adele song reminds me of a harrowed time concurrent with the song's release, so I disqualify, as relevant evidence, my difficulty climaxing to it.

I record a quick series of six more orgasms. In all of them I maintain one or two pitches per measure until near-orgasm, or, by the famous Masters and Johnson model of arousal stages (Excitation, Plateau, Orgasm, Resolution), the later Plateau stage, when I vary more. The pitches of these six, however, differ greatly from my first round, though are all very similar to one another. I have a strong, and I mean *strong*, tendency for the pitch G4. That is, in one sequence, the app estimates me at G twenty-seven times out of forty notes total. In another, twelve out of seventeen. My meter remains steadily at the rare 5/4 *Mission Impossible* time signature, though my tempo increases with each orgasm. In consecutive orgasms, I transition from "In Da Club" to the pace (ninety-five bpm) of David Banner's "Play" (a guilty, filthy favorite of mine) to that of Alice in Chains' "Over Now" (111).

I do not reach the end of my orgasmic capacity at this point, only the end of my interest in masturbating under a heavy blanket on the bathroom floor, though it seems important to say that I have often masturbated the same way that I listen to favorite songs: repetitively, often until I meet a dead-end of sorts, unable to continue.

In a 1991 study, neuroscientists asked subjects to listen to songs of their choice while lying in an fMRI scanner. In such songs, "the anticipation, violation, and resolution of our expectations triggers the release of dopamine in two key regions—the caudate and the nucleus accumbens, shortly before and just after the frisson." That is, frisson-inducing music stimulates the same neural reward pathways as other addictive behaviors, including, of course, orgasms. And when a pharmacologist blocked the brain's opiate signaling, he found that the study subjects experienced significantly fewer musically provoked skin orgasms.

As an adolescent in the 1990s, I used to record a single song over and over for the entire half of a blank cassette tape and repeat the process with another song on the other half. When I exhausted a song, I felt the way I did after I finished a box of Good & Plenty or, later, after I finished a cigarette, the way I sometimes do after a series of self-stimulated orgasms: satisfied and a little sad.

In 2003, two Israeli doctors, at the request of their subject, conducted, *A woman with a high capacity for multiorgasms: a nonclinical case-report study.* "Anonymous," the multiorgasmic woman studied, was capable of more than two hundred sequential orgasms at a time. Of her post-orgasmic feeling, she reported: "the orgasmic capability always makes me feel 'superior' and special and gives me a kind of 'well, I always have that to rely on' feeling. It is comforting to know that I have this to give to myself." I relate, and concur.

My lover and I are also multiorgasmic women. Though neither of us fully realized this potential with partners before meeting each other. We both feared being seen as oversexual, which is no surprise considering that in the nineteenth century, as treatments for the supposed affliction, "leeches were applied to the vulva and anus, the clitoris was cauterized, and the first known therapeutic function of X-rays was to irradiate and destroy the clitoris in these women." I did not know this until I encountered accounts in my research, though obviously I have lived with the legacy of such beliefs all my life.

And so finding each other has also been a discovery of what Donika calls "the infinite feedback loop of pleasure," wherein her orgasm, and the according sounds, spurs mine and then mine hers and so forth, until we are simply tired or decide to stop. And the vocalization is an integral part of this momentum. We each attest to the other's volume but have little self-consciousness of our own.

I can confirm that her sounds have a definitive frisson-like effect on me, not unlike "the fevers," or the feeling I get from the final movements of the Rachmaninoff, to which I have been listening on repeat while writing this. Though different in quality, I feel an equal pleasure when I hear the interest in her voice as I tell her about my bathroom experiments. Thus far, she has reacted to my work, and this assignment, with a curiosity that rivals my own. When she laughs at my fort, I join her, though my laughter is tinged with relief.

Much has been made of the male of many species' mating calls. In Darwin's 1871 *Descent of Man*, he coined the term sexual selection by describing the mating songs of birds and the way the most sexually appealing traits spread among populations. Then he applied this model to a theory of the origin of human music: "It appears probably that the progenitors of man, either the males or females or both sexes, before acquiring the power of expressing their mutual love in articulate language, endeavored to charm each other with musical notes and rhythm." A romantic idea, if also a scientific one—that all music is born of seduction and sexual appeal.

It has been suggested by other scientists that all humans are born with perfect pitch and that as the only primates who do not (any longer) communicate through song, all our melodic communication has been relegated into the realm of music. As a music lover, this theory is attractive to me, though as a human lover, I am hesitant to believe it. Very early in our relationship, Donika and I spent five weeks apart and nurtured our new bond exclusively over the telephone, on nightly calls. That is, our courtship happened aurally. I fell for her while listening to her murmuring voice, which became familiar—in its tones and rhythms, the faint drawl of her years in the South, her high and low laughs—long before I came to memorize the contours of her body. How can I not describe that communication as melodic? To say that our mutual seduction depended solely on the *meaning* of our murmured words, to divorce it from the music of our sounds seems akin to separating the sound of a poem from the meaning of its words. Impossible.

Birdsong has long been studied for its communicative properties and been found to signify sexual attraction, social bonding, territorial signaling, and sometimes multiple uses simultaneously: for instance, "The impressive coordinated behavior of plain-tailed wrens may represent the interaction between sexual advertising and group territorial dynamics." Less familiar are the rhythms of the Southeast Asian firefly, who signal in perfect phase with one another for hours on end; or the songs of some cicadas; or the synchronous claw waving of male fiddler crabs.

Humans depend on rhythm too. A University of Vienna

study asked paired participants to articulate nonsense phrases and match their voices, without any further instruction. Eighteen of twenty pairs synchronized with relative ease, and in repetitions quickly found a shared rhythm. Reading this, I can't help but think of those late-night phone calls, the easy seesaw of our conversation, our shared laughter. Also, the ways our bodies move together like practiced dancers, improvising to the same song. We, too, find shared rhythms easily.

Does recording our sex occur to me? Of course it does. My urge is clamp a hand over the mouth of that thought, much as, for many years, I used to clamp my hand over my own mouth at orgasm to stifle the sound. If I can hardly bear my autoerotic sounds, how will it feel to hear those made in the company of my lover? Consider the mild discomfort hearing a recording of your voice on, say, a voicemail. Multiply that discomfort infinitely. My lover has told me that I am a noisy at orgasm (which she relishes), and though I suspect she is right, I have never heard myself. I am happy for this deafness. Some things I don't want to notice, to reflect on, to *consider.*

Because lack of inhibition is dear to me. So much of my early sexual interactions were governed by performance, and, partly as a result, devoid of pleasure. As are those, I suspect, of many adolescent girls. Such is the conditioning of heterosexual hegemony. A fundamental reason why my sex with women is so much better than that with men is the freedom it grants from performative scripts. With her, more so than any lover before, I follow my pleasure without fear of shame. My attachment to that freedom is greater than my curiosity in the music of our sex. The intimacy of our sex feels profound; it is unprecedented, and precious. I fear testing its resilience, the degree to which it might be disrupted by the more scrutinizing aspects of my mind.

And what would she think of the suggestion?

Predicting the responses of our partners, like falling into music, seems a deeply held biological priority—aurally, in the brain, and, I would venture to say, emotionally. Indeed, the conclusion drawn from the Austrian study was that "increased regularity of intervals between words arose specifically to facilitate synchronization, presumably by allowing participants to accurately predict the timing of their partner's speech and coordinate their behavior accordingly." In other words, we find shared rhythms to facilitate syncopation.

And so a theory of the origin of musical rhythm: it evolved as a method of achieving vocal synchronicity. But why synchronicity (if not urged by the conditions of a study)? One theory says signaling in chorus gives sexual advantage, at least in the case of meadow crickets. When prompted to "choose" between a recording of single male cricket and a duet of two male crickets, female meadow crickets reliably chose the latter.

Another idea: the ability to find shared rhythms is attractive because it suggests other, analogous strengths. One theory posits that men's ability to synchronize together would draw more migrating females to a settlement, simply because they were louder together. I can't help but wonder if there is an explanation here for the timeless draw of musicians, however deadbeat in other respects: if a man can keep rhythm, if he can sing with other men, perhaps some ancient instinct recognizes a talent for survival, sees the rapt audience as some modern equivalent of a promising early human settlement. Even more convincing: "High quality synchrony may have also indicated something about the capacity of a particular group for cooperation, which may have had additional benefits in resource acquisition and territorial defense."

This final theory—that syncopation (and therefore rhythm) evolved as a means of facilitating cooperation—makes the most sense to me. Synchronized singing has been proven to result in increased trust and cooperation, and many forms of synchronization, from walking to bimanual object manipulation, have "demonstrated to increase interpersonal affiliation, as well as the probability of engaging in helping behavior." That is, syncopation bonds us.

I am as avid a dancer as I am a lover; I don't need a paper in *Biology Letters* to demonstrate the pleasure of social dance. But it does: finding and syncopating the rhythms of our dance partners' bodies prompts the release of oxytocin, and MRI scans show that watching others dance activates the same neurons in the observer's brain. That is, dance promotes empathy and helps us to connect—a result of the shared rhythms that govern our movements and grant us the potential to predict our partners' next moves.

If you have ever made love to music then you, too, know how bodies syncopate to a rhythm. Donika and I have fucked to Trey Songz, Rihanna, Roberta Flack, and The Dream, our movements interrupted only by her remarks on the lyrics (*What does he mean "knee-deep"? Knee-deep in what? And why only to the knees?*).

Before I met her, I spent six months intentionally celibate. It was the longest period of my adult life that I've spent single. I was hoping to gather some new information about the ways that I syncopate with other people. By learning something new about my own rhythms, I wanted to learn how to recognize, and to trust, those I found with another person. If our instincts for recognizing partners who might be skilled at cooperation are as primal as this research suggests, then shouldn't I be able to access some refined perceptive ability? Maybe my motivation for that period of solitude and for writing this essay are the same: to learn to listen more closely.

I have told the kind administrators of the residency that I will be collaborating for a few days with a fellow writer. I don't tell them that the fellow writer is also my girlfriend. And I haven't yet decided the degree of the collaboration. The idea of suggesting that we record our sex still terrifies me. I fear her reaction to the suggestion, yes. Also the self-consciousness that such scrutiny might encourage, and what intimacy might be therein lost.

Deeper still simmers a fear in what I might find, or not find, as if the experiment is a test we could fail, a test that could bear proof that our love is not different, not more than an ordinary chorus of hormones that will fade as quickly as it came. I sensed this risk from the beginning, I think; it is part of what drew me closer.

Historically, much less has been made of the female primate's copulation call. Unlike the male's, it happens during coitus, as well as just before or after. When I subjected a recording of a female rhesus macaque's copulation calls to my musical app—again, a flimsy approximation, as the rhesus macaque's copulation calls occur in primarily sliding pitches—she also appeared to repeatedly reach A4 and D5. She climaxed at C5, however, the only place where that note appeared in her short sequence. While her screams did not sound musical to me, the surprise note at the end may well have spurred her partner on in the manner of Rachmaninoff and Adele.

Human females, multiple studies have shown, emit more vocal sounds during sex, but largely for the benefit of their male lovers, who overall find sexual vocalizations more exciting than females do. One study showed that 68 percent of women faked orgasm to hurry men's ejaculation. Expediting male orgasm is, in fact, a much more popular motivation for sexual vocalization during coitus than physical pleasure, across all studies of heterosexual women.

But a 1994 study found women's sexual vocalizations during self-stimulation were not random or performative but appeared "related to the actual contractions of the superficial perivaginal striated muscles that can usually be observed on the skin surface around the vagina. These in turn probably correlate with each wave of erotic pleasure."

As my lover and I are both women, I suppose our sexual vocalizations have more in common with pleasure than performance. Neither are our orgasms any signifier of the end of sex, so vocalization would be a poor method of hurrying.

"So I'm thinking that we might actually do some collaborating for this essay I'm working on," I say into the phone a few days before she arrives in the Midwest.

"Yeah?"

"Yeah."

"What exactly does that mean?" she asks.

"I thought maybe I could try to record us."

"I thought that's what you meant."

"Would that be okay with you?" My heart is beating at well above a resting heartrate bpm. (Maybe around ninety, that of Big Pun and Ashanti's duet "How We Roll"?)

"Yeah," she says. "That'd be okay with me." I can hear her smile from six hundred miles away.

The first night, at her nearby hotel, I leave my phone in my purse on the floor. We have not seen one another in two weeks and there is a scrim of shyness between us. While not unpleasant (because I know that it will pass and I even savor it as an aspect of the excruciating but pleasurable symptoms of early love), I suspect that the red pulsing screen of the Music Memo app will exacerbate it, and also that it will skew our more "regular" vocalizations. Later, between orgasms, I observe the abandon our vocalizing has quickly reached and regret the decision.

The next afternoon, on the tautly made hotel bed, a blade of afternoon light slicing through the cracked curtains, I observe my body's obvious response to her sounds. Frisson, yes, chills, yes, thrills, yes, and considerable lubrication. The only part of me that touches her is my mouth, though the interaction touches every part of me. It is, of course, impossible to separate the effect of any one sensory stimulation. How can I say that it is her vocalizations and not the pulse of her orgasm against my tongue that sends a net of electricity sprawling across my back? I cannot. How can I measure the subtle but definite increase in intimacy from her simple yes to this experiment? I cannot, though I feel it when our eyes lock as she comes again.

What I can say is that she tends to circle around middle C. That her climaxes are often a flurry of pitches and that as her volume rises, her pitch goes sharp. That she had a minimum of eleven orgasms in thirteen minutes. And that listening to an audio recording of her climaxing produces none of the discomfort that listening to myself masturbate did.

I listen to all twenty-five minutes and eight seconds of our Music Memo on a pair of headphones while my lover reads a book of poetry in a nearby chair in my studio. Just before I began listening, she read me a poem about penises that made us both laugh. The poet listed a series of penises she had known, alternately with tenderness, dismissal, chagrin, and nonchalance. "One was a mouse," she explained in one line, and I yelped with pleasure at the unexpectedness.

Science, of course, confirms that the brain centers stimulated by melodies are also those centers associated with language, and that scans show similar phenomena at the reception of unexpected language and musical notes. Yes, the frisson I feel at the now familiar progressions of Rachmaninoff are easily comparable to the thrill that moves through my body when I read her poems, or the sentences of any favorite writer. And those I feel in response to the sounds she emits when I move inside her.

As I listen to her crescendo of moans on the headphones and watch her scowl with concentration as she reads in the chair, I imagine the smudgy pathways of my brain, the step of its gray expectation, the jog in direction at an unexpected image or sound, and the synapse that fires, sends its invisible lightning bolt through my body, sparking as it scrapes the curb of my hip and flashes down my thigh.

Listening to myself is so much harder than listening to her.

I am glad for the natural relay of pleasure that our lovemaking often takes, which spares me the task of parsing out our simultaneous sounds, or my own contrasting reactions to them. As the recording transitions into my "turn," there is a shifting sound as we rearrange our bodies, accompanied by soft laughter. It turns out that I favor G4 as much in my murmuring—*One more?* I ask her after a series of orgasms, to which she laughs and proceeds—as I do in in my self-pleasuring.

Unsurprisingly, I listen to about twenty bars of G4 before I have to turn down the volume, but by the time my recorded self nears orgasm, she is even louder than before I turned the volume down. I am shocked by how loud she is. My lover looks up from her reading when I cover my face. When my first recorded orgasm finally ends, I uncover my face and sigh with relief. My sigh is mimicked immediately by a sigh from my recorded self, in exactly the same note. I am, it seems, very reliable. And very, very loud.

"I'm so loud!" I exclaim at around orgasm four or five, pulling one earbud out.

Donika nods. This is only news to one of us.

"I guess it's not out of character," I say.

She shakes her head and smiles.

When she turns back to her reading, I sneak a look at her while feigning interest in my work. I want to memorize this moment—sunlight dappling the floor, her long legs crossed at the ankle, the small rasp as she turns the page of her book—in which I feel utterly at ease, able to share my delight in multiple things with her: my strange study of our lovemaking, the recorded fact of it, her total acceptance and actual pleasure in this obscure corner of reflection. If there is a test, I know we have passed it, whatever my hard findings. This moment, alone, is different. It is full of things I have not known before.

I am surprised, though not very, when I consider the Austrian study to find that my meter in this recording shifts from the uncommon but reliable 5/4 of my self-pleasure experiments.

Like the Austrian study participants, together we maintain a shared tempo, 3/4. I isolate clips of our individual orgasm progressions to confirm this and do. We also keep a fairly regular bpm of around fifty-nine. I measure these numbers against Adele and Rachmaninoff and find no parallels. And though Leonard Cohen's "Hallelujah" is closer, the more perfect match turns out to be k.d. lang's rendition. Hallelujah, indeed.

The most unpredictable element does seem to be the pitch of my orgasms. Though my Masters and Johnson stages of Excitement, Plateau, and Resolution all tend to the familiar G, my penultimate stage of arousal, Orgasm, is sometimes E4, sometimes an alternation of A4 and C5, sometimes ten bars of E4. It is the unexpected pitches that render Adele and Rachmaninoff and Leonard Cohen's "Hallelujah" so pleasurable, and that bring me delight in language. Is it a factor in this pleasure as well? I don't know, but my lover did have three orgasms of her own while pleasuring (and listening to) me, as she quietly but audibly announces on the recording after my ear-splitting finale. Are there happy accidents in nature's design? I tend to think not.

When I return to the Rachmaninoff after listening to our sex, I think again of Darwin's postulation that all music originated in sexual attraction. It's not hyperbole to say that it makes sense to me in a new way, the concept that this universal language for emotional phenomenon between humans should have originated in the interaction it so superiorly describes.

I'm not convinced that this origin is particular to sexual attraction though. Alternate theories of musical origin cite the musicality of vocal-gestural communication between mothers and their children, commonly referred to as Motherese, which uses melody, rhythm, and movement patterns to aid in the infant's acquiring of language. This employment of "musical" elements with intention and meaning makes it easily as viable a potential origin for music as mating calls. As one expert I interviewed, composer Emily Doolittle, states, "Really, I don't think human music evolved out of any one thing—or even that there is any one thing that music is." Like me, the bonding-related theories make more sense to her than the strictly sexual ones. "Mating calls, group bonding, and parent-infant communication all have to do with intimate interpersonal bonding, in different contexts—which of course sexual communication does, too," she tells me. The urge to designate a single source for something so linked to fundamental forms of communication and connection among species does seem a particularly human one. One result of my research is that it has reminded me how similar our designs, and the comfort therein. To my delight, when I played some orgasmic clips of our sex for a gay composer at my residency to verify my musical interpretation, he said in response to my admission of embarrassment, "Oh it's nothing to me! Just like listening to animals in a zoo."

Have I come to some conclusion about the connection between the music that most inspires our pleasure and the music our pleasure inspires? Tenuous, at best. I am more confident in this connection between the pleasure art brings us and that of our bodies, the common thrill of surprise. I am more interested in the way that our particular love, musically noted and experientially, resembles a song in its refrains and surges, its patterns and diversions, its similarity to all art that moves me with its symmetry and brokenness. I am most convinced by the ways that musical elements arise out of and facilitate bonding. And I am most interested in love's inexhaustible ability to surprise me. The unexpected—expressed in music, yes, but also in touch, in a few short words spoken six hundred miles away—strikes me in a tender place, frissons me, and finds me new.

From a few steps back, the lifelong progression of my intimate relationships resembles that of a frisson-inducing song: it has occurred in patterns, predictable over time, but ends with an unexpected shift: her. A shift that moves me physically and emotionally. It has been said of literature that a good ending to a plot must be both inevitable and surprising, and it seems to me that the same is true of both music and love.

The night after I listen to our recording, the night before she leaves, we make love for hours. I don't record it. I don't count either of our orgasms. I listen only to the sound of our bodies' slick movement; her moans; the rush of her breath, muffled as she bites my shoulder; my hand keeping time inside her, regular as a metronome; like no other song I have heard. After, we curl against each other to fall asleep and instead fall into each other one more time. And this time, when I come? I hear myself. Like the dazzling long-held howl of some animal so close by it must be inside.

Manifest

Camille T. Dungy

I CAN SAY: THAT IS A HAWK. BUT NOT: RED-TAIL, red-shoulder. I can say: deer. But not: white-tailed. I can say robin. I can say raven. I can say bird, but not: bunting, wren, warbler. Sometimes: gerbera daisy. Sometimes: crimson glory rose. But not the name of the creeper that edges my neighbor's lawn or the flowering stands near the car park.

I can say blackberry in every season: fruit, flower, and vine. I can say poison oak. I can say: watch out for the thistle. But not what the berries are that grow at the base of the park's redwood trees (I can say redwood. I can say Sequoia sempervirens).

I can say: California poppy, nasturtium, tiger lily. Eastern fox squirrel (like me, not native). I know so much about this part of California, but if I had to make my way to you by naming everything that I encountered, I'd never make it home.

I want to say border collie, not just dog. I want to say king snake, not just snake. I want to say aloe and agave, not just cactus, which would, anyway, be imprecise. I notice, now more than ever, what I don't know, and what I want to know, and what I want to share with you, Callie Violet. I want to name the world correctly. One day this will be your language, and I will have been the first to present it to you.

There is a story I heard, when you were the tiniest baby, about a waiting room in someplace close to Heaven. After death, that's where people go to wait to be forgotten. This was a place people wanted to stay for a while. No one wants to be immediately forgotten. Family reunited in the room, if I remember the story correctly. I imagine enemies would confront each other there too.

When we mourn, we give memory a name, and in this room those memories were corporeal. It feels like a long time ago, when you were the tiniest baby and I listened to the story while we drove from one place to another in the car. For a while, the bodies thought it was nice to be in the waiting room. It was nice to be remembered.

But after a while, names lose meaning. Living speakers stop associating some real body with the body's name. In the waiting room in the place that was close to what we might call Heaven, if I remember the story correctly, a man who drowned in a New England well waits to be forgotten, while every day a tour guide on some idyllic college campus walks by the well and repeats, with less reverence than she bestows upon the well stones, the still-not-completely forgotten man's name.

Naming is a kind of claiming. In the Judeo-Christian tradition that is your inheritance, Adam named all the birds and beasts of the world, including Eve. Even after his exclusion from the Garden, even after the all-consuming loss he suffered when he acquired the deeper knowledge that brought on his expulsion from Eden, and hardship and death, Adam possessed the names of everything with which he'd once shared uncomplicated communion. The ability to name even a lost world keeps that world alive. I imagine this was both painful and potent for Adam who, like the drowned man in the story I only half remember, must have wanted some days to return completely to a world he remembered. That world was gone, though. In reality, if not in memory, his past was irrevocably erased.

You are named Callie Violet after my grandmother Callie Madge and your father's grandmother Violet. You are my grandmother's first great-grandchild, and there was no question that you would be the next Callie. My grandmother's grandmother was also a Callie, and now our family spans three centuries through women who have borne one name.

It was the continuity I wanted. Persistence personified.

Some people are surprised I named you after someone who is still alive. What if the angel of death came for the old one, got confused, and took you instead. I want to say this never occurred to me. But sometimes I worry that I left no room for you, my daughter, in this old woman's name.

When you came to be outside my body, the name we bound you to seemed limiting.

I call you Abena because you were born on a Tuesday. I call you Abeni because the name means we asked for her and she has arrived. These are Fante and Yoruba names, for these, too, might have been your people.

The next time I hold you, I call you Butter Bean because, when you were a newborn package of squirm and gas smiles—my stinky little Cochina—you, like three of your great-grandmothers before you, were the color of a butter bean.

There is no escaping history.

Your aunt calls you Minukee, a Louisiana Creole endearment with afro-indigenous roots. She calls you mon petite chou, my little cabbage, my precious little girl.

Because you coo-coo-coo in the morning, you are my Mourning Dove. Not just any old bird.

Your godmother calls you the Boo Boo, because that is what her father called her and so that is how she knows to show you love. Your grandfather calls you CVDB. I call you CV. I call you Argentina, because I do not want you to cry. Your father calls you Little Bit.

The act of naming who you are to us may never end.

I walk with you daily because the confines of our apartment are too small.

I point out the trees we walk beneath: plum, crab apple, lemon, mulberry. Eat this, not that, eat this not that, I tell you, as if it is never too early to teach you what might cause you most harm.

I want you to know a violet when you see one, Callie Violet, and though they are lovely, just as you are lovely, I want you to know the calla lilies growing in every other garden have nothing to do with your name.

Rhododendron, rose, I say, daisy, daisy, chrysanthemum.

White flower, purple flower, pretty yellow flowers, because I can't name all of them.

The walk is long, the hill is steep, and I am often out of breath.

Ma ma ma ma ma ma mama is your latest sound, and I've known better than to think that when you made that sound you made it for me. But today you looked at me when you said *Ma ma mama*, and when I came toward you and lifted you off your play mat, you giggled and repeated the words that had brought me to you: *Ma ma mama*. And just that quickly, I had a name.

The jury is still out on whether your infant brain can consciously drive action in the way that my brain receives the things I see. A jellyfish swimming in my direction is not consciously moving toward me, a mosquito who favors my skin over your father's may be responding to the higher levels of carbon dioxide I release, not making a statement about my relative sweetness. In both cases, the hardline objectivist will assure me that what might feel like intentional attention is not. Electrical impulses, hormonal imperatives, these drive action. Not emotion or reason or thought.

These same hardline objectivists are liable to tell me that

animals do not *feel* in the same way humans feel. Without the capacity for language, a dog or a whale or a stork is incapable of human emotion. To say a stork is sad when it loses its mate is to risk anthropomorphizing, to lose scientific objectivity, and to falsify the intellectual potential of the stork. I will not make distinctions between emotional capacities based solely upon what we know of language. I know the orphaned elephant wakes with nightmares, *knowing* what happened to her herd, and *mourning* that loss. This is why the caregivers of orphaned elephants sleep with the foundlings, so they do not have to wake up afraid and alone. I know that whales express gratitude when released from a bind. I know that captive baboons store anger and express it, intentionally, with the calculated hurling of poop.

I know that you are only now acquiring language, after hearing us speak it during your six months out of my womb and forty weeks inside. I know that the *Ma* sounds, like the *Da* sounds from earlier this month, are merely your way to explore the range of sounds available to you. When the sounds first started, I had no illusions that you meant anything by the expressions. But I know, also, that you are smarter than I have the capacity to understand, and I know that when you look at me and make a sound, and when I recognize the sound and respond, and when you repeat my new name without losing eye contact, this is not an accident. And I am filled with unspeakable gladness.

One of the easiest ways to strip a person of her power is to take away her right to choose her name.

The Interesting Narrative of the Life of Olaudah Equiano, or Gustavas Vassa, chronicles an eighteenth-century man's journey from an African (Igbo) boyhood through the seas and hands and lands of Europe and its colonies. In the book, the young protagonist is forced to answer to at least four different names. In his own autobiography, Frederick Douglass writes about resisting renaming. So do Solomon Northup, Harriet Jacobs, and characters imagined—with the help of a narrative written by Josiah Henson—by Harriet Beecher Stowe. Abolitionist literature is riddled with stories of people who recognize that freedom is measured, in part, by the freedom to choose one's own name.

When we take a man's name, he disappears. Sleeping car porters in the early twentieth century were referred to, by the white passengers in the segregated train cars where these porters worked, as "George." This is if they were referred to by any name at all other than "boy" or "you there" or some more brutally dismissive term. A man in prison is sometimes known only by his number. In many morgues, a body without a history is called John or Jane Doe.

At some point you will decide what the world will call you. Callie or Callie Violet or some other, as yet undetermined, name. I can't know what the future will name you, but when I call you Sweet Pea or Turtle Dove, Abena or Pumpkin, Callie Violet or my sweet girl, I do it always in the same tone, so you have learned to turn when I speak. I think you turn not to the names but to the sound of my voice when I speak your many names, the sound I hope you already recognize means you are truly and completely loved.

I love when you notice me, when you direct a new skill toward me as if to purposefully engage me in your growth. When you learned to kiss me, I felt as if every expression of love I'd ever directed toward you had been returned sevenfold. Now you pull my face toward yours and with your mouth wide as a whale shark, smooch my chin or cheek or forehead, whatever part of my face happens to be near. This must be what my mouth feels like on your face, my lips covering huge portions of your skin. Yesterday, you pulled back and reapplied your smooch several times, as if to duplicate my *muah muah muah*s. Sevenfold times sevenfold times sevenfold, that blessing.

When you meet someone new, you meet them as a blind

person might meet someone who matters. You lift your little hand to the new face and work it over the eyes and the nose, the mouth, the cheeks. You learn the contours of the primary points of interaction, and when you are satisfied with what your hands have learned, you smile, maybe even coo. This is how you say hello to strangers and to whatever it is we parents and guardians are to you. Lovers? We kiss you so much, cuddle you and caress you, we *love on you*. Sometimes your kisses catch me full on the lips, and I wonder when I will need to teach you not to show your affection in this way. I try to turn my face lest my hunger for your displays of affection appear indecent.

We are not supposed to conflate these two worlds of physical affection: the kisses and intimate touches of the lover of the body and the kisses and intimate touches of the lover of the babe. But it is like that. I take big whiffs off the top of your head, let your hair tickle my chin. I want you close close closer. When I am with you, mon petite chou, I feel good good and close and happy. I'm not talking about a kind of sexual good good feeling, though what I am talking about is mixed up in the same general neighborhood, which is why this feels like such a dangerous thing to be saying, to be feeling, to be acting upon. I'm talking about a *good* good feeling. A forever kind of good feeling. A "whatever you need, whatever you want, take it, I don't ever intend to be too far from you again" good feeling. A "you make me feel—you make my brain and my heart feel—better than I've ever felt before" feeling. People pay with their lives for feelings like this, these high kinds of feelings, and I get them from smelling your little palm when you cup my nose by way of greeting.

When you devour my face, taking hold of me on the far side and pulling my head toward yours, the force is sometimes so strong I can hardly believe you are only a six-month-old baby. Sometimes, when you hold me like that, or when you resist being held, my mind flashes to stories of smothered children, and I understand how intentional those crimes have to be, how actively a person would have to work to overpower even an infant's resistance. This is what happens when I am with you, Mourning Dove. I can be intensely in the presence of our pleasure when your mortality manifests, a specter undeniable as my joy when you slay me with kisses.

I think I was expecting you to kiss like a guppy might kiss, swift cold pecks that were nearly imperceptible. But, little whale shark, you devour me.

On February 4, 1846, a ship called the *Brooklyn* left New York with 238 voyagers, mostly Mormons from the East Coast. After being blown nearly to Cape Verde, after being caught in the doldrums in the South Atlantic, after rounding Cape Horn without incident then being gale-blown south again, after detouring nearly four hundred miles from their desired dock at Valparaiso and stopping over in the Juan Fernando Islands, after taking on fresh water, fruit, and salted fish, after burying one dead woman in a cave on the island, after more time on the Pacific, after laying over in the Sandwich Islands, after leaving one woman and her mortally ill infant son on Oahu, after many more days on the open ocean, after nearly twenty-four thousand miles, on July 3, 1846, the *Brooklyn* docked at the small settlement of Yerba Buena, its passenger load more than doubling the settlement's population, which was about one hundred and fifty people at the time.

The Mormon settlers arrived just as United States forces seized control of California. Within a year, the settlement of Yerba Buena was officially known by its current name. Now when we say Yerba Buena in relationship to the San Francisco Bay, we don't mean the community that grew up around what we call Mission Dolores in the city we now call San Francisco but the small island through which runs the tunnel portion of the San Francisco-Oakland Bay Bridge. In 1846, there were village ruins on this island, abandoned pots and pestles. Tuchayunes buried their dead in the hillside, sitting up, knees tucked near their chins. But these are not things the people who came off the *Brooklyn* would have known.

The new arrivals might have called the island Goat Island, as some did at the time and for many years after, though there had already been a fairly effective slaughter of the goats that had earned the island that name. Soon they might call it Wood Island to memorialize ships wrecked against its shoals. Spanish-speaking settlers called it Isla de Yerba Buena. Some U.S. surveyor must have liked the sound, for Yerba Buena Island remains the official name. No one for a long time has called the outcropping Sea Bird Island, nor have they used the word the Tuchayunes would have used to call it by that name. The Padres at Mission San Francisco de Asis had already killed most of the Tuchayunes with overwork, unfamiliar diet, and European disease.

It was to ward off ill health that the Tuchayunes used the California mint, the "good herb," whose vines trailed all around the Mission settlement and also draped the island in the bay. People say tea steeped from yerba buena tastes like a cross between mint and pine. Perhaps someday I'll make some of this tea for you.

Babies are like chocolate. Like that first bite of a phenomenal steak. That rich and delicious. Umami and sweet. Umami most of all, that fifth, most crucial, taste we Westerners loved but didn't have a name for until the word *umami* came along. To get to umami we have to stew meat *all the way down to the bone.*

I'm not talking about oppression, suppression, or power plays, though I am aware of how all these things could manifest and corrupt the love that I love. I am talking about love. Consuming love. I'm talking about acknowledging our animal desires, both yours and mine. When you kiss me, Sweet Pea, I want to eat you up. Reading a passage about running or eating cinnamon activates the same parts of our brain as would be activated if we were actually running or eating cinnamon. When I say I am going to eat your little baby thighs and little baby stomach, the parts of my brain that activate when I eat something delectable must go wild. You kiss me, and I am hungry for more kisses.

Since you came to live inside me, much of my sense of propriety is gone. It's as if there were many doors to our apartment, and every door is open, and anyone can walk inside. Strangers talk to me about their own incontinence and I tell them about my weeping breasts. Women I don't know walk into my bathroom to double-check my strategy for mitigating hemorrhoids. Nothing is private. Nothing is sacred. There is nothing I keep to myself. Being your mother has required one act of vulgarity after another, and I'm so strung out on you I couldn't care less.

I don't know if I can define myself anymore, now that I'm your mother. You've consumed me. Being your mother cooked me right down to the bone.

Your grandmother Julie, far more restrained than your mother, has devised a greeting that doesn't involve kissing but allows for eye contact and smiles. When your grandmother Julie was here, she taught you to press your forehead to hers. She never threatened to eat you up. We all have our own ways of telling you we love you.

You picked the gesture up in one day, and every time Grandma Julie was near, you'd run your little hand over her nose and brow ridge, and then you'd bump your tiny forehead right against her head.

She was proprietary about this demonstration of affection. She would tell you and anyone around that this was how *she* greeted you. None of the rest of us gets your forehead pressed against our foreheads. It's your secret handshake with Grandma Julie. Your father and I get the wide-mouthed kisses. Soon, you'll be waving like your grandmother Dungy when your grand-mother Dungy is around. Already you are flapping your little hand, rotating at the wrist and collapsing the fingers toward the pad of your palm, in the specific way your grandmother Dungy gestures hello, my love, and goodbye, my love, and I'll see you soon, my little darling.

What is language but the way we communicate with each other? You are already multilingual, aware of the proper greet-ings for the various microcultures you come in contact with. As we would be if we were in a foreign country and heard someone call us in our native tongue, when we are in your world, we are always delighted that you make the effort to greet us in a way we understand.

Around you, I *am* in a foreign land: the land of infancy with its particular laws and language. With its specific names for things. Its confounding customs. Like an American who lives for a while someplace where the plumbing consists primarily of pit toilets and buckets for hand washing, I've learned both that I need not be grossed out by human waste and that there are more-or-less sanitary means to discard it. So much of my energy is taken up learning new information that I am tired tired tired all the time. I have nearly given up dreaming, and when I do dream, even my dreams seem foreign to me, and so I cannot rest when I am sleeping.

Tired as I am, I am that much more susceptible to emotions. I think that must be why, most of the time, I feel like I'm strung out. Living in your country has exhausted me beyond the point of reason.

I worry about the end days more now than I did before you were born. Your father has humored me and put track shoes, old jeans, and a T-shirt in a go-bag. In case of earthquake or firestorm, I keep food, water, and a basic first aid kit in an accessible place.

I am teaching myself to identify edible native plants. The

berries on bay laurel can make a substitute for coffee. Acorns can be soaked and leached and mashed into a nutritious paste. Miner's lettuce, which restaurants are serving in twenty-dollar salads, comes up along the creek path after rains. I've always liked to season my own salads with nasturtiums. Though it's native to Mexico and South America, nasturtium has made itself at home in Northern California. The yellow-orange flowers add a peppery taste to greens and brighten the plate.

Juan Bautista de Anza, Junipero Serra, Fermín Lasuén, and the other colonists who walked to Northern California, planting missions and settlements and cutting the road we still call El Camino Real, sowed mustard seeds along the way, enacting the parable from Matthew, chapter 13: *The kingdom of heaven is like a mustard seed, which a man took and planted in his field. Though it is the smallest of all seeds, when it grows, it is the largest of garden plants and becomes a tree, so that the birds come and perch in its branches.* California, in the blooming season, is vibrant with mustard's many-headed bracts of yellow flowers, on which I have often seen birds perch.

The Mediterranean grasses that cover the hills of California, historians think, came on the fetlocks of livestock.

Mormons were the first to grow wheat here.

Wild fennel, which must have been cultivated in some early settler's garden, grows all around.

Sausal Creek runs behind our apartment and up into foothills where once were rooted Sequoia sempervirens so dominant men piloted ships into the mouth of the San Francisco Bay by taking their measure. Along the creek path, native and exotic blackberries grow wild. Fruit trees thrive in the places where loggers and the farmers who came after the loggers once chucked their pits. An abolitionist from Iowa first brought the plums and the peaches.

Fennel, blackberry, mustard, plum: I point these out to you on our walks. We can eat these if we need to, I say. As if naming what could save us might save us one day.

Most states and territories in America were inhospitable to adherents of the word of God as spoken to Joseph Smith and practiced by members of the Church of Jesus Christ of Latter-Day Saints. Americans, busy claiming America in the transcontinental drive that caught the west up in its wake, struggled with the Mormons who were allegiant to their church and wanted a place to grow it.

Manifest Destiny was merciless. Not in New York, not in Missouri, not in Illinois, not in Iowa could the Mormon people stop and not be pestered. But California held promise, which is why those 238 believers boarded the *Brooklyn* in February 1846.

Some historians presume that if the Mormons who trekked out of the Midwest hadn't stopped in Utah, on land no one else wanted to claim, the Church of Jesus Christ of Latter-Day Saints might not still exist today. But in Utah, the Church and its people found some measure of peace. Now, by many accounts, the Mormon Church is growing faster than the Christian Church did in the second and third centuries AD.

When Church fathers called the Californians to come build their homes in the desert, some of the new immigrants traveled east across the mountains. But many of them stayed, planting the Church in California as well as in Utah. California now has the largest population of Mormons of any state outside of Utah. The second-largest Mormon temple outside of Utah is in Los Angeles. The sixth-largest is in Oakland.

The Oakland Temple is vast, with manicured grounds, green lawns, and gardens. It sits one and a half miles straight up a hill from our apartment and has spectacular views of the entire San Francisco Bay. The sidewalk on Lincoln Avenue, leading to the temple from the valley where we live, is unbroken. A smooth path for the stroller. That sidewalk and those views are the reason I push you toward the temple on clear days.

You have perfected the barrel roll and now you are sitting up without assistance. Sometimes, when I need a break, I can sit you down someplace and walk a little ways away. Once sitting, you'll stay for a while, looking at books, playing with toys. Sometimes you seem a sovereign nation, my Argentina. When you cried all night in that first month, before I learned to burp you properly, before you had a physical vocabulary for showing us your needs, I used to remind myself that one day you wouldn't want me to hold you at all, let alone for hour after hour, and then I would miss the smell of your head as it nestled all day and all night just below my chin. I knew you wouldn't be mine to hold forever, and sometimes that made me want to cry right along with you, Mourning Dove.

Today, after you called my name, I sat you in your crib where you could watch your mobile. No more *Ma ma ma ma*, just a silent gaze circling with the plastic safari animals tethered over your head. That quickly, I was replaced in your attentions. If I were the jealous type, the mobile would have been removed before it could have done us any more harm.

I heard a story recently about a couple who grew jealous of their daughter's mobile. They had so completely fallen in love with the way the baby gazed into their eyes that they didn't want to share her attention, even with a musical crib mobile. Irrational, yes, but something in me understands.

When the elephant passed your head for the fifteenth time, you grabbed it and went along for the ride. Your upper body followed the mobile around the crib, while your heavy, diapered bum stayed put.

It all happened quickly and slowly, so I had time to multiply into many mothers: the one who would rush toward you like a rescue team and another who would stand by the wardrobe, mouth agape, watching as, *kerplop*, you fell onto your back on the mattress, nearly smashing the soft part of your head on the crib slats. I had time only to think, 'Oh my god oh my god oh my god' and 'That's what you get for grabbing after something

that cares nothing for you.' There was humor in your predica-
ment, but also there was the fact that your fall nearly slammed a
wood bar into the anterior fontanelle, where your outsized brain
waits inside your as-yet-unfused skull.

How can I name what I felt when I saw you not hurt? Not
this time.

Lincoln Avenue is steady and steep, and we walk up without
stopping. I use the Temple Viewing station, with its map and
information placard, as my excuse to rest, so I am breathless
when I learn about the *Brooklyn*.

I read the bronze placard, look out over Oakland, San Francisco Bay, Yerba Buena Island, and San Francisco. You sleep in
your stroller, and I watch you awhile. Then I read the placard
again. I read one name and then another. A name and then
an age and then another name. Your weight, and your stroller's
weight, and my extra weight, I pushed all that up Lincoln Avenue, and now there is this new weight, this old, old weight. It
takes my breath away.

Sarah Sloat Burr lost a boy, an unnamed one-year-old, and
gave birth to another, John Atlantic, during the voyage on the
Brooklyn. Forever after that, if she called him John Atlantic,
would she remember the dead son she shrouded and slipped into
the ocean, recalled by the living boy's name?

Was it meant as salt or as salve, his naming?

Jerusha Ensign Fowler (twenty-seven), traveling without a
husband, left the East Coast with her parents, a sister, a brother,
and sons ages six, five, four, and one. She arrived at Yerba Buena
with no father, no sister, and no baby boy. Their bodies were left
behind in the water.

What mixture of celebration and mourning must have accompanied her landing?

Jane Cowen Glover brought Joseph Smith Glover (age one)
safely to California. Relief may not be the right word to describe

her response to their arrival. When the *Brooklyn* nearly foundered in an Atlantic storm, the passengers sang hymns and prayed, assured that God would guide them safely through the voyage. Some people's prayers were answered, some of the time.

Had she not died (pregnant) on the voyage, Laura Hotchkiss Goodwin would have witnessed the safe arrival of one-year-old Albert Story Goodwin and six other children, ages three to eleven, but she died, so her seven children reached Yerba Buena without her.

I try to imagine the lives of the women and children named on the placard.

Hardline historical objectivists would warn against emotional anachronism. What drove these women could not be the same things that drive me today.

You cry out, my little Argentina. I pull the blanket up under your chin to protect you from the hilltop wind.

Compelled by the story revealed in the names, I read the manifest again.

The hope these women had for themselves and their children's futures: is there any other way to think of it than all-consuming? They must have been out of their minds with complicated desires. Sarah Duncan McCullough Griffith brought her two-year-old boy to California, and Caroline Augusta Perkins Joyce brought her one-year-old daughter. In addition to a five-year-old, a seven-year-old, a thirteen-year-old, and a fourteen-year-old, thirty-four-year-old Eliza Hindman Littleman boarded the *Brooklyn* with four-month-old identical twins. What was it for her to nurse those two in the ship's cramped quarters, water festering and roaches in the meal she needed to keep her milk production high? Did she feel good nursing the twins, even in the midst of that squalor?

When Octavia Anne Lane Austin left New York with children ages two, five, and seven, she couldn't have known there was gold at this end of the world. It wasn't that kind of materialism that drove her to California.

Alice Wallace Bird was one month old, so she had no say in the matter. What of Ann Eliza Corwin Brannan, who had a two-month-old son? Can anyone say what it was she hungered for?

There was new life, yes, but also much common, unspeakable horror. Thirteen people died in transit. Eight of the dead were babies. Scarlet fever took the first. Consumption, diarrhea, dehydration.

Sarah Winner, six months old when the *Brooklyn* set sail, never made it to California. Oren Hopkins Smith, ten months old when the *Brooklyn* set sail, never made it to California. Mary Ann Shunn Burtis Robbins, already the mother of three children under seven, bore and buried Anna Pacific Robbins in the ocean for which she was named. When she loved her living children, did she hug them so tightly, sometimes, she nearly squeezed the life from them?

Phoebe Ann Wright Robbins (thirty-four) lost five-year-old George Edward Robbins and one-year-old John Franklin Robbins somewhere at sea. A baby, born off the west coast of America, was a living memorial to her aunt's and mother's losses. Georgeanna Pacific Robbins. Was she salve or salt on their wounds?

You cry again, obviously rooting. I love that word, *rooting*. As if by seeking your mother's milk, you are planting yourself in this world.

I take you out of the stroller and bring you with me to a bench where I can hold you while I look across the houses of Oakland and out into the bay. You nurse while I steady my gaze on Yerba Buena Island, known in a decimated people's decimated language as Sea Bird Island, known later as Wood Island because of lost treasure. Arbor Day plantings of the nineteenth century installed invasive species that have mostly squeezed out the native plant the Spanish once called yerba buena.

I don't know what I know now that I can name these losses.

I soothe your cries and look out over the bay toward where, sometime in 1846, Georgeanna Pacific Robbins must have cried for much the same reason and in much the same way. As she nursed her, did her mother call her darling, sweet pea, little honeybee? Georgeanna? Pacific? When she looked out at the ocean where she lost those other children, what was there to say?

I don't know if there is a name for this in any language, this hope and hurt and hunger I hold when I hold you. The story of the *Brooklyn* makes me breathless with sadness and a relief that borders on joy.

I haven't lost you yet, I think. I haven't lost you yet. I haven't lost you yet. Oh my god oh my god oh my god.

Let's Talk About Sex, Baby

Amber Flame

I FEEL THE SUNLIGHT LEAKING OUT OF ME. FOR DAYS each morning since my return, I slipped into the same clothes. I think to press the heat to me just a little longer; maybe it's just that my loneliness leaves me cold. I never understood the old people in their RVs each Arizona winter, going forty miles per hour in the passing lane—but I get it now. I never thought I would miss the sun after running away to the Pacific Northwest as soon as I turned eighteen, vowing never to return. Last week, I looked up property prices in Tucson. The joke is that the name my mother gave me keeps me warm, prone to over-heating even, but this year I can't seem to get winter out of my bones. Returning to my empty house, I imagine I feel a draft everywhere. Every night I awaken, slicked with sweat, anxiety-mind again spinning possibilities: this isn't normal—is it? Internet self-diagnosis leaves too many options for the cause of chills and night sweats. Is this perimenopause coming for me? What a bitch! I'm still too young for that, right? Is it COVID? Is my throat sore? Do I have a fever? Is it the flu? No. It's the sunlight. Leaking.

"How exactly does sex work?" My twelve-year-old asks me this on a Tuesday night after a long traffic-laden commute home. Or perhaps this conversation began when they say their boyfriend wondered what a vagina looked like (really, how female bodies pee without a penis, god what are they *not* teaching these kids), and my kid told him to imagine a hot dog bun.

And I suppose not every moment has to be a teaching moment, but I really couldn't let that stand, could I? Let's talk about sex, baby.

The first day I was gone, I floated on my back in a saltwater pool, watching a cloud take the same shape as me, then grow into a winged creature, an anatomical heart, and then dissipate into nothing. Warm and alone, finally, I could feel the depressive weight still, the grief, still—and for a moment it didn't feel like fathomless depths below me. I was floating. Out of the whirlpool of my thoughts to soaking in sunlight, instead. And the hunger for touch so desperate that, with my eyes closed, I could mistake it for a warm embrace. Perhaps the heat leak sprung that night as I tossed the hot sheets off and then pulled them back on, over and over, in the chill blast of the AC. You're allowed to sleep. Go to sleep. My skin, refusing to be soothed, glowing. A beacon. A summoning.

"So you've heard of lube?" The kid wants to know how it doesn't hurt, and, well, we're here now, aren't we. The concept of lube leaves them unfazed, but they are thoroughly disturbed by the reality of natural lubrication. The kid identifies as asexual and is still grossed out by the thought of French kissing. "Perhaps you are asexual now because of your age. You are still really young to be any kind of sexually active," I say, because clearly the curiosity, though awkward and uncomfortable, is there. Privately, I marvel at an AFAB Black human in this world who only knows about rape, assault, molestation, incest, sexual trauma intellectually. I cannot think of a single other one in the family with this lack of experience.

I stayed on the thirty-fifth floor downtown, my nighttime arrival giving no true indication of the panoramic view that was glorious from first light to sundown. The small, last-minute Airbnb was just comfortable enough to stay in but not enough to keep me holed up in the room. Mild agoraphobia sometimes overtakes me without the motivating factor of parenting, work, or community. Too easy to mistake the virtual world for connection, for days to pass without encountering a single person outside the screen. Too much empty space in our house for me to try to fill—I can easily replace a walk around the neighborhood with wafting from room to room; I'll get my steps in. So pick a vacation spot too luxurious and I would come home as melanin-deprived as I left. And if there was one thing I was determined to get out of this trip, it was a tan. I woke up early on the second day, still insomniac, and out I went. It was hot. Hot in January! Every inch of me gushed about it, aching with thirst, guzzling water unsated. When I sat in the shade, spooning sticky-sweet shave ice, I thanked myself for this gift. It sounded like a prayer.

"Alright, now let's talk about queer sex." Because clearly queer is a cultural identity, not a sexual one, my kid is also—as they would put it—gay as fuck. This is mostly expressed through memes and tropes, but they are truly everything I could want in my kid and more. I love that they get to be exactly and only who they decide to be. It's what we fought for, right? We untangle *blow job* from *prostitution* ("What? It's a *job*, right?!") and study comparative drawings of male and female reproductive systems ("Why do the nuts look like earbuds just dangling down like that?").

When it has been 323 days since my ex last desired me, or when I have been gone for four days, I think I can rekindle my passion with a loverfriend. It's as if I forgot how to desire someone else since adopting a monogamous lifestyle, easier to fall back to/into something known. I lack faith in meeting someone new while navigating a world where a conversation with a stranger could be deadly. I didn't say the hope for connection with someone familiar is why I picked this place to escape to; this isn't the only reason. However, the idea that the best way to get over someone is to get under someone else hums in my head. We spend the day driving around and sitting on the beach. She takes me to see the stars, incredibly bright, in full 180-degree glory. I am so thirsty I buy coconut water and electrolytes, check my shoulders and cheeks for telltale raw pink. But I've been cold all day.

"Oh gross. That's even worse than a penis!"

"Fingers are *worse* than a penis? How?"

"I dunno, that's just like, really disturbing."

"More disturbing than butt sex. Interesting. How did you think lesbians have sex, besides oral?"

"Like, dildos and toys and stuff!"

"Well. Yes, and."

"Ewwww!"

Now, I feel a bit defensive. As a dyed-in-the-wool lesbian, I *love* hands. However, this conversation isn't about me. I make a joke about long fingernails and leave it be. One day perhaps they'll know the joys the beautiful hands of a dyke can bring. Or not. It's up to them.

When I say I am grieving, no one thinks of the breakup. After all, it's been nearly a year, so they assume I am talking about my dead mother, about the big and sprawling grief. How every year February rolls around again with the anniversary of my mother's death, not how once falling in love lit me up despite that month's cold weight. We've all lost so much in this pandemic, heartbreak is frustratingly small and petty in scope. How to explain the body betrayal of orienting your daily life to a partnership with someone who changes her mind? How to account for the dimming of every joyous thing? I am so tired of it, I want to be over it, to move on as I've been promised I will. How do you grieve someone who isn't dead? It wasn't until the day before I returned that the revelation happened. Lulled into a meditative state by the crashing waves of the ocean, the warm sun, the cool wind, and the utter absence of anything else to do, something inside unclenched. Surrender. The truth is what it is: I'm just sad. I must feel it and make space for as long as it takes.

"Welp, I can definitely say I've done my homework for sex ed!" The kid has grown increasingly squirmy and is clearly ready to shift subjects, but I want to say one more thing.

"I don't know if your friends' parents talk to them so openly about this stuff, so if they are asking you for information it's important to know the facts."

"You mean instead of just learning from TikTok."

"Oh, yes, please, don't do that."

"I won't. I'll tell them I'll ask my mom."

This is a major parenting win. I feel like a goddamn superhero. They kiss me and walk off, already deep in a text exchange with their bestie, and I marvel at their ease and confidence, their surety in being loved and wanted by the people in their life. I wonder if I ever had that, and if so, why I lost it.

I went to a warm place seeking some relief I could not name. I am weary of this particular sadness and wonder aloud if I only long for my ex because she is no longer mine. Her specialty is withholding, and so I seek other sources of heat. Since my return, the thermostat is set for the temperature of Hawaii in January. I buy a pink velvet sofa, rugs, space heaters; I pull out soft, fuzzy, shapeless things that retain my heat. My home becomes a beautiful invitation for future guests, but every room is mine to occupy. In the mirror, I see myself growing pale again, the sunkiss sloughing off my skin with every shower, but summer is on its way. It takes two weeks to unpack my suitcase; when I do, I imagine future trips, new loverfriends. My skin flushes at the memory of pleasure hands have given me.

Acknowledgments

THIS BOOK BEGAN DURING A CONVERSATION OVER dinner with Esther Perel, the brilliant sex and relationship psychotherapist and author, at the Boston Bookfest. Her enthusiasm and belief in the need for a project like this gave us the firepower we needed to imagine and begin. Thank you to Debbie Porter for that dinner invitation and so much support over the years.

Thank you to our agent, Andrew Blauner, and to our acquiring editor, Leigh Newman, for believing in this book from the start.

Thank you to everyone at Catapult for incredible creativity and support. Thanks especially to our amazing editor Alicia Kroell, who molded this book with imagination and grace, and to design phenoms Nicole Caputo and Laura Berry, who made the message beautiful. Thanks also to our dream team of promotion and marketing champions: Rachel Fershleiser, Megan Fishmann, Lena Moses-Schmitt, and Selihah White.

Thank you to the many organizations that have supported this project in one way or another, including AWP, the Boston Bookfest, Hugo House, the Hofstra Cultural Center, and the Virginia Center for the Creative Arts.

Thank you to our friends and families for your support, love, caretaking, and generosity. From Margot: thanks to all the friends and teachers who've shown me what it looks like to want something and go after it; in particular, Jenn van Dijk, Ming-Lien Linsley, and Jessica Ludders—you've carried me through the years. From Kelly: thanks to my N., my heart, and thanks to my sons, who are everything I've ever wanted, always.

Most of all, thank you to the writers in these pages for your bravery, your trust, and your words.

About the Contributors

Elisa Albert is the author of the novels *Human Blues*, *After Birth*, *The Book of Dahlia*, and the short story collection *How This Night Is Different*. Her stories and essays have appeared in *n+1*, *Tin House*, *The New York Times*, *The Literary Review*, *Michigan Quarterly Review*, *Bennington Review*, *Los Angeles Review of Books*, *TIME*, on NPR, and in many anthologies.

Kristen Arnett is the author of *With Teeth: A Novel* (Riverhead Books, 2021) which was a finalist for the Lambda Literary Award in fiction and the *New York Times* bestselling debut novel *Mostly Dead Things* (Tin House, 2019) which was also a finalist for the Lambda Literary Award in fiction. She was a Shearing Fellow at Black Mountain Institute and was longlisted for the Joyce Carol Oates Prize recognizing midcareer writers of fiction. Her work has appeared at *The New York Times*; *TIME*; *The Cut*; *O, The Oprah Magazine*; *Guernica*; *BuzzFeed*; *McSweeneys*; *PBS NewsHour*; *The Guardian*; *Salon*; and elsewhere. Her next book (an untitled collection of short stories) will be published by Riverhead Books (Penguin Random House). She has a master's in library and information science from Florida State University and currently lives in Miami, Florida.

Molly McCully Brown is the author of the poetry collection *The Virginia State Colony for Epileptics and Feebleminded* and the essay collection *Places I've Taken My Body*. With Susannah Nevison, she is also the coauthor of the poetry collection *In the Field Between Us*. Brown has been the recipient of the Amy Lowell Poetry Traveling Scholarship and a United States Artists Fellowship, and her work has appeared in *The Paris Review*, *Tin House*, *Virginia Quarterly Review*, *The Yale Review*, and elsewhere. Raised in rural Virginia, she teaches at Old Dominion University, where she is an assistant professor of English and creative nonfiction and a member of the MFA Core Faculty.

Angela Cardinale's work has been featured in *McSweeney's, RAZED, Lost and Found: Stories from New York, The Chaffey Review*, and the *Mojave River Review*. She also led a writing workshop with incarcerated students, whose resulting work was included in *Inside/Outside*, an exhibit at the Wignall Museum. She lives with her two teen boys and coordinates online education for a community college in Southern California.

Tara Conklin is a writer and former lawyer whose first novel *The House Girl* (William Morrow) was a *New York Times* bestseller, number-one IndieNext pick, and Target book club pick and has been translated into eight languages. Her second novel *The Last Romantics* (William Morrow) was published in February 2019 to wide acclaim. An instant *New York Times* bestseller, *The Last Romantics* was a Barnes & Noble Book Club Pick and IndieNext Pick and was selected by Jenna Bush Hager as the inaugural read for The Today Show Book Club.

Sonia Maria David is a member of the Council of Urban Professionals Fellowship program for 2022. She is a pleasure advocate and DEI professional. Sonia double majored in political science and religion at the University of Vermont for her BA and earned her MDiv at Harvard University, with a focus on the interconnection of race, religious identity, community, culture, and inclusion. A New York State native, Sonia is passionate about creating tight bonds and deep connections with her community; writing is her lifelong passion. She is writing a book about leading a defenseless life as a black woman.

Jennifer De Leon is author of the YA novel *Don't Ask Me Where I'm From* (Simon & Schuster), which was chosen as a Junior Library Guild selection, and the essay collection *White Space: Essays* *on Culture, Race, & Writing* (University of Massachusetts Press), which is a recipient of the Juniper Prize in Creative Nonfiction. She is also the editor of *Wise Latinas: Writers on Higher Education* (University of Nebraska Press), an anthology that won an International Latino Book Award. An associate professor of creative writing at Framingham State University and faculty member in the Creative Writing & Literature Master Program at Harvard University, she has published prose in *Ploughshares, Iowa Review, Michigan Quarterly Review,* and more. Her next YA novel *Borderless* is forthcoming in 2023. Also on the way are two children's picture books—*So Many Gifts* and a biography of Nobel Peace Prize winner Rigoberta Menchú. Connect with her @jdeleonwriter on Instagram and Twitter or at her website: www.jenniferdeleonauthor.com.

Camille T. Dungy's debut collection of personal essays is *Guidebook to Relative Strangers* (W. W. Norton, 2017), a finalist for the National Book Critics Circle Award. She is also the author of four collections of poetry, most recently *Trophic Cascade* (Wesleyan University Press, 2017), winner of the Colorado Book Award. She was awarded a Guggenheim Fellowship in 2019.

Melissa Febos is the bestselling author of four books, most recently, *Girlhood*, winner of the National Book Critics Circle Award in criticism, and *Body Work: The Radical Power of Personal Narrative*. She is the recipient of awards and fellowships from The Guggenheim Foundation, the National Endowment for the Arts, MacDowell, Lambda Literary, The Barbara Deming Foundation, The British Library, and others. She is an associate professor at the University of Iowa.

Amber Flame is an artist and performer whose work has garnered artistic merit residencies with Hedgebrook, the Watering Hole, Wa Na Wari, Vermont Studio Center, and Yefe Nof. Flame served as the poetry writer-in-residence (2017 to 2019) at Hugo House in Seattle and is a queer Black dandy mama who falls hard for a jumpsuit and some fresh kicks.

Amy Gall is a writer whose work has appeared in, among other publications, *Tin House*, *VICE*, *Poets & Writers*, *Glamour*, *Interview*, and the anthology *Mapping Queer Spaces*. She is coauthor of the book *Recycle*, a collection of collages and text, and the recipient of a fellowship from the MacDowell Colony. Amy earned her MFA in creative writing from The New School and is currently working on a collection of linked essays about queer bodies, sex, and pleasure.

Aracelis Girmay is the author of three books of poems, most recently *The Black Maria* (BOA Editions, 2016), for which she was a finalist for the Neustadt Prize. She is the editor of *How to Carry Water: Selected Poems of Lucille Clifton* (2020).

Nicole Hardy's memoir *Confessions of a Latter-Day Virgin* (Hyperion 2013) was a finalist for the 2014 Washington State Book Award. The Modern Love essay that inspired it—"Single, Female, Mormon, Alone"—was also featured on the *Modern Love* podcast and noted in 2012's *Best American Essays*. Her essays have been published widely in outlets including *The New York Times*, *The Washington Post*, and *Marie Claire*, and adapted for radio and stage. Her other books include the poetry collections *This Blonde* (2009) and *Mud Flap Girl's XX Guide to Facial Profiling* (2006), a chapbook of pop culture–inspired sonnets. She earned her MFA at the Bennington College Writing Seminars.

Laura Joyce-Hubbard is a Northwestern University MFA candidate and fiction editor for *TriQuarterly*. Her nonfiction and poetry appear in *Creative Nonfiction*, the *Sewanee Review*, the *Chicago Tribune*, *The Rumpus*, *Boulevard*, *Ninth Letter*, *Hippocampus Magazine*, *Tupelo Quarterly*, and elsewhere. She has received fellowships from the Ragdale Foundation and the National Endowment for the Arts to attend a residency at VCCA. She won the 2021 Ned Stuckey-French nonfiction contest at *Southeast Review* and the 2020 Essay Prize in the William Faulkner Pirates' Alley Writing Competition. Laura was a pilot in the U.S. Air Force and commercial airlines and still waves hello/goodbye to her spouse each week from the home they share with their teenage sons in Highland Park, Illinois.

Sonora Jha is the author of the novel *Foreign* (Penguin Random House India, 2013) and the memoir *How to Raise a Feminist Son: Motherhood, Masculinity, and the Making of My Family* (Sasquatch Books U.S.A. and Penguin Random House India, 2021). After a career as a journalist covering crime, politics, and culture in India and Singapore, she moved to the United States to earn a PhD in media and public affairs. Sonora's OpEds, essays, and public appearances have featured in the *New York Times*, BBC, *DAME*, *Electric Literature*, and elsewhere. Her new novel, *The Laughter*, is forthcoming from Harper Via in early 2023. She is a professor of journalism and lives in Seattle.

TaraShea Nesbit's second novel, *Beheld*, was a *Publishers Weekly* Best Fiction Book of 2020, a *New York Times* Notable Book of the Year, and was longlisted for the 2021 Massachusetts Book Award and the 2021 Ohioana Book Award. Her bestselling first novel *The Wives of Los Alamos* was a finalist for the PEN/Robert W. Bingham Prize, a *New York Times* Book Review Editors' Choice, a Barnes & Noble Discover Great New Writers Selection, an Indies Choice Debut Pick, and winner of two New Mexico-Arizona Book Awards. Her writing has been featured in *The New York Times*, *Granta*, *The Guardian*, *Literary Hub*, *Ninth Letter*, *Salon*, *Fourth Genre*, *The Iowa Review*, *Los Angeles Review of Books*, and elsewhere. She is an associate professor of creative writing at Miami University.

Keyanah B. Nurse, PhD, is a writer and historian by day, femme fatale by night. She completed her doctorate in African diaspora history at New York University in 2020, and uses her academic training to write compelling personal narratives about Black sexual politics. Her work on polyamory, race, and gender has appeared in *HuffPost* and *Honeysuckle Magazine* and on the *Multiamory* podcast. She is currently at work on her debut memoir about navigating marriage and polyamory as a Black millennial. Follow her on Twitter at @KeyanahNurse.

Torrey Peters is the author of the novel *Detransition, Baby*, published by One World, which won the 2021 PEN/Hemingway award for debut fiction. It was also a finalist for the National Book Critics Circle Awards, a finalist for the Brooklyn Public Library Award, and longlisted for the Women's Prize for Fiction. A collection of four novellas titled *Infect Your Friends and Loved Ones* will be published by Random House in 2023. She has an MFA from the University of Iowa and a master's in comparative literature from Dartmouth. Torrey rides a pink motorcycle and splits her time between Brooklyn and an off-grid cabin in Vermont.

Amanda Petrusich is a staff writer at *The New Yorker* and the author of three books. She is the recipient of a Guggenheim Fellowship in nonfiction and has been nominated for a Grammy Award. Her criticism and features have appeared in *The New York Times*, *Oxford American*, *Spin*, *Pitchfork*, *GQ*, *Esquire*, *The Atlantic*, and the *Virginia Quarterly Review*. Her most recent book, *Do Not Sell at Any Price*, explored the obsessive world of 78-rpm record collectors. She is an associate professor at New York University's Gallatin School.

Larissa Pham is an artist and writer in Brooklyn. She has written essays and criticism for *The Paris Review Daily*, *The Nation*, *Art in America*, the Poetry Foundation, and elsewhere. She is the author of *Pop Song: Adventures in Art and Intimacy* (Catapult, 2021), a finalist for the National Book Critics Circle John Leonard Prize.

She has received support from the Jack Jones Literary Arts Retreat and the Bennington Writing Seminars.

Rena Priest is a poet and an enrolled member of the Lhaq'temish (Lummi) Nation. She has been appointed to serve as Washington State poet laureate for the April 2021 to 2023 term. She is the 2022 Maxine Cushing Gray Distinguished Writing Fellow, an Indigenous Nations Poets Fellow, and recipient of an Allied Arts Foundation Professional Poets Award. Her debut collection *Patriarchy Blues* was published by MoonPath Press and received an American Book Award. Her second collection, *Sublime Subliminal*, was published as the finalist for the Floating Bridge Press Chapbook Award. She is a National Geographic Explorer (2018 to 2020) and a Jack Straw Writer (2019). She holds an MFA from Sarah Lawrence College.

Joanna Rakoff is the author of the international bestselling memoir *My Salinger Year* and the bestselling novel *A Fortunate Age*, winner of the Goldberg Prize for Fiction and the Elle Readers' Prize. Rakoff's books have been translated into twenty languages. The film adaptation of *My Salinger Year* opened in theaters worldwide in 2021 and is now streaming. Her new memoir, *The Fifth Passenger*, is forthcoming from Little, Brown in 2024.

Karen Russell won the 2012 and the 2018 National Magazine Award for fiction, and her first novel, *Swamplandia!* (2011), was a finalist for the Pulitzer Prize, winner of the New York Public Library Young Lions Award, and one of *The New York Times'* Ten Best Books of 2011. She has received a MacArthur Fellowship and a Guggenheim award and is a former fellow of the NYPL Cullman Center and the American Academy in Berlin. Born and raised in Miami, Florida, she now lives in Portland, Oregon, with her husband, son, and daughter.

Domenica Ruta is the author of the *New York Times* bestselling memoir *With or Without You*, the novel *Last Day*, and coeditor of the anthology *We Got This: Solo Mom Stories of Heart, Grit, and Humor.*

Susan Shapiro is the bestselling author of several books her family hates, including *Unhooked*, *The Forgiveness Tour*, and the popular writing guides *The Byline Bible* and *The Book Bible*. She freelances for *The New York Times*; *Washington Post*; *Wall Street Journal*; *Wired*; *New York*; *Elle*; *O, The Oprah Magazine*; and *The New Yorker* magazines online, and her memoir *Five Men Who Broke My Heart* was recently optioned for a movie. An award-winning professor, she teaches at New York University, The New School, and for private classes and seminars now on Zoom. You can follow her on Twitter at @Susanshapironet and Instagram @profsue123.

Ann Tashi Slater has contributed fiction, essays, and interviews to *The New Yorker*, *The Paris Review*, *The New York Times*, *The Washington Post*, *Catapult*, *Guernica*, *Tin House*, *AGNI*, and *Granta*, among many others publications. Her essays have been Notables in *The Best American Essays* and she is a contributing editor at *Tricycle*. Current projects include a memoir about reconnecting with her Tibetan roots in her ancestral homeland and a book about bardo and impermanence in our lives. A longtime resident of Tokyo, she teaches literature at Japan Women's University. Visit her at www.anntashislater.com.

A Guggenheim fellow, **Terese Svoboda** is the author of nineteen books and two forthcoming novels, *Dog on Fire* and *Roxy and Coco*. She has won the Bobst Prize in fiction, the Iowa Prize for poetry, a National Endowment for the Humanities grant for translation, the Graywolf Nonfiction Prize, a Jerome Foundation prize for video, and a Pushcart Prize for essay. She is a three-time winner of the New York Foundation for the Arts fellowship.

Lisa Taddeo spent eight years and thousands of hours tracking the women whose stories comprise *Three Women*, moving to the

towns they lived in to better understand their lives. She has contributed to *New York, Esquire, Elle, Glamour,* and many other publications. She has won two Pushcart Prizes for her short stories,
one of which, "Suburban Weekend," was also selected as a favorite
piece of 2017 by *Granta.* She lives with her husband and daughter
in New England.

Abigail Thomas has four children, twelve grandchildren, one
great granddaughter, two dogs, and a high school education. She
is eighty years old this year. Her books include *Safekeeping, A Three
Dog Life,* and *What Comes Next and How to Like It.*

Merritt Tierce was born and raised in Texas and earned an MFA
from the Iowa Writers' Workshop. A 2019 Whiting Foundation
Award winner, she was a 2013 National Book Foundation "5
Under 35" author and received a Rona Jaffe Foundation Writers'
Award. Her first novel, *Love Me Back,* was shortlisted for the
PEN/Robert W. Bingham prize for debut fiction and won the 2014
Texas Institute of Letters' Steven Turner Award for Best Work of
First Fiction. She wrote for the last two seasons of the Netflix
show *Orange Is the New Black* and is currently developing various
abortion-related projects for film and television. Merritt served as
the executive director of the Texas Equal Access Fund, a nonprofit
abortion fund based in Dallas, from 2011 to 2014. She volunteered
and worked for the TEA Fund from its founding in 2004, and
cowrote the abortion play *One in 3* with screenwriter and activist Gretchen Dyer and Pulitzer Prize–winning journalist Victoria
Loe Hicks. *One in 3* played to sold-out houses for most of its three-
week run and stimulated a local conversation about the reality of
abortion in women's lives.

Michelle Wildgen is the author of the novels *Wine People* (Zibby
Books, August 2023), *You're Not You, But Not for Long,* and *Bread
and Butter* and the editor of the food writing anthology *Food &
Booze.* A former executive editor with the award-winning literary

journal *Tin House*, she is a freelance editor and creative writing teacher in Madison, Wisconsin.

Jane Wong is the author of *How to Not Be Afraid of Everything* (Alice James, 2021) and *Overpour* (Action Books, 2016). Her debut memoir, *Meet Me Tonight in Atlantic City*, is forthcoming from Tin House in 2023. She is an associate professor of creative writing at Western Washington University and lives in Seattle, Washington.

Teresa Wong is the author of the graphic memoir *Dear Scarlet: The Story of My Postpartum Depression*, a finalist for The City of Calgary W. O. Mitchell Book Prize and longlisted for CBC Canada Reads 2020. Her comics have appeared in *The Believer*, *The New Yorker*, and *Event Magazine*. She teaches memoir and comics at Gotham Writers Workshop and is the 2021–22 Canadian Writer-in-Residence at the University of Calgary.

Permissions

MARGOT KAHN is the author of *Horses That Buck*, the biography of world-champion rodeo cowboy "Cody" Bill Smith, and a collection of poems, *A Quiet Day with the West on Fire*. She is coeditor, along with Kelly McMasters, of *The New York Times* Editors' Choice anthology *This Is the Place: Women Writing About Home*, and her essays and reviews have appeared in *The Rumpus*, *Lenny Letter*, *Publishers Weekly*, and *Bust*, among other places. An Ohio native, she lives in the Pacific Northwest with her husband and son.

© Mary Grace Long

KELLY McMASTERS is the author of *Welcome to Shirley: A Memoir from an Atomic Town*, an Orion Book Award finalist, and the forthcoming memoir *The Leaving Season*. Her work has appeared in *The New York Times*, *The Paris Review Daily*, *The American Scholar*, *Literary Hub*, *River Teeth: The Journal of Nonfiction Narrative*, and other publications, and she has been the recipient of a Virginia Center for the Creative Arts residency and a Humanities New York grant. She teaches at Hofstra University in New York.

© Sylvie Rosokoff